Biblical Faith
An Evolutionary Approach

GERD THEISSEN

Biblical Faith

An Evolutionary Approach

FORTRESS PRESS   PHILADELPHIA

Translated by John Bowden from the German
Biblische Glaube in evolutionärer Sicht,
published by Christian Kaiser Verlag, Munich 1984.

© Christian Kaiser Verlag 1984

Translation © John Bowden 1984

First Fortress Press edition 1985

ISBN 0–8006–1842–4

1276J84   Printed in the United Kingdom   1–1842

To my father
on his seventy-seventh birthday
21 February 1984

Contents

Contents

Preface

When we interpret the Bible in the light of the modern humane sciences (literary criticism, sociology and psychology), we soon come up against the question whether such approaches can in fact do justice to the theological content of biblical texts. One widespread answer is to limit the new methods of interpretation to peripheral aspects of the biblical tradition, so as to be able to interpret its central theological statements independently of them. As sociological and psychological analyses always cover only partial aspects of the texts, this approach is quite plausible. However, there is another answer to the question raised above. We can try to press research into the Bible from the perspective of the humane sciences even further, in the hope that the central content of the Bible will emerge in a new light. That is the approach which I have adopted in this book. The most comprehensive scientific framework we can use in modern times is the theory of evolution; so the aim of this book is partly to analyse and partly to interpret biblical faith with the help of evolutionary categories. It will have been successful if it communicates what to me has proved to be a surprising experience, that precisely when we refuse to stop short at the innermost 'sanctuaries' of the tradition with our modern scientific questioning, the tradition shows up in quite a new light.

The theory of evolution provides a fairly flexible framework for this enterprise. Those who accept it as a paradigm of contemporary thought have no reason to make it absolute: evolutionary theory, too, has undergone evolution. It corresponds to the present state of our knowledge and our mistaken ideas – and no more. It is a structure by which our knowledge can adapt to reality (and probably has only limited validity). But it is one of the most fascinating constructions of human reason, an attempt to give an explanation of the framework which determines our life.

I am aware that not everyone shares this fascination. 'Evolution' is a word which often has negative connotations, particularly for those interested in theology. So I want to remove some misconceptions from the start.

The fact that in this book I shall be illuminating and interpreting human history (including biblical faith) by means of a theory which derives from biology does not mean that I am claiming an unbroken continuity between biological evolution and human history. On the contrary, my central argument is that human culture is and calls for a 'diminution of selection', thus going against the tendencies of organic life. I reject any biologism, i.e. the naive transference of biology to human culture.

Nor does this book share that unwarrantable optimism which is often bound up with evolutionary philosophical systems and which is characteristic of the theological reception of the theory of evolution in some quarters. With the aid of categories drawn from the theory of evolution I shall be protesting as clearly against the modern dismissal of what the Bible calls 'sin' as against the illusionary assumption that world history could not end in catastrophe.

Some readers might expect that a clarification of biblical faith in the light of the theory of evolution would describe continuous lines of development from the beginnings of Israel to primitive Christianity. I shall be disappointing this expectation too. Certainly I shall be pointing to some lines of development, but even more I shall be stressing the phenomenon of discontinuity, of the break in history, the new beginning which cannot be derived from elsewhere. For example, the monotheism of Israel is not the result of an 'evolution' understood as a continuous development; it is a revolution in the history of religion.

After these comments I hope it may sound credible for me to claim that I described the first sketches of the approach developed here as 'anti-evolutionary'. And even in the book as it now is, the nucleus of this theology remains a protest against the harshness of the 'principle of selection'. Above all, concern with evolutionary epistemology (stimulated by reading Karl Popper) has convinced me that a comprehensive theory of evolution need not be 'biologistic'. In this way I have gradually overcome the antipathy against applying what were originally biological terms to history and religion, an antipathy which is particularly understandable in Germany.

Many people have contributed towards the development of the approach presented here by their stimulation and criticism. First and foremost among them is my wife. Her positive reception of ideas which in other quarters had been subjected to vigorous theological criticism was an important factor in the writing of this book.

I am especially grateful to Jürgen Hübner. By sharing a seminar with him on the theme 'Principle of selection or principle of solidarity?', I have been able to profit from his specialist knowledge in biology and other natural sciences. I found his sophisticated view of the relationship between the natural sciences and theology, knowledge and faith, a valuable corrective. He read the manuscript through critically and prompted a series of corrections. I am also much obliged to Ulrich Duchrow for an equally critical reading of the whole manuscript. He has made me aware of the implications of this book for social ethics, of which I was not aware when I was writing it. I would need to write a new book to develop them. But this also enabled me to make a good deal of it more precise. Reflections arising from a shared seminar on 'Faith in Christ and Community Structure in the New Testament and in the Oecumene' have found a place above all in Parts Three and Four.

I have taken the Old Testament into account as well as the New. To this extent I have attempted a 'biblical theology'. Rolf Rendtorff and Rainer Albertz have given me much advice. Helga Weippert read critically the chapter on monotheism. I learnt a great deal from her comments, and some important expansions of it go back to her remarks. Finally, I would like to thank Frau Schmidt-Thomé for her careful typing of the manuscript.

This book is dedicated to my father on his seventy-seventh birthday. There is a connection between that and its subject-matter. As a teacher of mathematics and physics, my father has always been concerned with the relationship between the natural sciences and faith. This book is intended to be a contribution to that theme. Perhaps it would never have been written had I grown up in another home.

Heidelberg, October 1983

PART ONE

Evolution and Faith:
An Outline of the Theory of Evolution

There has been a profound change in the relationship between science, religion and the public. The following imagery may help to make this clear. Once religion was the party in power and science was the opposition. As the opposition party, it made use of a middle class which was becoming aware of its position to emancipate itself from the forces of the past (including religion). It brought the promise of a better life. By contrast, the evils of the past were blamed on religion, which had already had a long rule. In the meantime science has come to power. The technology and administrative apparatus which it has created govern our life from cradle to grave. Now science is suffering the fate of any party which has been in power for a long time: it is being blamed for all our ills. An innocent, everyday comment will show what I mean. My neighbour, a truck driver, reacted to the news of the death of someone he had known by asking, 'Why don't the doctors find a cure for cancer?' He did not ask, 'Why does God allow that?' A 'change of government' has come about in the consciousness of ordinary people, and it is not easy for science to function as a ruling party. Disillusionment with life soon becomes disillusionment with science, which has done so much to shape our lives. This gives rise to one of the basic problems in the relationship between science and the public. Now scientists have to court recognition from a society which has a tendency towards emotional detachment from the foundations of its own culture – from science, technology, economics and rationalized administration.

What is the situation of religion? Let me develop the imagery a bit further. Religion has largely accepted its move from the government benches to the opposition (that is, in areas where it has not taken on influential representative roles). But like every opposition party, it has sensed new opportunities, as dissatisfaction with the government has increased. Perhaps its delight has been premature. The established opposition parties – the traditional churches – have had to recognize that alternative opposition movements have arisen quite independently of them, new forms of religion, whose influence may have got as far as the back pews of the church, though it rarely reaches the pulpit.

For this very reason the present situation is a temptation for religion. Or to be more precise, it is a double temptation, since those concerned for religion can respond to the present situation with two quite different strategies.

First, in view of the increase in new irrational tendencies they could make a 'great coalition' with the technological world, prematurely brushing all the differences under the carpet. They could offer religion to scientific thought as a proven way of domesticating irrationality and guiding it along ordered channels.

Alternatively, they could take the lead in the opposition movement against the world of technology, presenting the fashionable criticism of science and technology. In that case, instead of a 'great coalition' we would have an extra-parliamentary opposition, which could claim that imagination, sensitivity and irrationality have always drawn upon its resources for their opposition to a rationalized world.

I want to argue for a third way. In a technological society religion should be the constructive opposition of a cognitive minority which is aware of its share of responsibility, even if it is not actually in power.

In the first chapter I shall demonstrate three contradictions between scientific thought and religious faith which exclude the possibility of a 'great coalition' in normal circumstances. That should lead to a pointed reformulation of the problem.

The second chapter seeks to outline the theoretical framework within which we shall be discussing the problem of the relationship between knowledge and faith, i.e. evolutionary theory in so far as it can be applied to phenomena of human history. Here it is necessary to clarify the relationship between biological and cultural evolution.

The third chapter will then demonstrate, with the aid of evolutionary categories, that from a more comprehensive perspective knowledge and faith can be shown to have much more in common, particularly in the three following contradictions which, to begin with, I shall deliberately exaggerate. Despite these contradictions, which rule out a 'great coalition', there is a 'state of life' within which science and faith can fruitfully supplement each other.

I

The Problem: Three Contradictions between Scientific Thought and Faith

1. Hypothetical scientific thought versus apodeictic faith

Most people think that science and faith are contradictory because they produce contradictory statements about the world and history. However, that is not the real problem. Both scientific and religious statements about reality keep changing. They may come closer together or grow further apart. They can be interpreted and 'translated'. However, even if we were to assume that the content of all the results of science could be reconciled with faith, a basic contradiction would remain. Scientific statements are hypothetical and the statements of faith are apodeictic.[1] Scientific statements are always 'if-then' statements; they depend on premises, methodology, an empirical basis. After he had visited Lüneberg Heath, a physicist was asked whether the sheep had been shorn yet. He did not reply apodeictically, either Yes or No. He said: 'As far as I could see, the sides of all the sheep presented to me were shorn!' He made his statement dependent on what he had observed. And that is true of all scientific statements. None of them claims unconditional validity. All are valid only until the next investigation refutes them. However, faith is apodeictic. It confesses what can be depended upon utterly in life and death. It calls on people to sacrifice their lives. No one is a martyr for a hypothesis, other than by dying for the freedom to express such a hypothesis. However, faith requires people to be ready for martyrdom. It is concerned with the unconditional, i.e. with a truth from which one cannot withdraw under any conditions. In short, scientific thought is hypothetical and faith is apodeictic.

2. Scientific thought is subject to falsification; faith goes against the facts

Scientific thought subjects itself to empirical data and historical examples. Strictly speaking, one instance is enough to refute or to modify a scientific hypothesis. Thus science is deliberately open to objections which may arise from the subject-matter. Faith is different. Granted, it is based on experience. It, too, has an 'empirical basis'. However, every faith has features which go against the facts. Every faith contradicts reality in some way. That is inevitable, if faith is to be an unconditional 'Yes' to life. Think of all the horrors that could contradict this 'Yes'! Think of all the oppressive experiences against which it has to be affirmed: all the probabilities and certainties, including the certainty of one's own death! Scientific thought is corrected by reference to facts; faith must contradict the oppressive force of facts. Science subjects itself to the 'facts', faith rebels against them. In a single sentence: scientific thought is subject to falsification, while faith goes against the facts.

3. Scientific thought delights in dissension; faith is based on a consensus

The two basic contradictions between science and faith mentioned above lead to two different kinds of institutions: science tends towards those which favour dissension, and faith towards those which protect consensus. As early as the second century AD the early church developed three social controls to protect consensus: the canon, i.e. a collection of writings which was regarded as authoritative; the *regula fidei*, a confession of faith to be made by everyone; and the episcopacy.[2] If we formalize these controls which protect consensus, we obtain three characteristics of community faith, which stand in marked contrast to the scientific process:

(*a*) Obligation to tradition: community faith depends on an existing normative tradition, while science has an obligation to innovate.

(*b*) Obligation to consensus: community faith has to make a solemn confession of statements with a particular content. There are binding credal formulations. By contrast, science is controlled dissent.

(*c*) Dependence on authority: community faith is impossible without the charisma of office. Particular people define what is 'valid'. By contrast, scientific thought is anti-authoritarian. What counts in it is not the weight of individuals, but the weight of arguments.

We must look at these three differences rather more closely.

(*a*) Obligation to tradition versus obligation to innovation

To think scientifically means to err in the direction of the future and to correct yesterday's errors by those of today. For today's scientific truth may well be out of date tomorrow. Therefore science puts a premium on originality. Anyone who differs from previously prevalent opinions is not necessarily a brilliant scientist (lunatics, too, are original), but every brilliant scientist has gone against accepted opinions and produced something new. By contrast, community faith puts a premium on fidelity to tradition. It has been given 'holy scripture' once and for all, and simply has to understand that scripture correctly. Of course scripture must constantly be reinterpreted anew. But to a great extent that also happens in science. What filters through from science to community faith often amounts to no more than crumbs from the table of science, which confirms the understanding the community already has of its faith. For of course every now and then (indeed, quite often) scientific thought arrives at conclusions which seem to confirm community faith.

(*b*) Obligation to consensus versus regulated dissent

Science is a matter of weighing alternatives, institutionalizing differences of opinion. Scientists search for rules to control these differences and call them 'methods'. These rules establish the criteria by which it is possible to assess the relative merits of alternative possibilities of explanation and interpretation. Thus at the beginning of his or her study every student is confronted with 'methods'; this often shocks them, as they are thirsty for results, content and opinions. However, no one can join in the scientific dispute over the truth without mastering methodology. Therefore decisive progress in science is always expressed in an extension of the methods at our disposal: the range of what can be discussed methodically constantly increases. By contrast, community faith tries to exclude disputes as far as possible by formal and informal support for consensus. For example, all ministers are solemnly bound in a public ceremony to be faithful to 'confessional documents'. And in principle that also applies to every member of the community: no one can become a member of the community without assenting to certain beliefs. This assent is often regarded as a quasi-moral obligation. The pressure of social expectations and interiorized preventive censorship play their part in ensuring conformity and consensus; in all groups and organizations those who hold office are subject to greater pressures to conformity than are others. They cannot be accused of any more serious offence than introducing unrest into communities. Dissent is undesirable. However, in science it is necessary.

(c) Dependence on authority versus 'discussion without domination'

Science is a matter of weighing up arguments without respect for persons. That means the ideal of 'discussion without domination' which science is obliged to carry on even where it denies it. It is true that many scientists use their power as examiners, experts or chairmen to protect their view of things from objections. However, science as a whole neutralizes these egoistic tendencies sooner or later. What colleague X would like to suppress will be taken up by colleague Y for that very reason – possibly for quite human motives. It is no coincidence that many dissertations begin with a scientific 'orgy of slaughtering predecessors'. In other words, nothing entertains the scientific public so much as the discrediting of authorities, provided that this happens on a high intellectual level. By contrast, community faith is oriented on authority. How many lay people are really well versed in their belief? They are content to trust that the minister has a solution to their problems; indeed today people find it easier to believe in a friendly minister than in God. But the friendly ministers, too, are not well versed in their belief. They trust in their theological teachers, who in turn look up to the senior professors who taught them. But in cases of doubt even these last may say no more than 'But our Lord Jesus Christ said...' We should see more than the negative side of this dependence on the faith of people whose authority is trusted; it is necessary for convictions of faith to be put forward convincingly by human beings. They do not carry weight without some 'respect for persons'. By contrast, scientific arguments lose none of their weight when they are put forward by alcoholics, despots or reactionaries.

To sum up: religious faith requires social support. It is always 'community faith'. It needs a community as a 'plausibility structure'.[3] Precisely because aspects of it go against the facts and it does not correspond with all the aspects of our experience of the world, it looks all the more for acceptance from the group. Everything is easier to believe when your neighbour believes it as well. Therefore all community faith bolsters itself up against objections by mechanisms of conformity (like obligation to tradition, the support of consensus and the charisma of office). That gives it stability and security.

By contrast, scientific thought constantly gnaws away at any consensus there may be. It wants to discuss alternatives and gives an opportunity to join in the argument to anyone who observes the rules of its methodology or can develop plausible new rules. Science may not bolster itself against objections. It must remain sensitive to objections. Regulations must be built into those societies in which it has been institutionalized (like universities) to counter the omnipresent tendency towards conformity.

There are tensions between scientific thought and community belief which should dissuade us from striving for 'a great coalition' between them. Science works with hypotheses and the falsification principle, and delights in dissent. Community faith is apodeictic; it goes against the facts and depends on consent.

Many people will protest against this contrast between scientific thought and faith, and rightly so. Are there not many structures of community piety in the venerable halls of science? Are not schools formed with recognized authorities whose aura 'conceals' theoretical deficiencies and inadequacies of method? Are there not successful cartels of praise and endorsement? What is happening when a successful senior professor enters the seminar and takes his place in a group which listens to him with respect and devotion? Science or community piety?

Indeed, do we not have to go further? Are structures of dependence limited to the external trappings of the pursuit of science? Is not every scientist indebted to pre-existing paradigms of research and thought? Is he not dependent on agreement over what is a scientifically reliable method? Is he not always in danger of being intolerant of what he thinks to be 'unscientific' views?

We should not deceive ourselves: in fact there is more indebtedness to tradition, more pressure to conform, more dependence on authority in science than a group of learned scientists, concerned to enhance their reputations, might be prepared to concede. And vice versa, there is more innovation, more discussion, more dissent in religious communities than the theoretical considerations I have sketched out would allow. In view of these discrepancies between theory and everyday experiences, must we not proceed 'scientifically' – and modify our theory? Is not perhaps what I have so far contrasted neither specifically 'scientific' nor 'religious', but simply 'human'?

So we are looking for a theory which can bring scientific thought and faith under the same 'denominator', as expressions of human life. The attempt that I shall put forward is based on evolutionary epistemology.[4] The fascinating thing about this theory is that for the first time it points to the possibilities and limitations of scientific thought not only within the framework of a philosophical conception but also within an empirically tested paradigm, which at present gives us the best chance of integrating our knowledge. This paradigm is the

theory of evolution.[5] It can interpret science and faith as different
structures for adapting to reality and derive its character as adaptation
from the interplay of variability and processes of selection.

My basic argument is that just as, in biological evolution, life has
developed through mutation and selection towards constantly new
forms of adaptation to reality, so too culture has developed different
forms of adapting to the basic conditions of reality – like science, art
and religion. Only when these complement and supplement one
another do they do justice to the richness of reality. Each of them is
an independent way of coming to grips with it. In this process, forms
can be established which are analogous to those in the processes of
mutation and selection. Therefore features common to knowledge and
faith can be established in the light of the basic categories of the theory
of evolution: 'adaptation', 'selection' and 'mutation'.

Before we can get down to this basic argument, I must clarify the
way in which it may be said that there are analogies between biological
and cultural evolution, so that we may be assume a continuity between
the two phases of evolution.

II

Biological and Cultural Evolution:
Analogies and Differences

Cultural evolution is not simply the continuation of biological evolution[6] but a higher form of it, so that one can speak of a hierarchical superiority of cultural evolution to biological evolution in humanity.[7] Nevertheless, there is a continuity between biological and cultural evolution – not only because as living creatures human beings are still subject to the laws of biological evolution, but because the same fundamental processes run their course in both cases. In both areas development presupposes: 1. the appearance of variation; 2. a selection from the variants; and 3. their preservation. This is the only way of arriving at successful forms of biological and cultural adaptation to reality.

1. The variability of forms of life

In biological evolution, the variability of forms of life comes about through mutation and recombination, i.e. through the change and exchange of genetic information.[8]

Mutations are changes in the sequences of nucleic acids. In all living beings, the same elements are present, reorganized by mutations. The genetic code is universal. As a rule the genetic information remains constant over successive generations and in this way guarantees that all instances of a species resemble one another. However, nature leaves a little free play, a margin for error, a possibility of variation. Most deviations within genetic information lead to the destruction of the organism or to a diminished fitness and therefore do not last. Very rarely, however, creative mutations emerge which enhance their functionality. The individuals concerned get a better chance of propagation than others.

A second source of variability is the recombination of genes by sexual propagation. On the one hand the different individuals of a species must have enough genetic information in common to be able to exchange genes and have common descendants. On the other hand, the exchange of hereditary dispositions within a species leads to an infinite variety of individuals, since in the combination of the genes of both parents there is such a variety of possibilities that in genetic terms each individual is in fact unique – with the exception of identical twins.

There are analogies to these forms of process in cultural evolution. Every cultural innovation is a kind of 'mutation'; while it takes over traditional elements, by combining them in a new way it creates something that was not there before: this may be a new theory, technology, art or ethics.[9] Every creative innovation takes place in the context of many vain attempts; each genius is accompanied by many 'crackpots'(whom later perspectives sometimes rehabilitate). In cultural evolution, too, most deviations from the accepted norm prove to be 'dysfunctional'. However, there would be no development without deviation from the already existing patterns of life.

Just as in biological evolution, genetic exchange in the form of sexual propagation represents an 'institutionalized' form of the production of variations, so in human history cultural exchange is a constant stimulus to new developments. Often an innovation becomes established only when it has found a practicable form as the result of such exchange. Thus writing was probably invented in Sumeria and Egypt, but it was only the people of Phoenicia, involved in exchanges between both cultures, who took the decisive step of using letters, the basis of the modern alphabet.

What is the decisive difference between biological mutations and cultural innovations? Mutations have no direction. They happen by chance. One cannot predict where and when and in what form they will appear. Granted, there are induced as well as spontaneous mutations – mutations induced by changes of temperature, radiation or chemicals. However, these mutations too have no direction, i.e. radiation does not produce mutations which enable the organism to tolerate radiation more easily. It simply increases the quantity of mutations[10] and thus indirectly the chances of arriving at a higher tolerance of radiation through blind trial and error. In the light of the result one can therefore see creative mutations as a response to a problem: it is as though a particular problem produced the form of life which was appropriate to it. But that is a *post-factum* anthropomorphic interpretation. In it we are projecting our experience of cultural innovations on to nature. For the 'mutations' of human history can indeed be interpreted as deliberate answers to problems. They are 'directed'. People are looking for a solution. However, this decisive difference should not conceal the fact that cultural innovations, too, have their 'chance' aspect. An inventor does not by any means foresee all the consequences of his invention. He often solves problems which originally he did not intend to. Many of his attempts at solution have an element of blind trial and error to them. In short, the range of human consciousness is limited. Therefore from a wider perspective, the 'directed' innovations of culture, too, seem to be chance and undirected mutations.[11]

Moreover, mutations are always somatic. By contrast, cultural innovations are fixed outside the body – in products, language, writing and imagery. In principle, therefore, they can be handed on to anyone. So cultural exchange is a long-term process. In a 'mixed marriage' between members of different cultures the genes are exchanged only when sexual intercourse leads to conception and birth. However, to the process of cultural exchange there is no end, and that also involves people who are not genetically akin. What biological and cultural evolution do have in common, though, is that exchange heightens the variability of forms of life and as a result creates possibilities for development. And much as cultural exchange is deliberately achieved and sought, it also has a natural, organic character: people rightly say that some customs simply 'lose colour'.

2. The selection of variants

In biological evolution it is the selection of directionless mutations which first provides a direction towards higher functionality. From chance variants those are 'picked out' that are best suited. Again, the term 'selection' is a crude anthropomorphism;[12] underlying it is the image of the breeder who by crossing certain specimens which he has deliberately chosen breeds particular properties from them. Natural selection runs its course without such a guiding hand. Selection first of all means unequal chances of handing on genetic information from one generation to the next. This chance is reduced or heightened in very different ways.

Contrary to a widespread prejudice, the strongest do not always have the best chance; those have it who are best adapted to the inward and outward circumstances of their life. Here 'adaptation' should not be understood as a tautology, as though adaptation were the basis for enhanced chances of propagation, and these were the essential characteristic of successful 'adaptation'. Rather, adaptation consists in the fact that the structure and repertoire of behaviour of an organism already contains a good deal of advance information about the environment, so that it can live in it.

In practice, the selection of the most appropriate variants happens in a variety of ways. It may be in aggression between species – the one who can plunder more effectively or escape its enemies more effectively has a greater chance of propagation than others. Another way is rivalry within species, whether through ritualized combat for access to sexual partners or territories, or through the sexual preference extended to more attractive partners. Finally, selection takes place through sickness and hunger, i.e. on the basis of different capacities to resist infections or different abilities to assess possibilities of food.

We should guard against the notion that selection consists in a direct fight for existence. Here, too, we would be projecting human circumstances on to nature: with human beings, every struggle for better opportunities quickly leads to aggression and hate. However, in nature, selection can go on peacefully. Flowers do not fight one another – and yet a harsh selection takes place among them. In biological evolution, variants with differing degrees of adaptation to the same environment compete without being aware of their rivalry (and without hate).

'Selection' within cultural evolution is distinguished by the replacement of the hard selection of biological evolution with 'soft' strategies.[13] Human beings 'select' the most effective cultural patterns of behaviour by learning processes in order to combat harsh selection through diminished chances of survival and propagation. We learn through 'reinforcement'. We can distinguish three forms of learning:

1. In trial-and-error learning, human beings choose the most successful modes of behaviour from a number of attempts and include them in their repertory of behaviour. This form of behaviour can already be found among intelligent lower animals: even among rats, behaviour reinforced by success leads to an increased probability of the occurrence of this behaviour. However, the human characteristic is that we can consciously recall past instances of trial and error. Human beings evaluate their experiences by retracing them in their minds.

2. In imitative learning, human beings take over finished patterns of behaviour from successful models, which are vicariously reinforced. That saves them time-wasting effort in trial-and-error learning. This form of learning can be found in man's nearest animal relative, the ape. A characteristic human feature might be that man can also orient himself on models represented by symbols (pictures giving directions, or idols).

3. In learning by solving problems (or learning through insight) human beings anticipate reality in an inner model and carry out various operations in their imagination, deciding in advance what operations are to be reinforced and what are not. Only then do they carry out the action. This also enables them to deal properly with new situations straight away and without a model to go by. Although the beginnings of learning by solving problems can be found among chimpanzees, who are highly intelligent, generally speaking this is a specifically human way of 'learning'.

In every form of human learning the 'reinforcement' of modes of behaviour takes the place of selection between individuals who behave in particular ways. This reinforcement may come about through recollection; it happens vicariously, or it may be anticipated in the imagination. Selection is replaced by 'reinforcement', which in the human sphere includes deliberate processes of selection (though among human beings, too, there is unconscious reinforcement). We can make a decision between different possibilities and work out the situation in the most appropriate way. However, we are still subject to the pressure to adapt to external reality. The difference is that we have at our disposal not only 'advance information' about the environment, but in addition a wealth of consciously learnt information which makes it possible for us to 'evade' the pressure of reality through successful adaptation, namely by changing our behaviour.

By this flexible capacity for learning, unlike all other highly-developed living beings, human beings have 'adapted' to live almost anywhere in the world. They can diminish the pressure of selection by constantly looking for new areas. Above all, by constructing artificial 'living space' they can increase the chance of each person finding a world to live in which is 'adapted' to his or her disposition and interests. Every profession provides such artificial living space, as does every house and every society. This increases the chance that every person can find 'systems of reinforcement' by his or her own choice. Human beings also diminish the pressure of selection by differentiation in behaviour.

Culture begins where human beings reduce the pressure of selection by intelligent behaviour, i.e. it also makes human life possible where it would have no chance of survival without its deliberate intervention. Culture is a diminution of selection through change and differentiation in behaviour. At the same time it creates new forms of the pressure of selection: 'hard' selection is replaced by 'soft' selection.

It is worth explaining this difference once again. Hard selection consists in the unequal distribution of physical opportunities. From the loser's perspective that means that selection takes place through the death of individuals and the extinction of species (or of variants within the species). From the perspective of the 'winner' selection means life at the expense of other life. One's own life and that of descendants is possible because rival life has no chance of survival.

In culture, this hard selection, which involves the physical existence of individuals and species, is replaced by 'soft' selection. This latter does not involve human beings themselves but their attitudes. Forms of human behaviour can 'die out' without the death of their representatives. In other words, patterns of behaviour can become established at the cost of other patterns of behaviour without the extinction of those who practise them. Individuals and groups have a chance to adopt new forms of behaviour. They can 'learn'.

Of course this is only a possibility. The capacity to learn, i.e. the chance to change behaviour, can save hard selection. However, for that very reason, the capacity to learn in turn becomes the most important criterion for physical survival in culture. Where it is absent, hard selection begins within culture. To express it in a formula: culture means a reduction of selection. However, ineptitude for culture again subjects us to the laws of hard selection. The more complex the culture, the greater the learning achievements which it requires, and the more numerous the individuals who do not seem 'adapted to culture'. An inability to adapt to culture can manifest itself both individually and socially. Individually it appears as psychosis and neurosis, mania and suicide, criminality and negligence. All these phenomena, which are clearly on the increase, are consequences of the refusal of more and more people to meet the demands of their cultural environment. They are the losers in society, among whom an ineptitude for learning and the reduction in opportunities to learn as a result of social deprivation can also lead to harsh selection, i.e. diminished possibilities of survival and propagation.

At a social level, a failure to adapt to a culture expresses itself in great social catastrophes: in an inability to find peace internally or externally. In wars we clearly find an undisguised, 'hard' pressure of selection: military, technological, economic and administrative superiority – qualities all based on intelligent learning – give some cultures greater chances of survival in wars than rival cultures. Diplomatic and social deficiencies lead to decline.

That, precisely, is the dilemma of human culture: it should serve to diminish the pressure of selection, but frequently it simply creates a new, merciless pressure of selection which often seems to us to be more senseless and cruel than natural selection. Granted, the capacity for intelligent learning puts us in a position to kill off hypotheses instead of people.[14] However, this very capacity also increases our power to destroy people. Human beings come to be threatened by their own culture, and beside this threat, the threats from the natural environment, which still exist, seem to fade into the background.

Because human beings now find their own culture a great problem, they often become unaware that human culture as a whole is also subject to the pressure of selection from reality. Human learning through reinforcement which is recalled, perceived or anticipated, is successful only when it leads to appropriate reactions to the whole of reality in all its conditions. We are often so preoccupied with adapting to cultural demands that we forget that cultural systems of reinforcement are themselves only ways of adapting to a reality which extends beyond humanity. It has taken the ecological movement to make us newly aware of this.

3. The preservation of forms of life

In biological evolution, mutation and selection lead to a development towards increasingly differentiated organisms only if improvements which have once been achieved are not lost again, and are protected from chance deteriorations. In nature there are remarkable processes which ensure the reduplication of forms of life. The transmission of properties once attained is relatively rigid – and has to be. For the greater the differentiation in the organism, the greater the probability that changes will bring deterioration.

Not only transmission but also separation protects the preservation of forms of life. If a few founding individuals are isolated in an area and cut off from others of their species, the exchange of genes with the population as a whole ceases. The chance selection from the gene-pool of the population which is present in the founder-individuals is given an enhanced opportunity of propagation. Divergent forms of life can be stabilized. In addition to genetic reduplication and separation there is only a very wasteful third way of 'preserving' something in biological evolution: blind and fortuitous repetition. If a mutation has failed to establish itself, it may well emerge again later – and prove itself to be functional in other circumstances. Of course one must be very cautious in describing this course of blind 'repetition' as a way of preserving forms of life.

Again, cultural evolution works with analogous processes: it substitutes tradition for genetic transmission, cultural identity for separation, and in this way can also preserve individual and improbable experiences. Nevertheless, in some respects it too is forced back on 'blind repetition'.

Tradition is the transference of non-genetic information from one generation to the next. It makes possible the exploitation of individual learning even after the death of an individual, and has led to an accumulation of knowledge and capacities which goes far beyond the capacity of any individual and which can be put into practice only by specialists. Enhanced chances of life by a secure transmission of tradition probably encouraged groups of people to regard tradition as something sacred. Perhaps there is even a human tendency (to which our genes predispose us?) to believe what we are told in childhood.[15] That certainly has a disadvantage: tradition becomes an end in itself so that prejudices and follies which it protects often cling on tenaciously. The advantage is that by their tenacious (and often irrational) clinging to tradition, human beings are also given the chance to keep in store ideas which might contain the solution for problems still unknown.

Furthermore, the separation of cultures also plays a part in the development of cultural variety: cultures must develop an identity of their own without which the traditions latent in them cannot unfold. Granted, in an age of global communication we are quick to regard mechanisms of cultural isolation as disadvantages. However, they can also have a positive function: only when cultures and societies have an inner equilibrium does the exchange of cultural information become a creative process (and not just the adoption of other experiences of learning).

Human tradition and genetic 'transmission' are fundamentally quite different. Tradition takes place through deliberate effort. It, too, is relatively rigid. However, in the same way, just as at one stage individual experience has found a way into it, so in principle each individual has a chance to change it by his or her contribution. Nevertheless, one should not have any illusions about the 'natural growth' of traditions. They too are often blind and mechanical. They demonstrate a remarkable capacity to resist intelligent attempts to change them: myths usually survive attempts at demythologization. And like biological evolution, cultural tradition, too, is directed towards 'repetition': there are experiences which can hardly be handed down, and which each generation has to have for itself. Tradition cannot replace them; at best it will elucidate them.

To sum up: cultural evolution replaces 1. chance mutations and recombinations through innovations, which are *a priori* aimed at the solution of certain problems, but which in a wider context still occur 'blindly'. It replaces 2. selection through 'reinforcement', which is recalled, perceived and anticipated – i.e. through a 'selection' in human imagination which anticipates the external pressure of selection and makes it less harsh. It replaces 3. genetic transmission with tradition, which draws on individual experience and therefore can be modified by it – and which nevertheless often takes place as mechanically as 'inheritance'.

The forms of the process of cultural evolution transcend those of biology. This transformation is brought about by the intervention of human consciousness to give direction to the process. Therefore the step from the biological to the cultural phase is an 'evolution of evolution'.[16] The decisive factors in evolution – variation, selection and preservation – change, for all the affinity of structure, which continues to remain. This structural affinity also emerges clearly when human consciousness comes up against limits. That is to be expected from the start: if the forms of process in biological evolution change within cultural evolution as a result of human consciousness, at the limits of consciousness they must again approximate to blind biological processes, without being identical to them.

In the next chapter I shall consider knowledge and faith as two different patterns of behaviour in cultural evolution, both of which underlie the specific forms of the process of cultural evolution. What is common in both these expressions of life must be discovered with the aid of categories drawn from the theory of evolution. In anticipation, it may be said that in faith the structural proximity to the forms of the process of biological evolution will be greater than in the case of knowledge. For faith struggles at the limits of human consciousness, even if it is more than just a 'limit-awareness'. We can therefore put it at different stages in the theory of evolution: on the one hand as a transitional phenomenon between biological and cultural evolution – as the echo of an archaic prehistory – and on the other as an anticipation of future possibilities of evolution, which have not yet reached the level of our consciousness.

III

Knowledge and Faith as Complementary
Expressions of Life:
Relativizing the Contradictions

Science and faith can be illuminated by the basic categories of the theory of evolution: in both instances there are processes of adaptation, selection and mutation. The three contradictions between knowledge and faith sketched at the beginning can be relativized by means of these categories. In anticipation I shall formulate a thesis about each of these contradictions:

1. Hypothetical scientific thought and apodeictic faith are different forms of adapting to an unknown reality.

2. Science controlled by falsification and faith which goes against the facts are different forms of coping with the pressure of selection exercised by reality.

3. Science which delights in dissent and faith which depends on consensus are different forms of the openness of our spiritual life to mutations.

I am aware that many people will find these theses bizarre and strange. All that I will say at this point is that categories from the theory of evolution have been successfully applied to that most differentiated of human activities, the process of knowing. In connection with evolutionary epistemology I might mention the names of K.Popper, K.Lorenz, G.Vollmer and R.Riedl.[17] Is it hopeless from the start to interpret religion, too, with the help of ideas from the theory of evolution? The first attempts in this direction are to be found in Anglo-Saxon scholarship: the psychologist D.Campbell,[18] the marine biologist Sir A.Hardy,[19] and the meteorologist R.W.Burhoe;[20] one might also add the German scientist H.v.Ditfurth.[21] The fact that these approaches are not noted in German theology or are virtually unknown there need not necessarily tell against them.

1. Science and faith as ways of coping with an unknown reality

Evolutionary epistemology regards the hypotheses of human knowledge as a continuation of that comprehensive process of adaptation of life to reality which governs all organic structures. Knowledge is the adaptation of cognitive structures to reality, the accommodation of thought to experience. Conversely: life forms knowledge.[22]

Organic structures and processes to some degree 'reflect' the environment when they act as though they were informed about its laws. Knowledge is therefore a continuation of life generally. But what is faith? From the perspective of evolutionary theory, a human being, too, can also be interpreted as a structure adapted to the basic conditions of reality. The only question is: which reality?

There are scientists who are ready to accept the interpretation of religious faith as a human structure of adaptation to reality. However, they understand reality to be what the scientists say about it. In that case religious faith is a structure of adaptation which has meanwhile become obsolete; it was all right for our forebears, who had a deficient insight into the true connection of things, but is no longer possible for modern men and women.

This is the point at which thinking in terms of the theory of evolution begins; it can make room for a better understanding of religion. It is not a matter of grounding faith in science but of demonstrating the complementary and compatible character of faith and knowledge. To anticipate, I might mention the three decisive theses:

(*a*) Like any other interpretation, the scientific picture of the world (including the theory of evolution) is not identical with reality, but is a form of adaptation to reality characteristic of mankind. Reality in itself is 'other' and mysterious.

(*b*) Evolution has made possible partially successful structures of adaptation which are given with life and which enable us to have experiences of resonance – experiences of harmony between subject and reality – in which we detect in reality something that corresponds to us.

(*c*) In the present state of our knowledge and error the theory of evolution gives us an impressive picture of the unity of all reality. Behind all the phenomena we have intimations of a central reality which determines and conditions everything.

(*a*) The intrinsic mystery of reality

Living beings grasp reality only as it appears to them, and not as it is in itself. Living beings find orientation in their world by 'assimilating' the influx of sense experiences, possibilities of knowledge and patterns of interpretation. Even human beings are no exception to this. They live in their specific world, which is bound up with their organic, technical and intellectual shaping of it. Their world may be the most complex and differentiated of all worlds. It may transcend the world of a frog or a cow in every respect. But even their world is bound up with the capacities of their senses and brains.[23] They have just one advantage: human beings are the first to know that the world they experience and reality are two different 'realities'. They have always suspected that. Religions and philosophies make a distinction between the world of appearances and the world in itself. But only modern physics has succeeded in demonstrating empirically that our categories of space, time and causality are structures for adapting to the reality around us which have only limited validity. Evolutionary epistemology was the first to provide an anthropological explanation for this state of affairs: space, time and causality are structures of adaptation with limited validity because they make it possible for *homo sapiens* in his current stage of evolution to find enough of an orientation in reality to be able to survive. Thus evolutionary epistemology confirms a first basic experience of any religion, namely that behind the familiar human world a mysterious other world opens up which appears only indirectly, brokenly and symbolically in the world that we experience and interpret. At this point there is no contradiction between religion and knowledge – even if faith goes beyond what we 'know'.

(*b*) The possibility of 'experiences of resonance'

Reality in itself is more mysterious than is indicated by what we can discover of it through the sciences. However, even what we do understand about it is quite amazing: again and again the world as interpreted by the sciences corresponds to our cognitive needs for order, symmetry and regularity. Evolutionary epistemology can explain this adaptation of the world to humanity as an adaptation of humanity to the world: we bring to it *a priori* thought categories which match objective reality because these thought categories have made it possible for human beings to cope with life successfully.

Before any experience whatsoever we are pre-programmed to arrange our impressions according to space and time, to look for causal connections, to note evocative forms and to combine them in analogies. Such pre-programmed patterns of assimilation – the *a priori* elements in our experiences – are the results of genealogical development in which environmental factors select the best attempts at adaptation from the many which have arisen by chance. Organisms with the best cognitive structures of adaptation had better chances of increase and became our ancestors. Apes with bad eyesight missed the branches on to which they wanted to jump and soon became dead apes. That ruled them out as possible forebears. In other words, because organisms whose neural structures were pre-programmed to look for regularities in the environment increased rather than others, and because we are their descendants, we are now *a priori* convinced of the regularity of nature. With considerable internal evidence we argue from a limited number of cases to all cases without being able to provide a rational justification for this inductive conclusion. Rather, belief in the possibility of inductive generalization from observations is 'innate' in us. It is a proven hypothesis about the basic structure of reality, a hypothesis which has not been put forward by any single individual but which has been tested by the genus in a long unconscious process of trial and error. We would not exist if this hypothesis did not in part correspond with reality.

Here is an illustration to clarify this correspondence between objective reality and subjective thought categories. The rules of chess are an *a priori* human construction, the free play of human imagination. Would we not be utterly amazed if we noted that reality outside our human world also acted in accordance with the rules of chess? Similarly, mathematical laws and rules are purely *a priori* constructions of our understanding. Here, however, we are continually amazed by the fact that natural processes can be described by these rules and formulae.[24] Must not any open-minded person find this correspondence between reality and our understanding of it quite amazing? I have suggested calling such experiences 'experiences of resonance'.[25]

The 'nomological' experience of resonance which I have just described is only one form of them. Another is the experience of animate nature. We and all living beings have the same genetic code within us – all organisms, plants and animals do, from single cells to the most sophisticated forms. We are parts of the same living stream and constantly experience it as something that makes us happy – for example when we recover from a long illness and our bodily functions are again adapted to the conditions of reality.

The experience of aesthetic resonance shows us reality (for the moment) as a lovely game which is an end in itself. Here too it corresponds amazingly with what we are. An *a priori* sensitivity to form, developed by evolution, is stimulated in us without being made the tool of instrumental ends: the forms of nature and art set something in motion within us which escapes everyday awareness.

We have an experience of resonance whenever we reach understanding with other human beings; this is especially intense in erotic fascination, in the awareness of belonging indissolubly together.

All this happiness is the result of an infinitely long process of evolution which has led to increasingly more adequate structures of adaptation. We grow up with an 'irrational' basic trust that our organic and intellectual equipment has an 'adaptation value', that it corresponds to the basic conditions of reality – in us and around us – before we have made a single conscious effort to correspond to it. All experiences of resonance therefore lead to an affirmation of life.[26]

All these are caught up in an existential experience of resonance. The fact that anything exists at all then appears as amazing as the fact that we ourselves are alive. The chanceness and unfathomableness of being finds its echo in our own chance and unfathomable existence. This experience may oppress some people. Often it is bound up with an intense feeling of happiness: in that case the existential experience of resonance is the emotional reaction to the successful adaptation which is already given with the mere fact of our existence and on which we may always rely in our lives. In it, human beings detect that the whole of their existence – from their organic structures to the most sophisticated patterns of perception – corresponds to objective data, indeed that all these subjective structures are ultimately called forth by reality lying beyond humanity and represent its weak echo. Experience of resonance are experiences of the contingent match between subject and reality – before any effort, before any achievement, before any 'work', as we theologians are fond of saying. In them the successful creatureliness of mankind rejoices.

(c) The 'central' reality

It might be asked what justification we have for relating the various experiences of resonance to a single reality. There are religious interpretations of the world which take account of various basic forces. The monotheistic conviction that a single reality determines all things has become historical. However, this particular conviction is confirmed rather than refuted by evolutionary thought.

At the moment the theory of evolution is the best paradigm for integrating the multiplicity of our experiences. Today, to put it in anthropomorphic terms, we see the whole process of reality as a quest for 'stable' configurations: atoms look for stable constellations of rare gases because these are favourable to energy. So they combine themselves into molecules and form permanent bonds. These bonds become chains of molecules, polymers, some of which by chance 'invent' the marvellous technique of reproducing themselves, so that life can arise – all the way to human culture with its abundance of models, shapes and forms. In the beginning was hydrogen: protons, electrons, neutrons and quarks. The multiplicity of reality was created by blind 'trial and error' out of a few basic elements and with the aid of a few basic forces. In this process, secure 'stable configurations' were constantly found up to the point when humanity came into being, consciously in search of permanent ways of organizing matter, life and society.

The extension of the theory of evolution both into the abiotic sphere[27] and into the sphere of human culture has shown us the unity of reality in a completely new way – even if we are still a long way from being able to incorporate all phenomena into this paradigm. The theory of evolution can only correspond to the present state of our knowledge and error. Later, quite new connections will probably occur to us. But when that happens, the unity of reality will probably become even clearer. For a look back to the history of science up till now shows that attempts to interpret reality as a unity achieved success only step by step. One important step was Newton's demonstration that the power which determines the courses of the planets is identical with the power which makes an apple fall to the ground. Another step was Maxwell's discovery that magnetism and electricity can be embraced within one and the same theory – and also that light is a variant of electro-magnetic waves. A third step was Einstein's theory of relativity, through which energy and mass can be interpreted as different manifestations of the same reality. Steps towards a greater unitary conception are continually 'reinforced'. We can guess at the next step: perhaps we shall recognize more clearly the unity of reality and time. The intuition is becoming increasingly inevitable that the mysterious reality-in-itself to which we are related in all our structures of adaptation is a single central reality, which discloses itself to us step by step under various aspects. Scientific theories are in fact only one variant of human structures for adapting to it.

Provisionally, we may say that knowledge and faith are different structures for adapting to reality. They supplement and confirm each other in respect of three basic experiences:

1. Behind the world that we interpret there is an intrinsic reality which we cannot yet grasp adequately.

2. Our life is a structure of adaptation to this reality which is always already partially successful.

3. All attempts at adaptation relate to a single 'central' reality.

A simile from an age-old tradition may illustrate the indissoluble connection of these three basic experiences.[28]

The eye is a structure in which the skin is adapted to sunlight. It is constructed in such a way that it is completely informed about all the laws of optics. We can infer from this organ of adaptation the reality to which it is adapted; indeed, we can say that light has produced the eye by positively consolidating chance changes of the skin so that it becomes more sensitive to light. Therefore it is possible to argue that where there are eyes there must also be light.

But we also know that this conclusion has only limited validity. There is more than 'light'. For the eye changes only a small frequency range of electromagnetic waves into visual impressions. It is blind to ultra-violet and infra-red rays. It is only a partially successful organ of adaptation: enough to give us the orientation that we need in order to live.

When we see with the help of the eye, we are certainly unaware that all optical information has ultimately one origin, the sun, whose light, reflected in various ways, from various directions and in various constellations, makes contact with our retina. We attribute colour, form and position to external objects. In practice, a causal attribution of light waves to the sun would be meaningless. Only through a conscious act of attention does it become clear to us that the sun is the ultimate origin of the waves of which we make use.

Suppose that we transfer this imagery to human beings: to our brain, the vehicle of our reason, our will, our imagination.[29] From the perspective of evolutionary theory our brain, too, is simply the same kind of organ of adaptation as the eye. From its rationality we can argue to an objective pre-existing rationality which made the evolution of the brain possible. Here, too, however, it is the case that our brains comprehend only a small part of that objective rationality and meaningfulness. For the brain, too, there is an infinitely large realm of 'ultra-violet' and 'infra-red' – not to mention other dimensions. Just as the eye was produced as a result of light, so we can now say that our understanding, too, was called forth by a far superior reality, which finds only an inadequate echo in the activities of our reason. Finally, it is also true of our understanding that it is mostly concerned with causal attributions which are relevant in practice: it sees only the world, and must turn its attention in a particular direction if it is to become aware of itself and understand itself as the outcome of an ultimate reality. Not everyone gets that far. Seldom has anyone found better words for this self-interpretation of human reason than Albert Einstein:

You will hardly find one among the profounder sort of scientific minds without a religious feeling of his own. But it is different from the religiosity of the naive man... (It) takes the form of a rapturous amazement at the harmony of natural law, which reveals an intelligence of such superiority that, compared with it, all the systematic thinking and acting of human beings is an utterly insignificant reflection.[30]

But what is that mysterious ultimate reality towards which all our organic, intellectual and religious structures develop attempts at adaptation? Religious tradition knows only one appropriate term for it: God. For religion, it is the unknown goal of all attempts at adaptation. All organic, intellectual, social, religious and aesthetic structures are hypotheses aimed at depicting, corresponding to and doing justice to that ultimate reality from some perspective. The whole evolutionary world-process – from the smallest microphysical entities to the galaxies, from individual cells to the brain, from the most scurrilous myths to the most sophisticated theoretical systems – strives towards finding increasingly more adequate structures for adapting to this ultimate reality. In other words, the world is a hypothesis to do justice to God. Scientific theories are only part of this comprehensive process. The whole of life is 'hypothetical'.

In his novel *The Man without Properties*, R.Musil has the hero, Ulrich, a mathematician in search of religious experience, making the following remarks:

Now all kinds of once-favourite ideas came to mind, from the earliest time of the first self-awareness of youth, which we find it so touching and shattering to look back on again later, including the phrase 'live hypothetically'. It still expressed the courage and the involuntary ignorance of life in which every step is a new risk without experience, and the wish for wider contexts and the hint of the possibility of being wrong, which a young man feels when he steps out hesitatingly into life... The will of his own nature to develop forbids him to believe in perfection; but everything that he encounters acts as though it were perfect. He suspects that this order is not as firm as it makes out: no thing, no I, no form, no principle is certain; everything is caught up in an invisible but never resting change; there is more of the future in the insecure than in the secure, and the present is no more than a hypothesis, beyond which one has not progressed. What more can he do than keep away from the world in the good sense that a scholar remains detached from facts which seek to mislead him, to make him believe in them prematurely?[31]

Here once again we find the basic principle of science: not to believe in anything too hastily. To begin with, such an attitude appears in sharp contrast to 'unconditional faith' - but not if we recognize that not only our knowledge but the whole of life is a 'hypothesis'. Faith is a matter of becoming aware of this situation – becoming aware of that comprehensive hypothetical process to which all being that can be known in the world is subject and which has found a successful form in scientific thought. Although everything may be uncertain in this hypothetical process (even if in fact there are many tested structures of adaptation which we may trust), one thing is in any case certain: all hypotheses, i.e. all partially successful structures of adaptation, are related to a pre-existing ultimate reality, which encounters us as resistance, which rejects or accepts our attempts. For without this relation to a pre-existing reality there would be no reason to correct anything. Without this relationship a hypothesis would not be a hypothesis. Precisely because everything may be hypothetical, this certainty is unconditional and apodeictic.

In conclusion I might stress that faith is more than becoming aware of the hypothetical process of life and the world. It can be combined with cognitive clarity. But it is similarly the emotional and motivational reaction to this state of affairs, even when it is not consciously articulated. Faith consists in the attempt to understand the whole of life as a response to that ultimate reality: as an always incomplete hypothetical way of corresponding to it.

2. Science and faith as ways of coping with the pressure of selection

The second contradiction between scientific thought and religious faith was that science works through falsification, allowing its theories to fail by the touchstone of reality, while faith goes against the facts. Faith encourages us to say Yes to life (and to the symbols which form its foundation), even against the facts. This contradiction, too, can be relativized in terms of the theory of evolution. Here scientific thought and faith both struggle in comparable ways against the pressure of selection from reality.

The theory of evolution enlightens us about connections which are remote from us when we are having happy experiences of resonance. It tells us that all successful structures of adaptation have come into being as a result of a long process of selection, in the course of which less successful forms of adaptation failed, and only the best-fitted survived. To put it another way: all successful knowledge, all happiness is based on the suffering of countless creatures. We ourselves experience the limits of successful adaptation in our lives: sickness, death, injustice, isolation – all these are experiences of absurdity in which reality contradicts our experiences of resonance and harmony with it. In all this we are shown the ultimate reality towards which all our 'hypotheses' and all our life are aimed, from a completely different aspect: as the merciless pressure of selection, as resistance, as a limit. This pressure of selection is at work on different levels.[32]

On the biological level it is the case that all life's structures of adaptation, all organs, all forms of behaviour and experience (so far as they are genetically conditioned) have come into being through mutation and selection. Only what is compatible with the basic conditions of reality can survive. Everything else has a lesser probability of propagation. It has less chance of living. Thus in biological evolution the ultimate reality proves to be a power which controls from the outside, often by means of cruel selection; it builds up and destroys, and through the process of mutation and selection, in endless series of generations, produces an amazing variety of adapted structures whose preservation we regard as something holy.

Comparable laws are at work in cultural evolution. Patterns of social behaviour, too, are subject to a kind of 'selection'. The new thing here is that patterns of behaviour can be given up or changed without the death or the extinction of those involved in them. Human beings can change their minds. They can be 'converted' to the better when they see that the way in which they are behaving will lead to disaster. But here, too, there are limits. Conversion always begins with individuals. However, it is hard for individuals by themselves to avoid collective patterns of behaviour and experience, even when it is obvious that these are leading to historical catastrophes. Think of all those people who had to watch helplessly fifty years ago while a whole society adopted the arrogant and inhuman system of Fascist behaviour with tacit approval – although many already had inklings of its collapse, that collapse which is still sounding in our ears and which one hopes will continue to resound for a long time yet in human consciousness. And how many people today are afraid that they will be caught up into a catastrophe which would mean the end of our culture because of the atavistic way in which states are behaving towards one another! Again we are faced with a power which comes upon us from outside, which permits systems of behaviour and lets them be destroyed when they are incompatible with the basic conditions of reality – with that objective power on whom the great prophets who preached disaster called as Yahweh in the historical crises and catastrophes of Israel and who, they trusted, even in the worst catastrophes would give them the chance of a new beginning.

The same pressure of selection, however, is also exerted by reality on each individual, and not just in the physical collapse of death. Even while we are alive, each one of us experiences the failure of our plans. The pressure of reality shows itself in crises of identity in which previous interpretations of ourselves collapse, proving to be false convictions which are hostile to life; these may be crises in work or crises in relationships. Again we are given a clear warning from the reality that determines us, which seems to say: 'You can't do that!' And again, religious awareness articulates these crises as a call to repentance and sees the chance of a new beginning in the collapse of old forms of life.

We must also include science in this series of experiences; indeed it has special significance in combating the pressure of selection from reality: it deliberately tests its hypotheses to destruction on reality. Assured results, absolute truths, irrefutable principles are expected from science. The scientific process consists in constantly re-examining and revising supposedly 'assured' results. In principle it is impossible to make a complete verification of universal conclusions based on empirical observation, since we can always examine, test and investigate only a limited number of cases. Assured results come only from the falsification of hypotheses. Science is a matter of erring in a forward direction. The decisive thing for us is that science does not attempt to evade the resistance of reality, but deliberately exposes its hypotheses to this resistance. It affirms this resistance.

In the end, behind the various forms of the pressure of reality, behind the pressure of selection (in the narrower sense), historical catastrophes, crises of identity and the falsification of our hypotheses lies the same central reality which sets limits to human arbitrariness and all life, which compels a harsh schooling in reality and often acts cruelly and inexorably. However, this very reality at the same time makes possible an infinite variety of organisms, cultural patterns, self-interpretations, interpretations and hypotheses, so that we are just as amazed at its apparently boundless generosity as we are hurt and terrified by its harshness. In the end this central reality is the 'creator' of the limited world in which we live, and which has taken shape in adaptation to it. Everything that takes place in us, all that we do, think and breathe is an inadequate experiment in corresponding to it. All organic, psychological and spiritual structures are attempts at adapting to it. This ultimate reality is 'judge' of all hypothetical outlines of the evolutionary process, judge of all organisms, actions, words and thoughts. It brings to grief anything that does not correspond with the basic conditions of reality which it controls.

If what I have said is true, there is an important structural affinity between scientific thought and faith: both accept the pressure of selection from reality and despite all its harshness see it as a productive force. Science affirms the falsification of its hypotheses. It is the only way in which knowledge advances. It endorses selection in the biological sphere: that is the only way in which chance mutations take on a 'forward' direction. Faith endorses the 'falsification' of life generally, which again and again comes up against limits imposed from the outside. It can regard the whole of life as an endless process of 'hypotheses' whose failure is oppressive but not absolutely meaningless. As individuals and as a species, we human beings make progress only when we draw the consequences of crises and catastrophes, when we refuse to allow ourselves to be fascinated and overwhelmed by the absurdity of life. In this sense faith goes against the facts: it still hopes in suffering, in crisis, in collapse, even against appearances. It is unconditional motivation to live. I am aware that this religious interpretation of suffering and absurdity is alien to the modern consciousness. That sees only meaningless waste where faith looks for meaning against the facts. This tendency to go against the facts may contradict the average modern everyday awareness, but it does not go against scientific thought. Rather, both have a common root: the recognition of a pre-existing reality, the pressure from which, exerted by selection, is harsh and inexorable, but which creates opportunities precisely through this pressure. In the last resort it is the same reality to which falsifying scientific thought bows and trusts in the protest of faith against the facts.

The common features extend even further: science and faith can affirm the pressure of selection from reality as a productive force because they overcome its harshness. This harshness lies in the fact that successful adaptation always takes place at the expense of other life. Selection is to the detriment of other forms of life and expressions of life. Science and faith both look for possibilities of achieving 'adaptation' in a way which is not at the expense of other people. Science allows hypotheses to die vicariously so as not to have to kill people. Religion is aware of sacrifice. Sacrifice has central significance even in archaic religions: people know that it is better to offer sacrifice vicariously for oneself and the community – animals, fruits of the earth, sometimes even human beings – than to be sacrificed oneself. Sacrifice was done away with by Christianity. The interpretation of the death of Jesus as a vicarious sacrifice fulfilled all the needs which had led to a thousand-year-long practice of sacrifice. True sacrifice is seen in readiness for repentance: one sacrifices behaviour rather than animals and people. So it can be said that science makes a vicarious sacrifice of false hypotheses and faith sacrifices destructive forms of behaviour, both with the aim of not having to sacrifice people. Thus science and faith correspond to the unwritten task of cultural evolution: the reduction of selection, the overcoming of the harshness of the principle of selection without annulling the productive power of the pressure of selection.

Of course there are differences between scientific thought and faith; scientific thought tests hypotheses, i.e. cognitive operations, against reality until they come to grief. This process relates only to the cognitive realm and not to the whole person. However, faith is a matter of becoming aware of the fact that all life continually comes to grief. It articulates that not only as a cognitive insight but with the emotional and motivational depths of existence. What happened unconsciously in pre-cultural evolution, the furthering of life through selection (which always means suffering), becomes conscious in human beings: the dull suffering of creation finds a representative voice in them. Human beings are the martyrs of being, who can be aware of their relationship to an ultimate reality even in failure; this is an insight of the tragedians, the Bible and existentialist philosophy which is indispensable for human self-understanding. Man is the only living being who has a chance of consciously articulating the relationship of life to an ultimate reality, so that he lives his life not only as it is but also with a clear awareness that it is the echo of a central reality, hidden from us, for which there is no better word than 'God', the old name for the unknown factor behind all our experiences of resonance and absurdity, the goal of all structures of adaptation and the origin of the pressure of selection. Compared with this name, all other terms like 'central reality' and 'ultimate reality' are only counsels of desperation.

3. Science and faith as openness to 'mutations'

We have relativized the first two contradictions between science and faith from the perspective of the theory of evolution. What about the third contradiction, that between scientific thought which delights in dissension, and faith, which is dependent on consensus? Or, to put it another way: the contradiction between the autonomy of scientific thought and the dependence of religious faith on tradition, social conformity and authority? New perspectives open up on this contradiction too, if we put it in a wider context.

Evolution takes place in a process of trial and error. Mutations are the trials. The 'errors' among them are excluded by selection, so that only the very rare productive mutations have a chance of establishing themselves. Life is basically conservative. It has many ways of protecting itself against chance changes which in most cases would impair the capacity of the organism for adaptation. However, there is a slight room for variations, without which there would be no development. Life is directed towards both non-conformist variations and the conservative power of persistence which can sustain itself against the majority of divergent variations. Both belong together functionally.

Mutatis mutandis, that also applies to our spiritual and intellectual life, to science and faith. In both, the conservative power of persistence and openness to new things are combined. However, there can be no doubt that science is much more on the side of the 'new' than religion, which for many people is the embodiment of the conservative power of persistence. Of course insiders know that a good deal changes in the church; and those who are most familiar with its ways would add that in the church everything changes but bread and wine. Underestimated changes often take place in the church and religion. In my view the decisive difference between religion and science is that in science there is continual progress. In religion everything seems to be determined by retrospect; an event which has already taken place once and for all is simply interpreted in a variety of ways.

This contradiction can be relativized to some degree if we put science and faith in a scale of expressions of human life, the degrees in which are only in the forms and speed of evolution.

The fascinating progress made in science and technology rests on the fact that in one limited area of human life we have succeeded in consciously planning and carrying out evolution. We do not vary our organs but our apparatus and means of experimentation. By these means we deliberately test hypotheses to destruction without having to put our own existence at risk. In the evolution of our knowledge only hypotheses and apparatus come to grief.

We are already in quite a different situation when we come to the social sciences. While there is unmistakably a linear development in the natural sciences and technology, progress in the sphere of the social sciences is much less continuous. Granted, by means of rational methods we continue to develop our social, political and economic institutions. But each step forward is threatened with a relapse into atavisms. The way to a social democracy has taken Germany, for example, through the political catastrophe of National Socialism. Why is our progress in this sphere so much less planned? I think that it is because our possibilities of methodically replaying the evolutionary game of trial and error are *a priori* limited. We cannot experiment. For if we experiment here, people, and not apparatus and hypotheses, come to grief. Those who experiment here are playing with human anxiety, distress and hunger. So we can only make theoretical experiments, i.e. construct models which contain as many as possible of the factors which are effective in reality, in order to anticipate 'what would happen if...?' What would happen if we were to change this or that law, raise this or that tax, and so on? Natural scientists can try out their models in a 'laboratory' setting free of risks. By contrast, in society we have to grope our way forward in a process of blind trial and error. We feel our way in the dark, always working with an existential risk. Nevertheless, there is progress.

Least visible is 'progress' in the sphere of life-style, art and religion; on the contrary, here there seem to be classical periods in human history which remain unattainable models for subsequent times. Here we find successes which cannot be repeated. One may find modern music fascinating. But Bach, Beethoven and Brahms remain unsurpassable high points. And there are still forms of philosophy, literature and art from antiquity which nothing seems to approach. Religious faith is not completely isolated in seeing a particular period of the past as 'normative'.

Now if we compare the various spheres of life and the different speeds in their development, it is striking that the more we can use a process of evolution that we can control externally, the quicker the development is. But the more we come up against the centre of our own existence in this process of evolution, so that we can no longer feel detached from it, the slower the course of the process of development, provided that it can be seen and experienced at all. The 'speed of development' in the various spheres of life also seems to be connected with the number of productive 'innovations'. It declines the nearer we come to central spheres of our existence. We can observe an explosion of knowledge in science; probably far more new discoveries have been made over the past century than in the whole of previous world history. In religion there are comparatively few 'new discoveries' (especially if one has in view only the normative 'innovations'). However, common to all spheres of life is the fact that these innovations (or 'mutations' of our spiritual life) appear spontaneously. Nowhere can they be completely planned; not even in science. This point will be developed further below: both in science and in religion life represents experimental attempts at adaptation to the ultimate reality which come about through unplannable 'mutations' of our consciousness. Already in science the great idea, the new paradigm, the 'mutation' of our cognitive structures can hardly be planned, even if it often presents itself almost automatically at a given time. And that happens although the sphere of science and technology is that aspect of the life-process in which we can plan some evolution, i.e. not only experience trial and error but shape it. The process of development in the history of religion escapes our planning to an even greater extent. But here again new beginnings constantly appear, 'mutations' of our religious consciousness in which our ideas, insights and motivations relative to the ultimate reality keep changing. The revelations and revealers in the history of religion are such 'mutations'. Only a few of them make a mark on history. Only rarely do charismatic movements become established institutions which are capable of having a long life. It is important to note that one cannot 'make', 'plan' or 'order' such new movements. In our religion we are still in some respects in the position of a living being which cannot plan an improved adaptation to reality but depends on mutations which appear spontaneously. In religion, as elsewhere in our spiritual life, we find such spontaneous 'mutations' in the form of charismatics, geniuses or revealers, whatever one calls them. No one can produce them. This soon gives rise to the impression that the great innovators fall from 'heaven'. The spirit blows where it wills. In my view the structures of dependence in religious belief are to be derived from this situation. I shall demonstrate this point from the threefold dependence of religion on tradition, consensus and authority.

(a) Dependence on tradition

Because we do not feel competent to plan new structures of adaptation to the ultimate reality, we hold on to previous ways of life and previous ideas – for want of anything better. Hence the amazing power of religious traditions to persist, in a way which has survived the attempts of modern theologians to demythologize them. This is often still evident in the way in which many people hand on religious traditions which they no longer understand. This not unproblematical power of religious traditions to persist is the obverse of their positive function: it sees that nothing of what appeared in those remarkable figures which are points of reference for the various religious communions is lost. We must note here that debased elements are handed down along with the rest of tradition. But the fact remains that what modern sujectivism may shake off as a burdensome dependence on other people, i.e. on previous generations, is one of the great opportunities of cultural, as opposed to biological, evolution. In biological evolution a mutation disappears if it does not establish itself. It must arise again spontaneously if it is to have another chance. Humanity, however, has a cultural memory, tradition, in which all trial and error, all 'mutations' and innovations can be preserved, independently of whether or not they have established themselves, whether or not they are fully understood. This cultural tradition feels obliged to preserve the memory of failed forms. Nor can it escape the crucified Jesus of Nazareth. For even if he does escape our understanding – who knows whether one day, later, the time will not be ripe for him? Who knows whether we may not one day discover in religious traditions that we do not understand possibilities which so far have not been realized?

(b) Dependence on social conformity

Religious faith always becomes 'plausible' only in a society which effectively protects its consensus by mechanisms of conformity. These mechanisms of conformity are often oppressively rigid. Nevertheless, they have a positive function: they stabilize the individual so that he or she can also withstand great tests of faith and courage. We dare to go against our environment where we know that we have the backing of our group. We suspect that reality is intrinsically open to many different interpretations. We dare to decide for one of these interpretations when it is supported by the attitude of a community. Thus mechanisms of conformity make possible personal identity, but at the same time they also ensure the preservation of the social identity of a community of faith. They ensure that not every new idea gets through untested. For in religion, too, most new beginnings go astray, just as in evolution most mutations have detrimental effects. One need only think of youth religions, by which people are led into totalitarian dependence. Mechanisms of social conformity are therefore necessary in every church (as in every community). But there is an important argument against applying them all too rigidly. The often inhuman 'exclusion' of religious deviations in the past once meant that in specific instances a religious view of the world was 'tested' in various closed societies. The risk of a total failure was limited: the history of religion experimented with 'high religions' in various cultures which existed relatively independently of one another. The failure of one of these experiments did not put the whole development in jeopardy. Today, however, a 'unitary culture' has come into being. The same technological structures are extending throughout all societies. We have a global network of communication. It is as though history were staking everything on one card. But it would be too great a risk to invest everything in one possibility. We must lay off the risk. We must allow more alternatives in all areas than we have done hitherto. However, because of the unification of the world in technology and civilization these alternatives can no longer be tested separately; they must be realized in one and the same society. In this situation, I believe that the claims of communities of faith to absoluteness are harmful.

(c) Dependence on authority

In my view, the dependence of religious faith on authority is to be derived from dependence on 'mutative' innovations. In different ways the great religions declare their dependence on their founders: on Jesus, Buddha or Mohammed. Among the many experiments in the history of religion the adherents of these figures have identified them as the embodiment of 'adequate adaptation structures' to the ultimate reality. And there is one good argument for following them: the forms of life which begin from them have been tested over a period of centuries. We know where they tend towards fanaticism and inhumanity, and also where they have led to positive developments. Historical experience can enlighten us more than any abstract theory. D.Campbell, the psychologist and evolutionary scientist, rightly thought that the great historical religions are better tested forms of life than all modern forms of therapy.[33] However, tested authority remains authority – and is therefore offensive to modern awareness, unless it comes to what is in my view the inescapable conclusion that we must also reckon with 'mutations' in human history, which to a greater degree than ever before disclose spheres of reality which are not generally accessible. Once we recognize this, it is no blind risk to follow figures in order to transcend the bounds of our own personality, the worlds in which we live, indeed the limits of the human condition.

We continually see that the dependence of religious faith on tradition, conformity and authority ultimately derives from its dependence on singular, charismatic figures who appear spontaneously and are comparable to the productive mutations which occur in biological evolution. No one can rule out the possibility that there will be new revelatory figures in the future. We cannot conjure them up; indeed it accords with the human situation that in the most central questions of life we must wait upon 'messianic' figures. The Old Testament and Judaism consistently embody this attitude. Therein lies one of their elements of truth.

We can now return to our basic question. In my view, the three dependence-structures of religious faith which we have discussed so far, and which modern subjectivity finds so hard to accept, are an appropriate form of being open to 'mutative' innovations in religion, whether past or future. As we cannot improve our existential structures of adaptation to the ultimate reality by a deliberate process of trial and error (as we would a scientific theory), we must content ourselves with preserving the memory of structures of adaptation which once proved successful and wait for the return of such 'revelation'. In a sphere of life in which such productive 'mutations' happen only rarely, 'conservative' recollection is the appropriate form of preserving openness towards them, above all if it is bound up with the expectation of new 'revelations'. In spheres of life with frequent innovations this attitude would be inappropriate: here one must deliberately counter the human tendency to keep to the familiar and the known. In science therefore we must encourage the original idea, the divergent thought, and dissent, in order to remain open to every new combination of theoretical elements, every flash of insight, every new paradigm, in short, anything that may occur to us.

However, these differences should not be exaggerated. Once again it should be recalled that science, too, has its 'conservative' aspects. It, too, must develop social controls to filter out crazy ideas before they become too widespread, and this means that sometimes good ideas are filtered out as well. In science, too, authorities multiply their errors along with brilliant insights. Science, too, is extremely reluctant to abandon tried theories, and sometimes that happens only when their advocates slowly die out (in the literal sense). The converse is also the case: religious faith, too, knows rebellion against dependence on authority. Even in the Old Testament we find the utopia of the law written on the hearts of all men and women (in Israel), so that no one has to teach anyone else. Here already the idea emerges that an adequate structure of adaptation to the ultimate reality can be achieved independently of social dependence:

I will put my law within them, and I will write it upon their hearts; and I will be their God, and they shall be my people. And no longer shall each man teach his neighbour and each his brother, saying, 'Know the Lord', for they shall all know me, from the least of them to the greatest, says the Lord; for I will forgive their iniquity, and I will remember their sin no more (Jeremiah 31.33-34).

To sum up: at first sight there seems to be an unbridgable gulf between scientific thought on the one hand, which works by hypothesis and falsification and delights in dissent, and faith on the other, which is apodeictic, goes against the facts and depends on conformity. These contrasts can be relativized from the perspective of the theory of evolution. Scientific thought and religious faith are related to the same central reality. Science approaches it with constantly differentiated cognitive structures of adaptation, which embrace not only cognition, but also emotion and motivation – aspects which scientific thought must ascetically neglect. Both use the strategy of trial and error and thus continue at a higher level the evolutionary game of mutation and selection. Both are expressions of the same living being, humanity, whose capacity to experience the same thing from different perspectives, e.g. from those of religion and science, is one of the foundations of creativity, tolerance, humour and many valuable attitudes.

In a brief excursus I must explore another possibility of relating knowledge and faith in evolutionary terms. My own approach was to bring knowledge and faith under the same denominator with the help of the most basic categories of evolutionary process. However, it is often assumed that they also represent different phases of development within cultural evolution: in that case religion is regarded as an archaic structure of adaptation to reality which has been replaced by scientific forms.[34] The theory put forward here, that knowledge and faith complement each other, would certainly contradict such a 'replacement theory' in principle, but for that very reason the element of truth in the latter should be stressed. Religion is indeed an archaic heritage, but at the same time it is a matter of constant interaction with this archaic heritage in a process by which it is revised and 'humanized'.

Religion has existed for thousands of years, whereas science is a relatively recent phenomenon which clearly emerged for the first time in Graeco-Roman antiquity. At first glance that would seem to provide support for a 'replacement theory' – with a long overlap in the phase of religious and scientific development. However, we must reflect that the move towards the high religions took place simultaneosly with the first appearance of science. When the Pre-Socratics were laying the foundations for a scientific exploration of the world, there was a breakthrough in the direction of monotheism in three areas of the history of religion: with Xenophon in Greece, with Zarathustra in Persia and with Deutero-Isaiah in the Babylonian exile.

These observations suggest a parallel development or even a co-evolution of knowledge and faith or science and theology (as thought-through and therefore systematized forms of belief). In addition to great tensions between both 'systems of adaptation' we can continually note phases when there is a balance, for example the synthesis between Platonism and biblical religion in the church fathers or the combination of Aristotelian philosophy and church tradition in the heyday of Scholasticism. In between there are phases where both systems of adaptation are in opposition.

Today the tension between the cognitive structures of adaptation in knowledge, which have leapt ahead very fast, and the 'conservative' structures of adaptation in religion, in which the metaphorical, emotional and motivational elements form a unity, is felt very deeply. The religious 'heritage' is in tension with the demands for adaptation posed by our modern civilization. Awareness of science is often suppressed, so that religion can be understood as a form of coming to grips with the unconscious aspects of human life. This provides an opportunity for religion: unless we come to terms with our archaisms, our life is crippled. Unless we discover alternatives to our present forms of life, we may possibly find ourselves at a fatal dead end. Unless we are aware of our archaisms we deprive ourselves of an opportunity of being able to cope with our 'modernisms'. Unless we come to grips with our archaic heritage, mankind denies its identity.

However, religion is also an opportunity for the future. Humanity emerges from the depths of an evolution which leads a ghostly and inspiring after-life in our unconscious, but we are constantly concerned with new and more sophisticated structures of adaptation to a reality which is still undisclosed to us, of which we have intimations even beyond our most progressive interpretations of the world as 'wholly other'. In order to express this intimation of a wholly other, we can make use of the archaic structures of adaptation in religion: they came into being at times when people experienced even more intensively the limitations to the world in which they lived and their possibilities for action in it. They are better adapted to limit situations than the modern awareness which often denies them. So religion is both an echo of archaic times and an anticipation of future developments.

The decisive thing is that people learn to approach reality with different forms of adaptation. At all events that is an expansion of human possibilities of experience and behaviour. But it is also a heightening of the possibility that reality in its riches will be illuminated more adequately. We do not know the whole person unless we know his or her religion. Nor do we know every aspect of reality if we limit ourselves to the scientific and cognitive forms of adaptation towards it. In this sense knowledge and faith enhance each other in a complementary way.

Of course, among the general public a naive 'replacement theory' still holds sway. Here religion acts like a government party which is out of office, grumbling away on the opposition benches while science emerges self-consciously as the party in power. However, that very fact proves that each depends on the other, like government and opposition in a democratic system.

One riddle remains. Why is it so difficult to see the common features which are grounded in the make-up of life itself? Why do scientists find it so difficult to see the religious dimension of their own actions? First of all it should be stressed that one can do science successfully without ever realizing that all science develops hypothetical structures which seek to correspond to an ultimate reality. The eye, too, is a highly complicated structure which corresponds to the laws of sunlight, but it knows nothing of that fact. Prior to the evolution of the cerebrum no life can be aware that in all its manifold expressions it is striving to be adapted to a pre-existing reality. Even cultural structures of adaptation need not necessarily be conscious and evident. Presumably music, art and religion are partially successful structures of adaptation into which we have only an inadequate insight. Music often proves to be a 'revelation'. But we do not know what it reveals. Rather, we have the impression of something which escapes our reflections becoming evident at occasional moments. Science has a much greater awareness of itself. But is it wholly transparent? Do we see through the game in which we are involved here? All scientists know the feeling of being unable to see the connections even within their particular sphere of competence. Can they then comprehend the overall connections of all scientific thought? How many scientists are aware that there is a connection between the retraction of a slipper animalcule and the rejection of a hypothesis? In that case, is it also surprising that they should also be unaware of the connection between the rejection of a hypothesis and the prayer, 'Not my will, but thine be done'? In short, one can be a very good scientist without following Einstein in seeing one's own scientific work as an attempt to correspond to a superior reason.

Now for the other side. Why do so many religious people find it difficult to accept scientific thought without qualification? Why cannot they see that faith and science are different forms of adaptation to the same reality? This is doubtless connected with the fact that science has often denied faith the right to exist. In a scientifically organized society it is as though the party in power were rejecting an opposition simply because it did not fit into this modern world. Here we should recall the scientific ethos, the obligation to give an impartial interpretation and explanation of all the phenomena of life without hindrance. Suppose that a researcher found in the middle of the primal forest a bizarre plant which did not seem to fit into its environment. He would say to himself: 'There must be some aspects of this environment of which I am unaware, for which this alien plant is an appropriate form of adaptation.' Even the most remarkable features must have a function. In our world, religion is such a plant. It has nothing to fear from an impartial scientific investigation; if it cannot explain itself in the context of modern convictions, it may perhaps point to still undisclosed aspects of our reality. And what could scientific curiosity stimulate more than the suspicion that things could be quite different?

To return once again to the imagery I used at the beginning of this chapter. Nowadays religion is on the opposition benches and science forms the government. It would be good if religion could find a way out of its role as a smouldering opposition, and if science were less arrogant as the government. One need only recall that there are well-founded doubts as to whether it is in fact an ideal governing party. Scientists as a group produce hypotheses, attempt to falsify them, and delight in dissent – and the results are often chaotic. Their own understanding of themselves puts them basically on the opposition side. From there, both 'parties', opposition and religion, should combine to counter human arrogance, laziness and blindness: science, by constantly pressing us to correct our mistakes, and faith by constantly motivating us to correct our lives, to repent and change our ways; both, by constantly reminding us of the most elementary basic experience, which we all too quickly forget, that in all that we are and do we are dependent on a central reality which we come up against in our scientific thought and to which we respond in faith.

Both science and religion in fact have the suspicious tendency to establish themselves as a ruling party beyond the limits of their competence. Each then feels obliged to oppose the other.

Knowledge confers power, power over nature and over other people. Science continually becomes an instrument in the struggle which divides classes, peoples and social systems. With its help, groups in power attempt to maintain and increase their chances of power. With its help humanity heedlessly exploits nature. Here religion must remind us that all our doing – including the activity of science – is in the end adaptation to a pre-existing reality. All our thoughts and hypotheses must be subordinated and subject to it. The instrumental exploitation of knowledge for the exercise of power is only one possible way of doing science. Men and women also have an opportunity to understand science as a response to this pre-existing reality – and to see their limited understanding as the echo of an all-embracing reason. In that case science no longer has an instrumental function but functions as a response.

What I have said of science applies in a different way also to religion. Religion too confers power. It, too, constantly becomes an instrument in the fight for opportunities. Again and again it confers an aura of sanctity on particular interests. Again and again it legitimates unequal opportunities as divinely given destinies. Again and again it attempts to immunize its interpretation of reality against objections. Here science is obliged to provide an opposition to religion: it must uncover the interweaving of power-interests and religion. It must produce the awareness that religious images and symbols, like all human action, are 'hypotheses' – and not the absolute truth. It must make people aware of the often unconscious instrumental function of religion so that it can again become what it should be, a response to the reality of God.

Knowledge and faith depend on each other; they must correct each other.

PART TWO

Faith in the One and Only God: Biblical Monotheism in an Evolutionary Perspective

The Problem: Monotheism and the Transition from Biological to Cultural Evolution

Talk about evolutionary theory and biblical faith gives the impression that its subject matter is the rivalry of two theories about the origin of the world. One of these attributes the world to a single creative act of God, while the other attributes it to an infinitely long evolution from *homo sapiens*. The following discussion will not deal with this dispute between creationism and evolutionism.[1]

I shall approach the theme in a different way. The theory of evolution has undergone an amazing expansion. Today it is not just limited to the sphere of biological life but includes both the preceding abiotic evolution and also, albeit hesitantly, cultural evolution. In quantitative terms this last is utterly insignificant. If we compare the twelve or sixteen thousand million years of evolution as a whole to one day, humanity appeared round about the last minute. Of this one minute, humanity spent about ninety-eight per cent in the Early Stone Age, before it began to practise agriculture and cattle-rearing in the Neolithic Age.[2] In short, the cultural evolution has only just begun, if we take all the dimensions of evolution as a background and a point of comparison – and these dimensions are so inconceivable that the biblical calculation that to God a thousand years are as a day, is a crass understatement.

Our question is, What is the role of religion, and especially biblical religion, within this evolution? What contribution has religion made to the transition from biological evolution to the cultural evolution which has just begun? Is it a typical phenomenon of this transition? Here I shall not treat the theory of evolution and biblical faith as two rival theories about the origin of the world. I shall take a new look at biblical faith in the light of evolutionary theory, and at evolutionary theory in the light of biblical faith.

Once again it should be stressed that, quantitatively speaking, cultural evolution is a droplet in the sea of time. Qualitatively, however, it is a revolution. Language, the capacity to communicate with signs about any subject whatsoever, regardless of whether the subject-matter is there or not, is present or future, is a revolution. The capacity to develop technical apparatus instead of physical organs to adapt better to the environment and to control it is also new. Above all, the combination of the two capacities is new: communication by artificial products, by writing, print, radio waves and so on. This capacity first made possible a hitherto unknown continuity of tradition: individual experiences can be handed down securely over generations and enormous distances.

These are only a few characteristics of cultural evolution. However, they may all be reduced to a single denominator: the effect of culture is to reduce selection. As a rule culture is able to make life possible even where nature would drastically diminish its chances.[3] Technical inventions, the handing on of experiences, and social institutions help us to do that. To give just one example: medical progress exposes our descendants to much less pressure of selection than before. We need no longer play the cruel game of having to bring many children into the world so that in the end on the average two survive. That happened in all pre-industrial societies. Because the probability that our children will grow up is great, we can (and should) limit ourselves to a few children with the help of birth control. That has radically changed our view of life. Earlier, hardly anyone grew up without having stood at the grave of a brother or sister. From an early age death was a real possibility. Today things are different: specifically, that means a reduction in selection. We must realize that in comparison to previous evolution that is a revolution. Biological evolution takes place only through selection. Only selection gives a direction to natural processes and chance mutations so that they progress towards greater adaptation. By contrast, culture makes progress by reducing selection. A number of objections can be made to this theory, which I shall discuss briefly in anticipation.

The first objection runs: are not both phases of evolution so basically different that it is nonsense to combine them both under the term 'evolution'? Does not the application of categories from evolutionary theory to phenomena of human history wipe out the gulf between biological and cultural evolution? In contrast to some sociobiologists I am profoundly convinced of the existence of this break in evolution: humanity has introduced something new into evolution. But that does not contradict the attempt to incorporate human history into evolution as a whole. Was there not already a break in this overall evolution earlier, when life arose and gave the whole of evolution a hitherto unknown dynamic through quite new forms of process, through assimilation and reduplication, mutation and selection? Despite this break we speak of evolution as whole, and today we are coming close to plausible scientific theories to explain the transition from abiotic to biological evolution. A comparable break took place at the end of previous overall evolution in that fleeting moment when *homo sapiens* appeared and took evolution to a new level by means of his culture. Here, too, we look for natural explanations of the transition. People were once especially eager to find the 'missing link' between primates and human beings; now, however, it is dawning on us that we ourselves could be the 'missing link' between the animal world and true humanity.

A second objection is along the same lines as the first: how can evolution develop from itself something which goes against its previous dynamics? How can a development through the diminution of selection replace a development through the pressure of selection? Again I would refer to the analogy of the transition between abiotic and biological evolution: life in general is characterized by the (partial) breakthrough of previous forms of process. The physicist E.Schröd-inger[4] saw the characteristic mark of life as being that it is a process which diminishes entropy. According to the law of entropy, order declines rather than increases in a closed system, just as the mess on a desk gets worse unless someone decides to sort it out. However, the evolution of life leads to increasingly great and increasingly improbable order. Life succeeds in 'cheating' the law of entropy because it is an open system which in constant interchange with the environment builds up more order than it in fact demolishes. Just as life is a process which reduces entropy, so culture is a system which reduces selection. It is true of both that neither the law of entropy nor the principle of selection can be abrogated. However, their effects are removed in a partial sphere of reality.[5]

Whereas the first two objections put in question the continuity between biological and cultural evolution, the two following objections challenge their basic discontinuity. The third objection runs: is there not a harsh 'struggle for selection' between individuals and classes, peoples and nations, which is concerned with both biological and cultural chances of survival? Cultures which are superior in military, economic and administrative terms 'survive', while others are absorbed by them or destroyed. Nevertheless, here too humanity has the unique chance of replacing 'hard' selection by 'soft'. By intelligent choice and the adoption of promising modes of behaviour we can prevent the blind process of history from making this selection at the expense of individuals and groups, peoples and cultures. To put it in a simpler way: we can avoid or limit wars and class struggles. And we also generally recognize this task.

The fourth objection takes up the previous one: even in 'soft' selection, humanity succumbs to the pressure of selection exercised by reality. We have to put a premium on particular ideas and forms of behaviour. We have to expose our ideas and achievements to a harsh competition, with the result that culture may be experienced as a grinding process of selection.

However, here too culture proves to be a way of organizing life which reduces selection. It works in two apparently opposed directions: it makes possible constantly new differentiations between people – and at the same time increasing equality. To put it another way, it discloses constantly new mini-environments and at the same time creates greater equality of opportunity when it comes to occupying them.

Culture creates a new environment: a technological, social, aesthetic and spiritual world in which there are far more 'ecological niches' than in the natural human environment. Every profession, every science, every form of art, every hobby and every social group is such a niche. Everyone has the chance to build himself or herself a small world which corresponds to his or her needs and in which he or she may be successful. The greater the plurality of values, the greater the human tolerance and the imagination to see that everyone is to be assessed positively in some respect; and the greater the chance that everyone will experience positive consolidation, i.e. will have the experience of being accepted as competent and responsible members of society. Differentiation of behaviour reduces the pressure of selection from reality – an opportunity which is continually jeopardized by totalitarian tendencies.

On the other hand, culture brings about a social balance between individuals of different kinds. After a long and laborious journey it now recognizes equal rights for all – independent of status and achievement. It gives everyone a right to life – regardless of his or her fitness (and in societies without the death penalty regardless of whether or not he or she acts in accordance with its norms). It is concerned for material equivalence and strives for equality of opportunity. Above all, though, it rewards behaviour which protects the weak and takes their side. Action in solidarity diminishes the pressure of selection by creating greater equality – though here again culture is continually threatened by reversion to that atavistic pattern of behaviour which we came to know in Fascism.

Selection is an interaction between 'selective' environmental factors and variant forms of life. The reduction of selection in culture takes place on the one hand through the discovery of a new environment which allows a far greater breadth of variation in life than the natural environment, and on the other hand through the deliberate creation of a balance between the 'privileged' and the 'disadvantaged'. Both processes mean that fewer individuals experience the pressure of selection. However, it is important to note that human beings are still subject to the *principle* of selection, i.e. to the demands of a reality which does not accord the same chance to every form of life to survive and to spread. Only culture is a form of adaptation to reality in which this reality shows a tolerance of variations previously unimaginable.

Just as in the origin of life the law of entropy is 'overcome' through material exchange with the environment without being broken in respect of all of reality, so too culture overcomes the principle of selection through a new form of exchange with the environment, through a 'spiritual exchange of matter'. By means of intellectual operations it quarries information from the environment, and in this way arrives at permanent forms of life: at amazingly long-lived theories, 'eternal' works of art and stable technologies.

There are no natural limits to this 'spiritual exchange of material' with the environment. Human beings have an intimation of a mysterious central reality behind every spiritual world constructed by the assimilation of the experience that flows into them. In their cultural world, which is already superior to the biological world, they can already have the specific experience that reality tolerates more variations than might seem possible at first sight. Its 'tolerance of variation' grows with every progress. This experience points us towards a limit value. We have an inkling that were we to unveil the central reality completely, then it would reveal itself as a reality which has an unconditional tolerance of variation, in the face of which all human beings are of equal value. The opening for this more comprehensive reality is religion.

The thesis of this book is that if culture generally is a process which reduces selection, religion is the heart of human culture.[6] It is a rebellion against the principle of selection. It makes human beings open to a greater reality before which each individual has infinite value and is absolutely equal. Experiences with this reality are gathered together in exemplary form in the Bible. It is probable that they are had everywhere. However, it seems to me that nowhere does the rebellion against the principle of selection emerge more clearly than in belief in the one and only God who brought Israel out of Egypt, who revealed himself in Jesus of Nazareth and continues to be accessible to humanity in the experience of the Spirit. If people recognize that their whole lives must correspond to the central reality which appears here, then they are obliged to rebel against the principle of selection.

I chose traditional theological conceptuality to describe contact with this central reality when I spoke of revelation. This term is an apt one for our experience: revelation discloses to us something that was previously hidden. Provisionally this process can be described in evolutionary categories in the following way. All being is an attempt to develop stable forms through adaptation to the basic conditions of reality. Life and culture are a process which by trial and error seeks increasingly better structures of adaptation to reality. Religion, too, is a part of this process. Religious convictions are attempts to adapt the whole of life in all its aspects to an ultimate reality. The religious traditions have only one appropriate term for this reality, 'God'. All forms of religion – animism, polytheism, monotheism, all world religions, all confessional systems, indeed all life – are an attempt to correspond to God. The history of human religion, indeed history itself, is an unending story of trial and error.

At the end of these preliminary reflections let me formulate my theory once again. Biblical monotheism should be regarded as a project within the history of human trial and error aimed at achieving an adequate adaptation to the ultimate reality. My hypothesis is that it plays an important role in the transition from biological to cultural evolution (a process in which we are still involved). In it is formulated a resistance against the principle of selection, which, whether consciously or not, is a characteristic of all culture.

II

The Development of Biblical Monotheism:
A Historical Outline

The reader of the Bible who is unfamiliar with biblical criticism can
easily tend to think that from the beginning the history of Israel was
a struggle between an original monotheism and apostasy to other gods.
In reality, however, this view of history is the construction of post-
exilic groups who came to terms with the loss of land and temple, the
catastrophe of 586 BC, by regarding it as a punishment for continued
apostasy from Yahweh, the one and only God. Before the catastrophe
there was indeed a trend which argued for the worship of Yahweh
alone, without denying the existence of other gods. All in all, however,
like all other peoples Israel was polytheistic: people worshipped several
gods side by side.[7]

Yahweh had a special status among these gods: he was the god of
the land and nation, as Chemosh was the god of the Moabites, Dagon
the god of the Philistines, and Assur the god of the Assyrians, without
these peoples having a tendency towards monotheism or monolatry.[8]
Other gods were worshipped alongside the god of land and nation. In
Israel there were various El-deities like El Elyon (Gen.14.18ff.), El
Shaddai (Gen.17.1) or the god of Beth-El (Gen.35.7). Baal was
worshipped. In Jerusalem, there was an official temple to Baal (II
Kings 11.18) as well as the temple of Yahweh; indeed, alien gods were
worshipped in the temple of Yahweh itself – with the consent of the
priests of Yahweh (Ezek.8). As everywhere, so in Israel female deities
appeared alongside male deities, like Ashera (II Kings 23.7) and the
Queen of Heaven (Jer.44.25). The fortress of Kuntillet Ayrud from
about 800 BC (on the border between the Negeb and Sinai) has yielded
a provision jar with the inscription: 'I will bless you through Yahweh,
my (our) protector, and through his Ashera.' Even in the fifth century
BC in Elephantine in Egypt we find a military colony with Jewish
mercenaries who worshipped two other deities alongside Yahu: Anath-

Bethel and Asham-Bethel. There can be no doubt that during the monarchy Israel was polytheistic.

Nevertheless, the religion of Israel must have displayed special features. For the riddle of the history of religions remains that only in this people did the knowledge of the one and only God break through, to the exclusion of the worship of all other gods.[9] We can divide this development towards the monotheism of the Old Testament and Judaism into three periods. In the first period, between the beginnings of Israel (about 1200 BC) and the catastrophe of 586 the exclusiveness of Yahweh was established. Yahweh alone had to be worshipped, though the existence of other gods was not denied. In the second period – from the Babylonian exile (586) to the beginning of Hellenism (332 BC) – there was a break-through to monotheism and a recognition of the uniqueness of Yahweh. There are no other gods beside Yahweh; and Israel is the 'prophet' of Yahweh. The third period is characterized by the encounter with the cosmopolitan tendencies of a philosophical monotheism in Hellenism. If other people could also arrive at faith in one God, the question arose whether Yahweh is not the universal God of all humanity. Primitive Christianity is part of this discussion. So I shall distinguish three stages: the conflicts over the exclusiveness, the uniqueness and the universality of Yahweh.

1. The conflict over the exclusiveness of Yahweh

Exclusiveness can be one-sided or two-sided. It is one-sided if, while Yahweh is exclusively the God of Israel, Israel at the same time worships other gods. However, exclusiveness can also rest on mutuality: in that case not only is Yahweh the God of Israel (and of no other people), but Israel worships Yahweh exclusively – and no other gods beside him.

(a) The exclusive bond between Yahweh and Israel

First of all an exclusive bond developed between Yahweh and Israel. There are clear indications that Yahweh became the God of Israel through a historical process.

The name Israel is the first indication: it contains the theophoric element 'El'. The group of tribes designated Israel thus originally came together for the worship of a God 'El'. It is no coincidence that El is called 'the God of Israel' in Gen.33.20. There must have been a tribal group 'Israel' which only came into contact with belief in Yahweh at a later stage.[10]

The second indication is that there were other groups of Yahwehworshippers alongside the tribal group of 'Israel'. These included the Midianites. The Midianite father-in-law of Moses appears as a priest of Yahweh in Ex.18.[11]

The third indication is that the name Yahweh already appears on Egyptian lists before the time of Israel. These mention a 'land of the Shasu (-Bedouins) Seir' alongside a 'land of the Shasu Yhw'.[12] This agrees with the location of Yahweh on Sinai: Yahweh's abode was originally not the land of Palestine.

The fourth indication is that in one passage in the Old Testament it is clear that even according to Israel's own understanding Yahweh was not exclusively bound to Israel. Amos connects him with the early history of neighbouring peoples as well as with the early history of Israel: ' "Are you not like the Ethiopians to me, O people of Israel?" says the Lord. "Did I not bring up Israel from the land of Egypt and the Syrians from Kir?"' (Amos 9.7).

How did the exclusive bond between Yahweh and Israel come about? The Old Testament understanding of itself sees the exodus from Egypt as Yahweh's act of election *par excellence* (cf. Ps.114.1f. and the first commandment). The exclusive bond between Yahweh and Israel has its basis in this act of election. In fact it is probable that groups who escaped from Egypt brought belief in Yahweh to Palestine.[13] They were aware that Yahweh had saved them from the threat of the military power of Egypt, which was technically far superior.

When these groups arrived in Palestine about 1200 BC, they encountered the following situation: Pharaoh Merneptah had just devastated the land in a campaign. In a stele set up about 1219 he boasts of an annihilating expedition against a group of peoples with the name 'Israel': 'Israel lies fallow and has no seed-corn' (i.e. no descendants).[14] This is the first mention of the name of Israel. The campaign is not mentioned in the Old Testament writings. This campaign was the cause of the catastrophe which is said to have happened to the tribes of Leah, Reuben and Simeon (there are good reasons for supposing so).[15] However, we cannot go into that here.

More important is the fact that the groups which escaped from Egypt (either at the Sea of Reeds or in Palestine) were sociologically members of the category of Ḥabiru (the 'Hebrews') or had amalgamated with such groups. The Ḥabiru were a disadvantaged group of which there is evidence throughout the ancient Near East, without land or possessions, who were often conscripted for forced labour (like the 'Hebrews' in Egypt) or who spent their lives as robbers and outlaws, i.e. as 'people who did not belong to the established order, separated from it or excluded from it'.[16]

Presumably what now happened was that those who had escaped from Egypt and the survivors of Merneptah's campaign in Palestine amalgamated with other under-privileged groups. They had experienced comparable fates: homelessness, exploitation and a threat to their existence. They combined their traditions and recollections. As a result El (the God of Israel) was combined with Yahweh, the God of the group which had escaped from Egypt, but in such a way that Yahweh became established. For he was the only one who gave hope of escaping the military machine of Egypt and prevailing against the superior civilization of the cities. Thus the bond between Yahweh and his people came about in a situation of crisis and catastrophe. Yahweh was the God of those who had escaped and fled, who helped those who were oppressed beyond hope to survive.

The long transitional period between the settlement of Israel and its consolidation by the formation of the state – the period of the judges, which lasted about 200 years – deepened this connection between Yahweh and the tribal group of Israel. As there were no stable institutions for defence, the tribes had all the more to rely on an ideological 'mobilization' against the Ammonites, Midianites and Philistines who oppressed them; Yahweh himself had to help them against the superior power by sending them charismatic heroes. The monarchy emerged from attempts at defence against the Philistines with their superior civilization; David was a worshipper of Yahweh. The god of the land and nation became the personal god of the royal house. The temple of Yahweh planned by David and Solomon was a private sanctuary and a state sanctuary in one.

(b) The exclusive bond between Israel and Yahweh

Up to this point the exclusive bond between Yahweh and Israel was not matched by any exclusive bond between Israel and Yahweh: mutual exclusiveness was a new idea which only emerged during the monarchy. It occurs in a particular social context, i.e. as the revitalization of traditional values in the light of the development of society towards 'modern' social structures characteristic of the Canaanite city structures with their far superior civilization. Here we must distinguish beween developments in the Northern Kingdom and those in the South.

The Northern Kingdom not only had to incorporate a large number of Canaanite city states into itself (especially in the Plain of Megiddo); above all because of its geographical position it was much more exposed to the influence of the great Canaanite coastal states than Judah, which was rather out of the way. Therefore in the Northern Kingdom the ruling class pursued a religious policy aimed at integration: the Yahweh cult and the cult of Canaan were combined in many ways. Yahweh and Baal were worshipped side by side. A Yahwistic opposition movement rebelled against this. In the ninth century, Elijah, the prophet of Yahweh, for the first time posed the alternative 'Yahweh or Baal?' (the reference is to Baal of Tyre). At the same time he fought against the break-up of traditional social norms under Canaanite influence, as is indicated by the conflict over Naboth's vineyard. Both the religious and the social conflict belong closely together. The transition from an earlier tribal society to a centralized society controlled by royal officials is depicted as a conflict between Yahweh and Baal.[17]

In the eighth century, the two great prophets of the Northern Kingdom, Amos and Hosea, each continued one side of the early Yahwistic opposition to the ruling class. Amos formulated prophetic social criticism with a sharpness which was to have lasting effect, while Hosea castigated the religious devotion to the 'Baals'. Characteristic of both of them is their opposition to the ruling class: Amos was expelled from the royal sanctuary in Bethel. Hosea criticizes the kings of the Northern Kingdom (Hos.8.4ff.). This Yahwistic opposition had only transitory success against the ruling class: it supported Jehu's *coup d'état* (841-813). But this was only an episode. Hosea already regards Jehu as a murderer (Hos.1.4) and rejects his revolution.

The demand for the exclusive worship of Yahweh which was made for the first time in the Northern Kingdom in the ninth and eighth centuries has a specific social context: it is directed against the change in society brought about by the ruling class, who turned it into a state along Canaanite lines, aiming to consolidate their power. Old Yahwistic traditions were activated against these efforts.

Developments in Judaea, which was comparatively retrograde, took a different course. Here, too, Canaanite cities had to be integrated, like Jerusalem, which was first conquered by David. However, there was no conflict between Yahweh and El Elyon, the god of Jerusalem (or other gods of Jerusalem like Zedek and Shalom). El and Yahweh were identified with each other, the symbol of the peaceful course of the social integration between Israelites and Canaanites in the Southern Kingdom. Yahwism did not appear as an opposition movement. On the contrary, with its basic demands for the removal of cultic images, the sole worship of Yahweh and concentration of the Jerusalem cult, it became the foundation of state reforms of the cult,[18] though those which took place under Hezekiah (728-699) and Josiah (641-609) fell short of the demands of pure doctrine. These reforms were probably supported by fugitives from the North,[19] who like the Yahwistic opposition regarded the downfall of the Northern Kingdom in 721 as a punishment for disobedience to the demands of the Yahwistic movement. Amos and Hosea, the great prophets of Yahweh, had prophesied the catastrophe. God had confirmed it. The conclusion drawn from this was that a return to Yahweh could also save the oppressed rump state in the south. Yahwism thus became a programme of restoration, supported by sectors of the ruling class. Even where the great prophets of Yahweh in the Southern Kingdom seem to be in solitary opposition, they found unmistakable support in the ruling class. Jeremiah had a number of links with a powerful party at court. Isaiah and Ezekiel were members of the Jerusalem upper class.

The important thing to note is that these upper-class groups also took the social demands of Yahwism into their programme. The social criticism of Amos re-echoes in Isaiah. Deuteronomy, whose basic demands were the nucleus of Josiah's reform, contains many social laws. The strength of the Yahwistic reform programme lay in the fact that it sought to overcome the gulf between the classes and spoke to all strata of the people.

The Yahwistic programme of restoration was not a historical success. Some of its requirements began to be fulfilled under Josiah, but that too proved to be only an episode. In the final phase of the Southern Kingdom the group around Jeremiah, the prophet of Yahweh, seems to be a defeated minority, which unsuccessfully opposed the anti-Babylonian policies of the last kings.

Looking back on the pre-exilic period we can see that there was a Yahwistic movement concerned for monolatry. It was a minority. In the Northern Kingdom it appears as an opposition movement 'from below'. It did not prove successful in either place. On the whole pre-exilic Israel was polytheistic; it used small images of rods as amulets and had temple prostitution – and all this was an 'abomination' to Yahweh.

Two factors favoured this Yahwistic movement: national crises and social conflicts between traditional culture and Canaanite culture.

(a) National crises favoured a move towards one god. In the ancient Near Eastern environment of the Old Testament, the most interesting phenomenon is a temporary monolatry (i.e. a henotheism) in crises. In emergencies, all expectations were directed towards one god.[20] Israel lived in a state of permanent crisis, both in the period following the settlement and in the long period of political decline in the face of the Assyrians advance south-westwards. Conditions of chronic crisis led to a chronic monolatry. Here we should remember that Israel would experience crises from the start in a different light from other people: its God Yahweh was a god of those who had escaped from Egypt. He was the god of the fugitive Jacob. He was the God of the period of the judges, who rescued the people from a superior military power. In short, the experience of crisis did not contradict the character of the god Yahweh, and therefore any crisis could strengthen the bond with him.

(*b*) However, there were internal conflicts even in periods when foreign politics were more tranquil, and these could lead to a continually renewed revitalization of Yahwistic belief. Those who dissociated themselves from Canaanite culture adopted belief in the God of Yahweh as a sign of their own identity. Israel never forgot that Yahweh was a God of the wilderness and of nomads. Recollections of this were present in its tradition. However, they only became important in the context of dissociation from Canaanite city culture, and that was a contemporary issue.

1. Yahweh is regarded as a god of the wilderness. He has his dwelling in Sinai (Judg.5.4; Deut.33.2). Although he is the god of the land and the national god, he shifts his 'dwelling' more slowly than the Israelites who worship him. Only gradually does Zion become his 'mountain'. His 'settlement' is as impermanent as that of the Israelites: the recollection that he dwells outside the land is never lost.

2. The worship of Yahweh by Midianites, the 'Shasu Yahweh' and the Rechabites, who maintained the customs of life in the wilderness even when their people were settled in the land, shows a connection between Yahweh and nomadic groups. Israel never forgot that it had arrived in the land as nomadic groups: whereas Mesha king of Moab firmly believed that the Moabites had always lived in their land,[21] the Israelites told one another stories of homeless patriarchs.

It can hardly be argued that there is a natural tendency among nomads towards monolatry. The tendency towards monolatry is not a legacy of nomadism, but an expression of sedentary groups who, to distinguish themselves from other groups, recalled their nomadic origins. This brings into the forefront a god who has no affinity with the gods of the land and must appear as an alien among them. The strangeness of this god from the time of the wilderness explains why the alternative 'Yahweh or the gods' could emerge.

2. The conflict over the uniqueness of Yahweh

The breakthrough to consistent monotheism which denies the existence of other gods took place in the exile, when Israel threatened to
vanish from history. Precisely in this situation the knowledge broke
through that Yahweh is the one and only God, an insight which went
against a widespread 'logic' in ancient Near Eastern religions and the
other religions of antiquity. This logic said: when peoples fight against
each other there is a war between their gods. Chemosh fought for the
Moabites (cf. the Mesha stele) and Ishtar for the Assyrians. The defeat
of a people was also the defeat of its gods. Tiglath-pileser III (745-27),
for example, took off the images of the conquered gods and thus the
gods themselves to his capital in order to incorporate them into the
Assyrian pantheon and thus to subordinate them.[22] From then on the
conquered god served the victorious gods with his power – just as the
conquered peoples were enslaved by their new rulers. However, in
the total catastrophe of their state the Israelites arrived at their insight
that the gods of the victorious Babylonians were nothing and that
Yahweh was the only God, even though the Babylonians had proved
victorious over them.

Why could Israel come to terms with its own catastrophe in such a
novel way? The answer is obvious. The Yahweh movement provided
a convincing interpretation of the catastrophe. It was interpreted as a
punishment for despising Yahweh's demand to worship him alone.
Yahweh had acted in it. The prophets of disaster had prophesied it
and had been proved right. Before the disaster only a minority had
listened to them. But now their message had been confirmed: their
demand to worship Yahweh alone now had to be accepted by all.

As long as people lived in Palestine this demand for the sole
worship of Yahweh could exist alongside belief in other gods (of the
neighbouring peoples). It was hoped that Yahweh would always prove
stronger than these gods, i.e. would protect Israel from defeats.
However, in the final defeat it could no longer be argued that Yahweh
was stronger than other gods or that Israel was stronger than other
peoples. It was recognized that what the Babylonians were celebrating
as the victory of their gods over Yahweh was in reality to be attributed
to Yahweh himself. It was a mistake to suppose that this was the work
of alien gods. Only Yahweh was at work – and no one else. Thus it
was an illusion to assume the existence of other gods.

Faith in Yahweh as the one who guides and directs world history is
simply one theological presupposition for coming to terms with the
catastrophe. The second is belief in the creator of heaven and earth

who is present even in foreign lands and who can bring salvation there just as well as at home. This belief in creation is already bound up in Jeremiah with the saving gift of the land and becomes the background to prophetic accusations (cf. Jer.5.21ff.; 14.19ff.). According to Jeremiah, in the exile belief in creation becomes both the basis of new promises of salvation, i.e. a renewed 'settlement', and a theological argument against the idols and their images. The smith who makes lifeless images of idols must be ashamed before the one who has made heaven and earth (cf. Jer.10.12-16, an exilic addition?). This creator God, 'the Creator of the ends of the earth... gives power to the faint, and to him who has no might he increases strength' (Isa.40.28ff.) – to be specific, he gives the exiles hope that they will return to their land.

Whereas the radicalized idea of judgment among the prophets, directed against their own people, is a singular Israelite phenomenon, belief in creation is a legacy of Near Eastern peoples which Israel took over from its environment. In the polytheistic families of gods, however, the creator of the world is only one figure among others. He often fades into the background. Thus in the Ugaritic texts El and Baal stand side by side: El is the creator of the earth, father of humanity, creator of creatures. But in the foreground there is the dynamic Baal, on whom rain and fertility depend. In Israel both types of deity are fused: the God Yahweh who is at work in the present, who guarantees rain and fertility, is at the same time the God 'El Elyon, maker of heaven and earth' (Gen.14.19); here the fusion of two deities can still be traced in the juxtaposition of the divine names Yahweh and El. Yahweh, the God of the people, is at the same time creator of the whole earth. The way from the national to the universal God leads through faith in creation, which is taken over from the environment.[23]

Both theological presuppositions of Israelite monotheism, the idea of judgment and the idea of creation, belong closely together. Thus we find the two combined in Jeremiah. The God who made the earth, human beings and animals has given Nebuchadnezzar all lands (Jer.27.5f.). Even in the catastrophe which Nebuchadnezzar brought about, Israel is in the hand of this God. Two important sociological factors were added to these theological presuppositions to bring about the permanent success of the monotheistic revolution in the Babylonian exile.

First, we should note the internal conditions in the exile. Those who were deported to Babylon belonged to the upper class of Judah among whom the Yahwistic programme of Judah had already found an echo. These groups, which were disposed towards Yahwism, could develop in the exile without considering whether their programme could be realized.

They succeeded in taking a momentous step. Yahweh, the god of land and nation, responsible for public affairs and therefore already particularly associated with the upper classes who had been deported, became the personal God on whom anyone could call in need. After the destruction of the state, the state god became the god of each individual.[24] The god of the royal house became a 'personal god' of the people. This process is characterized by a change in literary form: Deutero-Isaiah uses the royal oracle of salvation to address and comfort the whole people.

A second factor lies in the changed external circumstances. The Babylonians were replaced by the Persians. This ruling power had almost got as far as monotheism. Only two gods remained from the divine pantheon of the old religions, the good god Ahuramazda and Ahriman, his counterpart. The Persians were tolerant. They restored the old cults. But they did not require the adoption of new cults, for example as a sign of loyalty to the new rulers. They allowed and encouraged the attempt to realize in Palestine the Yahwistic programme of reform which had come into being in the exile.[25]

Thus the exile and the time which followed was one of the most important and fertile periods in Israelite history. Granted, to our regret we hear little about the political and social history of this period. Rather, the creative energies of the people appear in its literature. The old history books were re-edited as large-scale aetiologies of winning and losing the land.[26] New programmes were developed, collections of laws were fixed and the sayings of prophets collected. Despite the severe catastrophe the people had a new mission. The content of this mission can be summed up in two phrases: there is only one God, Yahweh, and Israel is his prophet.

The uniqueness of Yahweh was thus assured. However, the community of Yahweh was particularist. It had to be. If all the nations were polytheist, monotheism could be maintained only by dissociating and turning away from all other peoples. Without mechanisms of social segregation the new faith would soon have been absorbed. This led to measures which we find hard to understand, for example to the dissolution of marriages which had already been contracted and an abundance of separatist tabus. However, one cannot endorse the breakthrough of monotheism without understanding these separatist tabus: a group which so radically goes against a previous consensus becomes a group apart. Without this segregation monotheism would not have been viable.

3. The conflict over the universality of Yahweh

This particularism inevitably ended in a crisis when horizons opened wide during the Hellenistic period, and a quite different Greek philosophical monotheism became known.[27] This philosophical monotheism was the product of an argument from the unity of the world to the unity of its origin; for epistemological reasons it therefore rejected the anthropomorphisms of the world of religious imagery. It was not against polytheism. Anyone who wanted to could worship one and the same God in the different gods. Popular religion was not put in question. In other words, this monotheism was not connected with a radical 'conversion' embracing the whole of life.

Nevertheless it changed the situation. It raised the question whether Jewish monotheism had for ever to be bound up with separatist practice. No one could claim that this monotheism could only be maintained *against* the other peoples. It no longer stood alone. But above all, even separatist Israel was convinced that the days of its separatism were numbered. One day all nations would acknowledge that there is only one God.

This produced the main theme of the second phase of the post-exilic period – from the emergence of Hellenism (about 330 BC) to the establishment of rabbinic Judaism in the second century AD. Just as the foundation for an exclusive bond with Yahweh was laid in the time of the settlement and the judges, and only later a correspondingly exclusive bond between Israel and Yahweh was called for, so now too the understanding of God preceded the social reality. The universality of Yahweh became the unshakeable foundation of Israel in the time of the exile. However, the great question was when a universal community open to all would correspond with this universal God. Hellenistic Judaism and the movements which arose out of it can be understood as different attempts to answer this question.

(a) The response of moderate Hellenistic Judaism

Many Jews acknowledged that the Gentiles, too, had recognized the true and only God – but in that case they were all the more to blame for not having drawn any conclusions from this recognition. The philosophers permitted polytheistic cults. Were not the Jews the only ones who were really consistent? Josephus, for example, puts forward this view in his apologia for Jewish religion. He concedes that Pythagoras, Anaxagoras, Plato and the Stoics all recognized the nature of God. 'But these, who philosophized only for a few, did not have the courage to present the truth of their doctrine to the masses who were preoccupied with false opinions. By contrast, our Lawgiver made his actions match his words' (Josephus, *contra Apionem* II, 169). Now if the Jews were the only ones to take their monotheistic conviction seriously in practice, they had to maintain their customs, including their separatist norms. In that case they were still a people 'set apart' by a faith which was unique to them.

(b) The response of radical Hellenistic Judaism

At the beginning of the second century BC there was a reform attempt in Jerusalem which endorsed monotheism but rejected separatism.[28] Yahweh was identified with Zeus - with God. Circumcision and food tabus were done away with. All this was not a syncretistic deviation on the part of Judaism; rather, it was a typical Jewish conversion movement. The slogan was, 'Let us go and make a covenant with the Gentiles round about us, for since we separated from them many evils have come upon us' (I Macc. 1.11). It was thought that this separation had not always existed. Unfortunately we have no direct evidence from these circles; if we did, we would probably find a religious programme worth taking seriously. It would presumably be based on views which have come down to us through Strabo: Strabo gives an amazingly positive account of Moses. Moses taught the true knowledge of God. God cannot be represented by any image. It was his successors who introduced dietary laws and circumcision (Strabo XVI, 2, 35ff.).[29]

What the radical Hellenistic Jews wanted was probably a return to these origins, a return to the true worship of God as taught by Moses. That is the only way of making sense of their argument that so many ills had come upon them since the Jews had separated from other peoples. The argument is in the spirit of the best Jewish tradition. The Yahwistic reformers had once argued in a similar way: the basis of disaster is a wrong religious attitude, apostasy to other gods. Who, then, could prevent other groups from saying that disaster lay in separation from the other nations, especially as the best representatives of these nations had arrived at the knowledge of the one God at the same time as the Jews? They found support in an all too weak civic upper class in Jerusalem. Rebellion from the country, the Maccabaean revolt, put an end to all attempts at reform. Yet one has to give them their due. The moderate Hellenists said, 'The Gentiles certainly have the true knowledge of God but they must follow us in our customs.' The radical Hellenists argued the other way round: 'We Jews have the true knowledge of God (in accord with the best of the Gentiles) but false separatist customs. *We* must change.'

(c) The response of primitive Christianity

Primitive Christianity, too, must be seen as an attempt to solve the problems which arose from the encounter between Judaism and Hellenism. Here, too, we find a reference to a time before the rules which were being criticized. Here, too, Moses could be played off against his successors (Mark 7); moreover, the order of creation is itself played off against Moses (Mark 10.2-12). Paul makes the law 'come in between' (Rom.5.20). Here, too, there was to be a universalization of Judaism. However, this differed from the reform attempts of moderate and radical Hellenism in two ways:

(a) The pattern of argument which ran, 'They certainly have true knowledge of God, but their customs do not match it', had previously been applied either to Gentiles (by the moderate Hellenists) or to Jews (by the radical Hellenists). Primitive Christianity used the argument against everyone: no one was fit for the one and only God. All men are sinners. All must repent, without exception. Paul argues this in the first chapter of his Letter to the Romans (Rom.1.18-3.20).

(b) The radical Hellenistic reform attempt was an enterprise carried on by the upper class and directed against the indigenous population of the country. Only the educated Greeks were to have rights as citizens in the newly founded Hellenistic polis. This made the indigenous groups *katoikountes*, i.e. second-class citizens. By contrast, the primitive Christian opening up of Judaism to other peoples was based on a development 'from below'.

III

Biblical Monotheism in an Evolutionary Perspective

Our question is: what contribution did the discovery of the one and only God make to the emancipation of humanity from its (biological) prehistory? How far is monotheism a step in the direction of a more human culture?

Three themes and theses will concern us in the following paragraphs: 1. Monotheism is not the result of a continuous development. 2. Monotheism is the expression of a protest against selection. 3. Compared with other religious convictions, monotheism represents a structure of adaptation which corresponds better both to the central reality and to humanity.

1. Biblical monotheism as a spiritual 'mutation'

Evolutionary interpretations of the history of religion are usually understood to be an explanation of the phenomenon of religion as the result of a continuous development. The model for such development is the growth of living beings which leads to increasingly subtle differentiation and integration. Within such a framework of thought, monotheism would be interpreted as the result of a continuous development from animism, polytheism, henotheism and monolatry to belief in the one and only God. Such a development cannot be proved. Monotheism appeared suddenly, though not without being prepared for. We must follow R.Pettazoni in noting that 'monotheism is not a formation of evolution but of revolution. The appearance of a monotheistic religion is always bound up with a religious revolution.'[30]

An evolutionary interpretation of biblical religion does not follow the 'model of growth'. Rather, development is a web of trial and error with many mistakes, discontinuities and breaks. 'Revolutions', too, are a way of bringing forth variants of life which may (perhaps) take us further.

Belief in the one and only God broke through in various places in a revolutionary transformation of our consciousness.[31] Two of these spiritual revolutions were significant for our culture: the monotheism of the Greek philosophers and the biblical belief in one God. They came about almost at the same time and independently of each other in Deutero-Isaiah, a prophet in the middle of the sixth century BC, and in Xenophon of Colophon, his Greek contemporary. In terms of the theory of evolution one can regard these spiritual revolutions as 'mutations' of our religious structures of adaptation to the ultimate reality, as an attempt to do more justice to it than, for example, belief in many powers.

I have used the term 'mutation' as an analogy. It is interesting that the witnesses to that monotheistic revolution in Israel also groped for comparable imagery. Conversion to the one and only God is interpreted as a radical inner change. Humanity is given a new organ; indeed, without this new organ men and women cannot do justice to the reality which has been newly disclosed to them. The following sayings from the prophets all relate to the inner move towards monotheism. Yahweh is speaking to the people (through his prophets).

'I will give them a heart to know that I am the Lord; and they shall be my people and I will be their God, for they shall return to me with their whole heart' (Jer.24.7).

'Behold, I will gather them from all the countries to which I drove them in my anger and my wrath and in great indignation; I will bring them back to this place, and I will make them dwell in safety. And they shall be my people and I will be their God. I will give them one heart and one way, that they may fear me for ever, for their own good and the good of their children after them. I will make with them an everlasting covenant, that I will not turn away from doing good to them; and I will put the fear of me in their hearts, that they may not turn from me' (Jer.32.37-40).

'I will gather you from the peoples, and assemble you out of the countries where you have been scattered, and I will give you the land of Israel. And when they come there they will remove from it all its detestable things and all its abominations. And I will give them one heart, and put a new spirit within them; I will take the stony heart out of their flesh and give them a heart of flesh, that they may walk in my statutes and keep my ordinances and obey them; and they shall be my people, and I will be their God' (Ezek.11.17-20).

The image of the new heart and the new spirit has a specific *Sitz im*

Leben. It symbolizes the transformation of those who were confronted with God in a new way as a result of the catastrophe and in the exile. Here it is illuminating that the real change is expected in the future. When God leads the exiles back they will receive a new heart. The decisive thing is that they should turn from all the gods. Yahweh says to them: 'A new heart I will give you, and a new spirit I will put within you; and I will take out of your flesh the heart of stone and give you a heart of flesh' (Ezek.36.25f.). The transformation of man and his turning away from many gods are different sides of one and the same event.

Those who for the first time in history arrived at a consistent monotheism recognized that if they were to do justice to the new reality which had disclosed itself to them they would have to undergo a kind of 'mutation' in order to be able to meet its demands – just as all living creatures have to undergo mutations when they come into a new environment which has quite new characteristics. For example, sea creatures have to develop new organs if they are to meet the demands of the dry land. Now with the development of the one and only God, a radically new 'environment' opened up with completely new 'demands for adaptation'. There was therefore need for radical change.

The discovery of this new dimension of our reality is already a 'cognitive' mutation. It found a way into the cultural memory of humanity in several different stages. Here there is no 'automatic evolution' (if by that we understand the continuous approximation to the new knowledge). B.Lang has described the history of this development in the following way:

> Once the Yahweh-alone idea has been created and emerges with a rather jerky suddenness, there are always people who are concerned for the influence of this form of religion and help it towards victory in the fight against Israel's polytheistic cult. Here the decline of an idea which is by no means intrinsically convincing is always at risk... The history of Israelite religion is full of gaps, but its basic outlines can be recognized; in it we can see a chain of revolutions which in quick succession lead from the fight against the Tyrian Baal in the ninth century through the idea of Yahweh alone in the eighth to the establishment of the sole worship of Yahweh in the late seventh century and monotheism in the sixth.[32]

2. Biblical monotheism as a protest against the principle of selection

In what direction has the discovery of the one and only God taken people? We cannot answer this question if we understand monotheism as an abstract idea. For an evolutionary interpretation of biblical monotheism it is crucial to note the situation in which it came into being: in the exile, when the Jews were confronted with the question whether they could continue to exist. In other words, it came about in a situation in which the Jewish people (not for the first or the last time) were in danger of falling victim to a historical process of selection.

What does that mean? Let us remind ourselves that human history knows just as brutal processes of selection as those of nature. Wars of extermination are instances of selection: those with military superiority survive. Their population and their culture has a better chance of dissemination. Those who are militarily inferior disappear – through physical annihilation or the dissolution of their own cultural traditions, i.e. their language, way of life and literature. The wars of the ancient Near East were in part wars of extermination. The conquered were wiped out. Thus King Mesha of Moab boasts that he has sacked the Israelite city of Ataroth: 'I fought against the town and took it and I slew all the people of the town, a spectacle for Chemosh and Moab.' The Israelites were no better and no worse than their neighbours. One has only to read Num.31.17f. There, after a victory over the Midianites, Moses commands: 'Now therefore, kill every male among the little ones, and kill every woman who has known man by lying with him. But all the young girls who have not known man by lying with him, keep alive for yourselves.' The young girls are spared because they can contribute to the physical expansion of the victors, but are too young to disseminate the cultural traditions of the people from whom they come. This is a reflection of the way in which war was waged in the Ancient East. This way of waging war had already been 'humanized' to some degree when the victors contented themselves with enslaving and deporting the besieged – or even limited their demands to the payment of tribute.

The Jews in Babylon who had been deported had just experienced such a war and an utter political catastrophe. According to the usual logic of the Near East their god Yahweh had also come to grief. For when peoples waged war on one another, this was at the same time a war of their gods.[33] Yahweh had been defeated. But instead of ridding themselves of their god – and recognizing the gods of the victors as being the more powerful, even – indeed, especially – after the catastrophe the Israelites proclaimed that the gods of the victors were nothing. They did not exist. Yahweh was the only God. The catastrophe did not show his impotence but his power. Why? Beforehand, the great prophets of Yahweh – Amos, Hosea, Isaiah and Jeremiah – had already foretold the catastrophe for the people as punishment for worshipping other gods alongside Yahweh. Now it had happened. The victory of the Babylonians over the Israelites was thus no victory of Marduk; it was a punitive action of Yahweh against his own people. Yahweh ruled over all peoples, even over the victors. Belief in particular national deities – in Chemosh, the god of the Philistines; Asshur, the god of the Assyrians; or Dagon, the god of the Philistines – was a mistake. There was only one God, a God of all the peoples, who had chosen Israel.

This interpretation of the catastrophe at the same time contained a great hope. People could tell themselves that if disobedience to the one God was the cause of the catastrophe, obedience towards him could overcome their catastrophic situation. Ezekiel, the great prophet of the exile, expresses it in this way.

> In exile the Israelites lamented: 'Our transgressions and our sins are upon us, and we waste away because of them; how then can we live?' (Ezek.33.10). The prophet replied: 'As I live, says the Lord God, I have no pleasure in the death of the wicked, but that the wicked turn from his way and live; turn back, turn back from your evil ways; for why will you die, O house of Israel?' (33.11).

So the breakthrough to monotheism in the exile embraces two basic insights: 1. There is only one God, who rules over all peoples, even over the victors; and 2. this God offers the possibility of repentance – and thus promises new life for the whole people despite the catastrophe.

Put in rather more modern terms, this prophetic message runs: radical change of behaviour is better than dying. And: radical change of behaviour is also possible for whole societies; it is allowed and commanded by that power which determines the basic conditions of all reality. That pessimism is unjustified which argues that people have hitherto always acted destructively and it can never be otherwise. On the contrary, they can receive a new 'heart', can change drastically.

The message of the possibility of a radical change of behaviour as a chance of survival no longer sounds as revolutionary to our ears as it did at the time. Modern societies believe in the possibility of a change of behaviour – a legacy of biblical tradition. However, the traditionalist societies of the time saw a change of behaviour as at best a sign of decay.

This message becomes even more revolutionary if we go back to the biological roots of our life. Non-human beings are largely pre-programmed in the way in which they behave. If modes of behaviour become dysfunctional because conditions in the environment change, the beings themselves must die out unless chance mutations lead to more appropriate forms of behaviour which enable them to survive. Here change in behaviour comes about through the extinction of the vehicles of dysfunctional modes of behaviour. Without death there is no change of behaviour - at least no permanent change of behaviour, which can benefit subsequent generations.

Human beings are the only ones to have an opportunity to alter their behaviour without having to die. For example, if we were firmly pre-programmed to the programmes of ethnocentric militarism which have governed the whole of history hitherto and which are glorified in the heroic epics of the nations, the downfall of our culture would be unavoidable. Sooner or later we would resort to our terrifying weapons – with patterns of behaviour which were intended for use with mace and axe, bow and arrow, sword and lance, but not with atomic bombs. Without radical changes in the basic patterns of our social relationships we would have no hope at all. We would fall victim to the age-old laws of selection. And these state that sooner or later living beings with modes of behaviour which are incompatible with the conditions of reality will die out.

The biblical prophets are among the first to see that collective disaster threatens us unless we are ready to change our behaviour radically. Through 'conversion' we deprive the laws of selection of their force.

That is not too difficult to understand today. It is harder for us to see the necessary connection between this call to conversion and monotheistic faith. Here we must consider a characteristic of biblical monotheism which distinguishes it in principle from the philosophical monotheism of the Greeks. The latter was syncretistic, i.e. it regarded all the gods as identical and simply as a manifestation of one and the same deity. One could therefore be a philosophical monotheist, but in practice worship many gods and continue to practise what they required. Here the break-through to monotheism is not bound up with the demand for a fundamental change of character.

By contrast, biblical monotheism belongs to a type of anti-poly-theistic belief. Belief in the one God is a protest against belief in many gods. There is a clear call to decide between God and the idols. The monotheism of Akhenaten,[34] Zarathustra and Mohammed has a similar structure. We should be clear what this polemic feature of biblical monotheism means in practice:[35] the multiplicity of related gods each with his or her specific functions are a reflection of society differentiated according to the distribution of work. Each god represents a sphere of life, specific values and needs. Each is assigned specific fields of action. Each represents particular groups of people – so that peaceful or hostile relations in the family of gods reflect the conflicts between peoples and societies. Anyone who casts fundamental doubts on polytheism in the ancient world *ipso facto* puts in question existing society and its pattern of behaviour and is seeking to impose one value over all others. Anti-polytheistic monotheism is always critical of society. The lives of Akhenaten, Zarathustra, the great prophets and Mohammed are stamped by conflicts with society.

In a syncretistic monotheism one can add different forms of behaviour together.[36] They need not contradict one another. By contrast, an anti-polytheistic monotheism knows only the decision for the one God as a decision against the other gods - and the values and pattern of behaviour which are attributed to them. To this degree this monotheism in the ancient world is always bound up with a call to repent – quite unlike our modern societies, where we often combine belief in God with traditional patterns of behaviour. The revolutionaries of yesterday are the traditionalists of today. By contrast, in antiquity anti-polytheistic monotheism and a change of behaviour necessarily went together.

We saw that the possibility of radical change of behaviour – instead of death as a consequence of unchanged behaviour – is already intrinsically 'anti-selectionist'. But the direction in which the change of behaviour goes is important.

Here, too, biblical monotheism has an anti-selectionist feature: bound up with faith in the one and only God is the hope of overcoming processes of selection 1. between societies and 2. in society.

1. Wars are selective processes between different societies. We might recall that according to the logic of war in the ancient Near East these were always also wars between the different gods.

As long as there were many different national gods, wars between the nations had to appear as something that was built into the structure of reality. Belief in the one God (instead of many national gods) did not in fact reduce wars. But it freed the imagination to conceive of a possible transcending of war. There is an oracle in the book of Isaiah (though it probably does not go back to Isaiah himself), which connects the recognition of the one God by all the people with the hope of eternal peace:

'And it shall come to pass in the latter days that the mountain of the house of the Lord shall be established as the highest of the mountains, and shall be raised above the hills; and all the nations shall flow to it, and many peoples shall come, and say: "Come, let us go up to the mountain of the Lord, to the house of the God of Jacob; that he may teach us his ways, and that we may walk in his paths." For out of Zion shall go forth the law, and the word of the Lord from Jerusalem. He shall judge between the nations, and shall decide for many peoples; and they shall beat their swords into ploughshares, and their spears into pruning hooks; nation shall not lift up sword against nation, neither shall they learn war any more' (Isa 2.2-4; cf. Micah 4.1-5).

I do not want to claim that anti-polytheistic monotheism is intrinsically oriented on peace. But the Jewish monotheism which came into being in the situation of a defeated people, ravaged by war, embraced the unique vision of an overcoming of war. When everyone recognizes the one and only God, there can be no more wars: this is a logical notion, if wars are wars between different gods. It is evident that this logic does not govern the behaviour of Jews, Christians and Moslems. But it is enough for the vision of the changing of swords into ploughshares, a vision which is still powerful enough to be regarded as dangerous and subversive in one of the most modern states in the world.

2. Suppression and exploitation are selective processes within a society. They provide some with a chance of life at the expense of others. Here, too, it cannot in any way be said that a monotheistic faith has an inbuilt tendency to criticize the ruling power. Akhenaten (about 1350 BC) can serve as an example to the contrary.

His monotheistic revolution was a coup d'état 'from above'. The Pharaoh wanted his God Aten to be established as the only God, in order to establish his own central position against all rival powers.[37] He failed. Biblical monotheism is different. It arose in a situation in which the vehicles of this faith had lost all power – except the power of dreams and memories. This monotheistic revolt is not a *Putsch* from above against the world of the gods but a rebellion 'from below'. The one and only God of the Bible is a God of those who have escaped, of fugitives and exiles, the deported and prisoners of war. This God may not be detached from the stories about him: the stories of the homeless Abraham, the fugitive Jacob, the enslaved Israelites in Egypt, the oppressed tribes of the period of the judges and the catastrophes of the Northern and Southern Kingdoms. If we detach him from this

history, he soon becomes the God of the rulers. By contrast, the God
of the stories of the Bible has a 'bias downwards'. We need read only
one of the social commandments of the Old Testament:

> 'You shall not pervert the justice due to the sojourner or to the
> fatherless, or take a widow's garment in pledge; but you shall
> remember that you were a slave in Egypt and the Lord your God
> redeemed you from there; therefore I command you to do this'
> (Deut.24.17f.).

We should note that biblical monotheism is necessarily bound up
with the command and the offer of a far-reaching change of behaviour.
Its central theme is the reduction of the pressure of selection through
a change of conduct, repentance instead of death. The biblical prophets
interpret this opportunity as a divine demand and grace. In other
words, if men and women want their lives to be adapted adequately
to the ultimate reality, they must repent – and put into practice
patterns of behaviour which hitherto have been completely unknown.

This message is topical today. The threat now is not of the decline
of an individual people but of the end of humanity. Probably we shall
only do justice to the basic conditions of reality if we change our
behaviour at some points. The direction may well be the same as that
in the prophets: reduction of conflicts between nations and within
societies.

3. Biblical monotheism as a structure for adapting to the central reality

Belief in the one God is a protest against the principle of selection.
Harmony with a central reality beyond the world in which human
beings live also gives a 'power to survive' to those who otherwise would
have no chance. Now one could not say that faith in the one God is
simply a sublime means of survival.[38] The disclosure of a new religious
dimension of reality would then be comparable to the discovery of a
new ecological niche, ensuring the 'survival' of forms of life which
would have gone under in their previous ecological niches. Natural
though this idea might be, it is false. For the one and only God is not
one 'ecological niche' alongside others, but the central reality behind
all ecological niches. He is a universal God. He is the ultimate
'environment' behind all specific environments. Given successful
adaptation to this newly discovered dimension of depth behind all
'environments', there could be no rivalry or conflict between human
beings over resources. The means of life contained in a particular

environmental niche are always sparse. Those who inhabit these niches will challenge one another and fight over access to them. But God is never 'sparse'. He is the ground of all resources. Innumerable living beings can 'have access' to him without exhausting his riches. He gives humanity the awareness of an infinite fullness at the basis of reality, by which any rivalry and conflict over distribution is limited.

This is the decisive step forward from polytheism to monotheism. As long as people worship a multiplicity of gods, the move from one god to another is simply a move from one 'ecological niche' to another. Each god represents a limited sector of reality. Rivalry and conflict between the gods reflect the human fight for distribution. That is quite obvious in the case of gods with territorial connections. But it also holds for gods with limited functions – gods who represent the spheres of sexuality, food and drink, war, law and order. Little would have been gained had one god gained the upper hand in this rivalry between gods – and found universal recognition as the ruler of all gods. Rather, the one God had to be the only God and embrace all spheres of reality, all territories and sectors of life, all peoples and groups. Only then does humanity extricate itself from that 'bond with the environment' which leads to competition with others because of our limited opportunities for survival. By contrast, where people arrive at the conviction that the decisive 'environment' for them is God, whose resources can be shared out among an infinite number of people without losing their value, they have found the Archimedean point from which they can shift the principle of selection which controls all life. They are still subject to this principle of selection, but they know that it does not represent the ultimate reality.

So everything depends on whether the newly disclosed comprehensive 'environmental dimension' appears as a completely new development in comparison with all limited environmental niches. The Old Testament expressed this wholly other by portraying God without images and without a family. In the following sections I shall show how both the absence of images and the absence of a family in the portrayal of Yahweh represent a decisive step forward beyond the bond with a specific and limited environment.

(a) The God without images

An archaic bond with the environment lives on in religion, which is put in question by the prohibition of images. If we leave aside strict monotheism (and original Buddhism, which is equally aniconic), we can note that the objects of religious veneration have precisely the same characteristics as the signals which trigger off a response in the specific environment of animals:[39] they are improbable, simple and evocative. One need only think of stones, mountains, trees, sun, moon and all the stars with numinous connotations. Anything that is striking becomes the object of religious veneration, except that unlike the signals which trigger off responses in animals, which are instinctual, these signals extend throughout the world (and are not limited to a few specific signals). Moreover, human reaction to such signals is not a specific action but a ritual, communicative form of behaviour which is not directly aimed at survival.

I must stress that this archaic bond with signals triggered off by the environment does not just lead to uplifting experiences of the holy; the archaic bond with the environment also means being attracted by the terrifying and hostile aspects of life which find expression in ghostly and grotesque images embodying the dark side of religion. This dark side still continues to survive in a debased way in belief in ghosts.[40] We are all more prepared to see ghosts when walking through a wood at night than in the clear light of day. We see suspicious figures behind the bushes, are terrified at the slightest noise, and our proclivity to anxiety increases. Darkness and forest trigger off an archaic set of responses in us, the mark of the experience of countless generations, the sense of enemies lurking in the night who can see exceptionally well where we cannot. Primaeval anxieties about beasts of prey in the jungle well up in us, anxieties latent somewhere in our 'tween-brain, which in some situations free themselves from the control of our reason (the cerebrum). 'The ghost is the projection of some beast of prey hunting in the night' (K.Lorenz).

A first step towards ridding ourselves of this archaic way of experiencing the environment is taken when human beings become sensitive to *all* signals which trigger off responses within the field of their perception. While they may respond to them with forms of reaction which are seated deep in their 'tween-brains, their sensitivity to types of forms is clearly connected with their cerebrum, or, to be more precise, with the non-dominant hemisphere in which their aesthetic (not to mention artistic and musical) capacities are seated.[41]

Making images of gods represents a more obvious detachment from the environment. Human beings differ from animals in being able to produce iconic representations. Their first creations are still deeply rooted in instinctual behaviour. We know from experiments with animals that signals which trigger off particular behaviour can not only be replaced but even enhanced by the use of dummies and decoys; when these artificially enhance the trigger signals they can produce bizarre deviations from the norm.[42] A bird can even come to prefer a gaudy dummy egg to its own egg – a tragic error. I presume that people for thousands of years have similarly revered such larger-than-life dummies and have allowed themselves to be impressed by them, in the form of divine images which they have made themselves. If we investigate archaic divine imagery we shall soon be struck by the exaggeration of certain features: one need think only of the goddess of love with sexual parts larger than life, the imposingly ruffled breast of the goddess of war, or the gigantic size of statues of the gods (this is particularly striking when they are depicted alongside human figures). Divine imagery serves to stimulate archaic and numinous responses to reality by larger-than-life substitutes. When we take this into account, we can see what a revolution the prohibition of images was. It was a violent wrench away from an archaic bond to signals triggered by the environment.

In biblical religion the word replaces the image.[43] God reveals himself, not in the image, but in the speech-event. In this way detachment from the environment is developed further. Whereas an image must be present to prompt behaviour, language has the means to make present what is not present: it preserves recollection of the past and hope for the future. It reports what is absent. Only a living being capable of speech can grasp the notion of something wholly other behind the world in which he lives. If God is this wholly other, the word is a more appropriate 'structure of adaptation' towards him than the image; indeed the command to adapt to the central reality to which all being is subject now takes on a new quality in human beings. For them, what elsewhere is 'adaptation', unconscious trial and error aimed at harmony with the basic conditions of reality, becomes the 'response' by which they deliberately react to the substance of the invitation from the central reality.

This shift from the image to the word took place in one of the great breaks in the history of religion. From the perspective of evolutionary theory it corresponds to a transfer of religious behaviour and experience from the non-dominant hemisphere of our cerebrum to its dominant hemisphere.[44] That is where our linguistic capacity is seated. That is where we must locate our awareness. It is the seat of those capacities by which we achieve our greatest freedom from ties to an archaic environment.

And yet religious experience and conduct continually remain tied to the more archaic levels of our being, to sensitivity to those qualities of the environment which trigger off in us a strange mood which we find it difficult to influence. Perhaps this dependence of religious experience on an archaic stratum partly explains the irritating 'phase-shift'[45] between religious and profane experience of the world: at one moment the world seems to us to be banal and everyday; at the next it is a shattering power which gets an almost personal grip on us. As we know from the observation of animals, the sensitivity of the living being to triggering signals emitted by the environment depends on a subjective 'mood'. For example, sexual signals are disregarded unless the potential recipient is disposed to receive them; for the male or female stickleback such symbols may be utterly non-existent, though objectively they may be there.[46] However, when the recipient is ready for them, such symbols become the 'most significant reality'. The parallel with human experience is certainly limited: we do not just react to certain signals which are important for our survival. We react to the varied signals of all of reality. However, here too we continually find that moods disclose reality to us. Our whole experience of the world is dependent on how we feel, which we find difficult to control. That is clear, for example, in aesthetic and religious experiences. A piece of music can on one occasion be experienced as 'revelation' and on another as no more than a structured mass of sound. At one moment we are living dully in the everyday world (without a thought of God) and at the next it is quite clear to us that our life is being lived against the background of an uncanny dimension of depth. For many people God does not exist outside a particular 'mood'.[47] It is therefore a concern of religion to reach out beyond this dependence on fleeting moods.

One way to transcend the fleeting character of religious 'moods' is to associate religious experience and conduct with words: natural places for the epiphany of deities are rare. Images of deities cannot be found everywhere. But the word can be learned and internalized. It can always be near. It is therefore no coincidence that in Deuteronomy the inculcation of monotheistic faith is bound up with the word:

'Hear, O Israel: The Lord our God is one Lord; and you shall love the Lord your God with all your heart, and with all your soul, and with all your might. And these words which I command you this day shall be upon your heart; and you shall teach them diligently to your children, and shall talk of them when you sit in your house, and when you walk by the way, and when you lie down, and when you rise...' (Deut.4.6f.).

'But the word is very near you; it is in your mouth and in your heart, so that you can do it' (Deut.30.14).

(b) The God without a family

The bond between religious experience and behaviour and the word represents a liberation from the natural environment; at the same time it represents an even stronger bond to the first 'cultural', linguistic environment of any human being, the family. This emerges from the admonitions in Deuteronomy: time and again the father is admonished to teach his children the meaning of the law.

Here we come up against a second root of religion, its shaping by the family. Freud was perhaps right to suppose that some people never get over the long period of childhood in which they were fully dependent on their parents, so that all their lives they look for those omnipotent figures who once emanated security in distress and abandonment and guaranteed the fulfilment of basic needs. As these figures cannot be found on earth (any longer), they are sought in heaven.[48]

It is plausible that the experiences of early childhood are determinative. There is a demonstrable analogy to this among more highly developed animals: conditioning. During a brief phase when they are susceptible to learning, some young animals can receive impressions which determine the whole of their future conduct. Probably there are comparable 'sensitive phases' in human development, though they are much longer and more flexible, in which the basic linguistic, cognitive and emotional pattern of behaviour and experience is shaped. So we cannot doubt the high emotional significance of the relationship of the small child to his or her first partner or partners.

Suppose we accept this analogy as a model: it may be that people have been 'irreversibly' stamped by their parents. But does that mean that a religious bond to gods is a relic of this conditioning? Is it the satisfaction in imagination of a basic human need, the roots of which very few people recognize as lying in the impressions of early childhood?

Suppose we consider the function of conditioning in animals.[49] The training by their parents of animals who are about to leave their nests is a crucial process. The offspring must be able to recognize its individual parents again from all other possible parents if it is to receive food; and without food it will perish. It has to learn the appearance of its individual parents. For it is not a matter of recognizing the member of a species by its general characteristics, but of recognizing an individual from a whole series of other individuals looking precisely alike, all of whom are potential parents. So the image of the individual parents cannot be 'genetically' pre-programmed as an inherited pattern of recognition. Rather, the capacity to distinguish individual parents (which is certainly pre-programmed) must have an empty space which can be 'conditioned' from outside. This plasticity of learning makes it possible to condition animals in all kinds of ways. If a human being comes into contact with them in that brief phase where they are sensitive to learning, they will even accept him or her as 'father' or 'mother'. Similarly, dummies can be substitute parents. In the brain of these animals there is a space which can be shaped by almost any external impressions, like wax by a stamp. This 'stamp' is not a universal state of affairs, but something individual.

Within evolutionary development this is a decisive step towards a more objective view of the world. It is the first time that living beings carry an individual image of external reality within themselves. Previously they followed general instinctive patterns and reacted to general evocative signals which could be simulated by any schematically constructed decoys. Now they react to a piece of 'individual' reality. In terms of the physiology of the brain, they take the step from the 'tween-brain with its pattern of instincts reacting to stimuli towards the cerebrum with its plasticity which adapts increasingly to objective data.

May we argue from this phylogenetic situation to human beings? In human life, too, is not experience of parents the gateway to the world? If we apply this approach to the development of the history of religion we might then arrive at the following hypothesis. Once the gods take on the features of families and are worshipped as mother or father or a heavenly couple, human beings are no longer controlled by the signals triggered off by relics, but by their first cultural experiences; by dealing with persons in a family relationship, with whom there is a family connection. This relationship takes the place of a vague general attraction to and fascination with stones, animals, sun and moon, the trigger-symbols of the natural world. In the history of religion, the appearance of father and mother deities was a step towards freedom from natural dependence. The old natural evocations continued to work, but now they became the context of the epiphany of the deity; the stone is no longer itself the god, but the 'house of God' (Beth-el). The volcano is no longer itself the deity, but his epiphany. Other evocative qualities become attributes: the 'bull' becomes the seat of the deity (Yahweh or El), the lion the vehicle for the goddess of love, the owl Athene's companion, the lightning the sceptre of Baal. Father and mother gods have trained human beings in reality.

The archaic stratum in religious experience and behaviour rooted in the depths of the 'tween-brain takes on permanence and duration as a result of these father and mother deities. It is moulded by the model of the most reliable of all inter-human relationships, that of the bond between the child and its parents. A relationship to the central reality shaped along these lines is independent of changes of mood and the fleeting moments of being positively addressed, important though these still are.

An interpretation of the ultimate reality in terms of father and mother is therefore to be assessed positively. Yahweh, too, originally had a wife by his side, like all gods: the Asherah (II Kings 23.7) or queen of heaven (Jer.44.25). This accorded with the logic of the family. It was a revolutionary step when the prophets broke through these categories of interpretation based on the family: the divine couple became the one and only God – without a sexual partner. The mother deities were radically suppressed. Israel took the place of the queen of heaven: from then on Yahweh had only one partner, the people. Moreover it was a problematical partner whose unreliability was castigated by the prophets. The very prophets who uttered polemic against the divine symbols which presented the gods in terms of the family – Hosea and Jeremiah – transferred the metaphor of marriage to the relationship between Yahweh and his people (Hos.1-2; Jer.3.1ff.). This transference is connected with their polemic against fertility cults: all associations with sexuality, procreation and fertility are to be kept remote from Yahweh, as remote as the ritual institutions which are hardly conceivable without an interpretation of the holy in terms of fertility: sacral prostitution, which was long practised in the temple of Yahweh (Micah 1.7; Deut.23.17f.), and the sacrifice of first children, which in the light of Ezek.20.26 must have been an ingredient of Yahwistic religion.

The fact that these mother deities returned, despite their suppression, shows how difficult it was to break through the symbolism of the family.[50] 'Wisdom' is the spiritualized form of the mother goddess (and compatible with monotheistic faith): God lives with her in a mystical marriage (Wisdom 8.3). She is God's partner (Prov.8), but not as an independent person alongside God. Rather, she is a hypostasis of a divine characteristic, a personification of his gracious side which is turned towards the world.

The return of the suppressed 'wife of Yahweh' was possible because in the meantime monotheistic faith had become so established that it could no longer be endangered by formerly polytheistic imagery. The categories of interpretation of the divine world in terms of the family were finally broken. How did this breakthrough attain its penetrative power?

We should recall that this development is not completely unique. The same thing happened in Greek philosophy. Here Zeus, the father of gods and men, becomes the sole ruler. In both contexts there is a basic recognition that the world is a unity – an experience which is increasingly confirmed as our knowledge progresses, but which is also accessible to pre-scientific thought. Again and again the unity of reality makes itself felt, regardless of whether it is experienced as a unity of the cosmos, as in Greece, or as a unity of history, as in Israel. However, only the symbolism of monotheism corresponds to this reality, experienced as a unity: one god, not a divine couple. The shattering of family imagery to symbolize the deity was an adaptation to objective reality which could no longer be interpreted in this way, as this was a pattern of interpretation more suitable to use among young children. The step towards belief in the one God without a family, without wife and children, without kith and kin, is an important step beyond the bond between human beings and their first social environment.

But it is even more: because the one God is imagined without wife, sexuality and procreation, he is thought of independently of the basic biological processes. His power is not the power of fertility. His love is not a sexual bond. He stands outside procreation and birth, sexuality and death, beyond 'biological evolution' and the sphere of the 'flesh', as the Bible calls it. Where it is a human being's calling to live in harmony with this God, it is clear that such a response to this God recognizes higher values than life and survival and enhanced chances of propagation.

To sum up: just as the God without images is a constant warning to us to free ourselves from the spell of natural images, so the God without a family is a constant reminder that human beings are called to free themselves from the way in which they are stamped by the family – to leave their father's house, as Abraham was commanded. The central reality to which human beings should correspond is something completely other. And it requires of human beings something 'completely other' than evolution hitherto: it gives them a chance to take a step beyond the principle of selection, through the disclosure of the riches of reality and through inter-personal solidarity. Only when it is clearly recognized that the reality which controls all things is not identical with nature and society can human beings 'leave' nature and family.

Thus the breakthrough of biblical monotheism is an 'evolution of evolution'. In it is manifested the fact that the ultimate reality supports groups which would have vanished from history had the usual processes of selection prevailed. At the same time evolution hitherto is transcended in a second respect: from the perspective of the living being adaptation means better use of the environment for its own chances of survival and propagation. Man is the first living being who can see independent value in the whole of reality and in adaptation to the environment, independently of all chances of survival and propagation. Adaptation becomes harmony with reality – without exploiting it. Granted, man is seldom free of 'exploitative intentions'. Scientific insights and technological control of the environment are closely connected. Knowledge can be understood exclusively as an instrument of power. But human beings are capable at the same time of adopting another attitude to reality. They can react to it responsively instead of instrumentally. This transition from an instrumental to a responsive attitude took place in religion. Granted, belief in the one and only God is also 'adaptation' to an unknown outside world, to the ultimate environment behind the limited worlds of humanity. But this adaptation is free of exploitation. Or, to put it more accurately, the commands of biblical monotheism prohibit the notion of an 'exploitation' of God – say for magical ends. The one and only God cannot be made an instrument of the will to survive. Rather, he requires adaptation even where adaptation puts survival at risk. He cannot be exploited, but takes humanity into his service. Before this God, people are aware that their life is subject to other criteria than those of survival and self-propagation.

Both these aspects of an evolution of evolution, protest against the principle of selection and the transformation of adaptation into response and responsibility, are closely connected. Anyone who has become free, so as no longer to have to experience reality in terms of survival and propagation, is also free from always having to increase opportunities at the expense of others. Such individuals are responsible not only for their own life but for all life, even for rival, weaker life.

PART THREE

Faith in Jesus of Nazareth: New Testament Christology in an Evolutionary Perspective

In an evolutionary perspective, the prophetic breakthrough to belief in the one and only God can be regarded as a 'mutation' of our religious life, a successful mutation, if we accept that it has led to a more adequate adaptation to the ultimate reality. This adaptation is not limited to the theoretical conviction that there is only one God, a conviction at which the Greek philosophers also arrived. Its practical aspect is also decisive. Faith in this one God means conversion and a change of behaviour. Because God is wholly other, he calls for a change in human behaviour.

Now Christian faith says that this God has finally revealed himself in Jesus Christ. In the midst of history there has been a valid demonstration of the necessary direction any change of behaviour has to take if it is to correspond to the ultimate reality. In the midst of history a possible 'goal' of evolution is revealed: complete adaptation to the reality of God. This very assertion of a final revelation in the midst of history becomes a problem for modern awareness.

I

The Problem: Revelation and History

In the light of historical criticism, the basic question for Christian faith is, 'How can a historically relative phenomenon be the vehicle of unconditional revelation?' Anyone who reads the texts of the New Testament in the light of historical criticism will keep coming up against this central problem: the hermeneutical conflict[1] between the New Testament's understanding as an echo of divine revelation and the modern analysis of it. There are three aspects to this conflict.

First, historical investigation discloses the relativity of the traditions about Jesus. Confronted with the miracles of Jesus, the crowd in the New Testament cries out, 'We never saw anything like this!' The historian adds: 'That often happened', or more accurately, 'People often told that sort of story.' He is satisfied only when he has found a context for the figure of Jesus by means of many analogies and parallels, partly to interpret them for modern man and partly to protect them from modernizing attempts at reinterpretation. The New Testament, however, insists that the figure of Jesus is unique and without analogy.

Secondly, historical research is concerned with the conditioning of historical phenomena. Its task is to interpret traditions in the light of their actual context, i.e. in the light of the social, economic, political and psychological conditions of the time. It tends to interpret texts as the reflection of a dependence on the history of tradition, in terms of social conflicts and a psychological dynamic. The New Testament, however, understands the traditions about Christ as the expression of an absolute divine revelation. The question is: what is revealed in the New Testament – the reality of God or social tensions and unconscious conflicts?

A third aspect of the hermeneutical conflict arises from the two which have already been mentioned. Of necessity, the interpretation of modern scholarship is immanent, i.e. it is based on analogies and correlations, on references to what is known and familiar. It goes very much against modern assumptions to suppose that a historical figure can leave the field of what is known and familiar and disclose a world which in principle is strange. However, that is precisely what the New Testament claims. For the New Testament, Jesus is the revealer *par excellence*. He makes accessible a realm which was hitherto inaccessible to human history and only became accessible through him.

There can be no doubt that there is a deep-seated hermeneutical conflict between our modern consciousness and the understanding the New Testament has of itself. Relativity, conditioning and immanence are almost *a priori* categories of modern consciousness.[2] However, an awareness of uniqueness, absoluteness and revelation in Jesus shaped New Testament christology. It has its common denominator in the conviction that with Jesus a new world begins, which does away with the old world. It is precisely this eschatological framework of New Testament christology which is involved in the hermeneutical conflict.

There are analogies to this eschatological awareness. In the New Testament period many people expected an imminent end to the world and suspected that this was beginning in the circumstances of their time.

There were reasons for this eschatological awareness: the current apocalyptic expectations were a reaction to the conflict between Hellenism and Judaism with all its cultural, political, economic and social aspects.

Above all, however, the eschatological consciousness could be understood as revelation only with some difficulty. The expectation of an imminent end was a mistake. Did God reveal himself in mistakes?

The hermeneutical conflict which I have sketched out is the fate of any theology in modern times. It is that 'enormously deep ditch', of which Lessing spoke in another connection.[3] There would be no point in relativizing it. That would not do justice to the claims either of the New Testament or of modern times. Rather, we must do what reasonable people attempt to do when they come up against a deep ditch. They attempt to build a bridge over it. They may end up in the ditch in the process. But that should not give anyone pleasure.

In the following section I shall attempt to interpret New Testament christology with the help of evolutionary categories. The decisive categories of 'mutation', 'selection' and 'adaptation' should serve as a model for coming to terms in an argument with the hermeneutical conflict between christology and the modern consciousness, and for building a bridge between them. In anticipation, let me sketch out the basic notion. The activity and proclamation of Jesus should be interpreted primarily as a 'mutation' of human existence. This puts him in the context of the history of nature and human history generally.

'Mutations' are the motive force behind all development. Jesus is one 'mutation' among many others. He is a phenomenon relativized in history. And yet the concept of mutation offers the possibility of conceiving something fundamentally new in history. For mutations are leaps in development beyond what has happened hitherto.

Secondly, the proclamation and activity of Jesus are to be interpreted as a protest against the pressure of selection, and therefore as a break with biological evolution. Here Jesus appears as the one who consummates the history of the Old Testament. Whereas the prophets arrived at the idea that a change of conduct and conversion is better than death, Jesus actually embodied the change in conduct that they called for. The principle of solidarity replaced the principle of selection. Symbolically that brought about the beginning of a new era in the cosmos and completed the history of the God who revealed himself in the experiences of Israel.

Thirdly, the activity and the proclamation of Jesus are to be interpreted as a successful 'adaptation' to the central reality. In him we see a possible goal of evolution, that gigantic process of trial and error which strives for increasingly adequate adaptations to the basic conditions of reality. These basic conditions are such as to justify unconditional trust – as unconditional as the child's trust in its father.

Granted, in the following section we shall be working with categories which are unfamiliar to the New Testament. Nowhere in the New Testament do we find the concepts of 'mutation', 'selection' or 'adaptation'. Nevertheless, every page in the New Testament expresses the conviction that a fundamentally new form of humanity has appeared which exceeds all previous human possibilities. A 'mutation' has taken place. The new feature is love. This is not to be understood, subjectively, as an emotional bond, which is the way we usually interpret it, but as solidarity with the weak, a contradiction of the processes in nature and history which are oriented on selection. In this love God reveals himself.

Perhaps the 'modern' images and similes of God from evolutionary theory show a way of overcoming the hermeneutical conflict between New Testament christology and modern consciousness. Some people will mistrust this way. That is understandable. The use of metaphors leads us into the obscure intermediate area between poetry and reality, imagination and reality. Metaphors often transcend boundaries which are set by strict reflection. However, metaphors and images are indispensable for theological reflection. That is clear from the parables of Jesus. Just as his images draw on material from the experience of his time, so it must be permissible to develop new theological metaphors and models with material from the experience of our time. For there are dimensions of reality in which we can find our bearings only with images and parables. That is no resigned irrationalism. On the contrary, images and parables are a possible way of continuing to deal with problems in arguments where abstract concepts fail; they enable understanding where otherwise only confessional positions would be adopted.

II

The Proclamation and Ministry of Jesus of Nazareth: A Historical Outline

Jesus[4] was probably born in Nazareth, a small village near the town of Sepphoris. All his life he moved in the hinterland of Hellenistic city culture and avoided the larger cities[5] – apart from Jerusalem, where he met his end.

We first encounter him as a follower of John the Baptist, an ascetic prophet who lived in the Jordan wilderness and proclaimed repentance and faith as deliverance from the imminent judgment on the world. Jesus had himself baptized, and probably shared the convictions usually connected with baptism, namely that baptism is bound up with the forgiveness of sins and calls for repentance. So Jesus understood himself as a sinner before God (or we would have to postulate that he attached quite a different meaning to his baptism).

After the arrest or execution of the Baptist he made an independent appearance in Galilee, gathered a group of disciples around him, and worked as a prophet and wisdom teacher. The tradition attributes both these social roles to him; in Matt.12.41f. Jesus compares himself to Jonah, the prophet who called for repentance but whose prophecies were not heard in Nineveh, and with Solomon, the great wisdom teacher, to whom the Queen of Sheba travelled. This understanding of Jesus as a prophet and wisdom teacher occurs in the proud awareness that 'More than Jonah is here' and 'More than Solomon is here'. The connection between the traditions and the content of the message of prophecy and wisdom is in fact characteristic of his preaching. It is also the case that despite its limitation to Israel his preaching also has a universalist tone: it can be addressed to anyone, just as Jonah and Solomon (according to Mark 12.41f.) addressed both Jews and Gentiles.

Thus in the following account I shall present Jesus as a prophet and wisdom teacher. However, we must make a further distinction.

According to the synoptic tradition, martyrdom was the fate of a prophet. So I shall give a separate account of Jesus as martyr. The wisdom teacher has the capacity to make teaching vivid in parables and imagery. In Jesus this feature is so marked that I shall devote a separate section to Jesus as poet.

1. Jesus as prophet

Like the Old Testament prophets, Jesus proclaimed judgment and salvation, and in so doing followed in the steps of his teacher John the Baptist. If we are to understand the character of the two New Testament prophets, we must note the continuation of Old Testament prophecy in post-exilic apocalyptic.[6] Prophecy had proclaimed Yahweh's action as analogous to the previous history of the people. The future corresponded to their experiences that far. With the exile two presuppositions changed: Yahweh was regarded as the God of all peoples, alongside whom there were no other gods. He had picked Israel out from all the peoples with the task of bearing witness to him as the one and only God. At the same time Israel lost its political independence. It became dependent on other peoples. In this situation Yahweh's action had to become universal action towards all peoples, and his judgment had to become a cosmic judgment on the whole world. The national past could no longer provide material to illustrate this action of God, since it always spoke only of one people. Rather, recourse had to be made to the mythical traditions of other nations: in apocalyptic we find Babylonian planetary speculations, Orphic visions of the underworld, Persian ideas of resurrection, mixed with the continuation of Old Testament imagery. Its central statement is that the whole of history is coming to an end.

The Jewish apocalyptists hoped that with this end Israel would attain salvation. John the Baptist challenged this assurance of salvation. For the pious in Israel, too, 'Now already the axe is set to the root of the trees' (Matt.3.10). People can save themselves only by repenting at the last moment. But what meaning could a radical change of behaviour have if the end was immediately in prospect? Was there still time to put one's repentance to the test? Here the Baptist offered something new which went beyond the Old Testament prophets: baptism. It could become a prophylactic sign of conversion, its symbol, which would be valid even if there was hardly time for any ethical test. One 'more mighty' than the Baptist would come soon and complete the baptism by water with a baptism by fire.

Jesus continued the Baptist's proclamation of judgment.[7] However, he did not require baptism. He limited himself to the demand for repentance. We shall see why. For Jesus there was time for testing. But this time was also the last period of testing. The goal of all time was the coming of a mysterious 'man' as judge.[8] This 'man' (or 'son of man') would break in suddenly and unexpectedly with his judgment, like the flood in the days of Noah and the catastrophe in the days of Lot (Luke 17.26ff.). His judgment would not affect peoples and groups, but every individual. Even if two shared a bed, it could be that 'one is taken and the other is left' (Luke 17.34). For the criteria of judgment would not be the characteristics of a political, national or religious group. Rather, the judgment of the 'man' would have a criterion: whether one had fed the hungry, given drink to the thirsty, harboured strangers, clothed the naked, looked after the sick and visited those in prison (Matt.25.31ff.). The ethical teaching of Jesus was decisive. The attitude of the 'son of man' in judgment would be oriented on attitudes to him and his words (Mark 8.38).

It is easy to see how with Jesus the mysterious 'man' takes the place of the 'mightier one' foretold by John the Baptist. Jesus identified this 'mightier' one with the 'man' of whom the book of Daniel already says that he will take the place of the kingdom of the beasts (Dan.7). This 'man' is not simply the 'mightier' one; rather, he is present in all those who are weak. He says: 'What you have done to the least of these my brethren you have done to me' (Matt.25.40).

The change in the preaching of salvation is even more radical. It is a feature which is not completely absent in the case of the Baptist: baptism and repentance provide a chance of escaping the coming wrathful judgment. However, whereas John the Baptist said that the axe was already set to the root of the trees, Jesus uses the same image of the tree to show that there is still time. The tree which bears no fruit should really be felled; however, at the request of the cultivator of the vineyard the lord still gives it a chance (Luke 13.6-9). It is one of the great riddles of the preaching of Jesus how this change from the proclamation of the Baptist to that of Jesus could come about. Perhaps the explanation is that someone who expects an annihilating judgment at any moment as the inexorable consequence of wrong human conduct can see any moment in which people and the world still exist as an unhoped-for time of reprieve; indeed, the simple fact that the sun rises and sets and the earth still stands can become a sign of the goodness of God, who makes his sun shine on evil and good alike and allows everyone the possibility of repentance.[9] In my view, the fact that the end of the world does not happen, although it is expected immediately, is confirmation of the fact that God is utterly different. He does not threaten life like the axe set to the root of the tree. He allows life. He continues to make it possible, although all life really deserved death. But if God continues to allow everything to exist, both good and evil – must not human beings similarly put in question the sharp boundaries between good and evil, friend and foe?

It is a basic experience of Jesus that life has a chance. God is gracious. Therefore now is a time of joy (Mark 2.19). Therefore the present generation experiences what prophets and kings longed for (Luke 10.23ff.). Therefore the kingdom of God is already beginning 'in our midst' (Luke 17.20). Therefore it is already hidden in the present like the seed in the ground (Mark 4.26ff.).

Then was the Baptist's dark vision of the end of the world an illusion? No, certainly not. The judgment had already partly taken place – but it had fallen on Satan, not humanity. In a vision (at his calling?) Jesus saw Satan falling from heaven.[10] From then on Satan could accuse no one. He had been conquered. And because the rule of Satan had been overcome, the kingdom of God could now already begin in secret (Mark 3.24-26); there were boundless visible signs of this change. The demons retreat: 'If I with the spirit of God cast out the demons, the kingdom of God has already come upon you' (Matt.12.28).

To sum up: Jesus continues John the Baptist's preaching of judgment and salvation. However, he gives it new accents. The preaching of judgment is changed because at its centre there now appears a 'man' as an eschatological judge who stands on the side of the weak. The preaching of salvation is changed because the kingdom of God is now already an offer of salvation.

Granted, the relationship between the proclamation of judgment and the proclamation of salvation are left unrelated. Nowhere does Jesus connect the proclamation of the 'man' and his judgment with the proclamation of the 'kingdom of God'.[11] However, there is a connection through a mythical event, the fall of Satan. If judgment is to come, Satan can have no part in it. He can no longer accuse and calumniate. His role is played out. He is cast out of the heavenly sphere of power. His place has been taken by the 'man': just as Satan fell like lightning from heaven (Luke 10.18), so the Son of man will one day light up the whole heaven like lightning (Luke 17.24). The awareness of already having won a decisive victory over evil therefore changes the idea of judgment. However, at the same time this awareness changes the offer of salvation: because Satan is cast down, the *basileia* (the kingdom of God) can already be proclaimed as a reality hidden in the present, which leaves time for conversion and ethical testing. Therefore Jesus can dispense with baptism as a sign of repentance. The anxiety that God will immediately fall upon humanity with his judgment of wrath is overcome.

2. Jesus as wisdom teacher

The background to the ethical teaching of Jesus[12] is the conviction that God has given men a chance to repent, i.e. to change their ethical behaviour. So just as the Baptist gave each individual a chance of salvation regardless of his or her social links (as a member of Israel), so the proclamation of Jesus poses an ethical test to all people independently of traditional social ties. Here his teaching often takes on a 'universalist' character. There are analogies from non-Jewish (and Jewish) traditions for much of its content, but as a whole it seems to be quite distinctive. It is aimed at people who have gained a larger degree of autonomy over against their environment.

A tendency towards such autonomy can already be seen in the simple summary of all ethical demands in simple maxims. Love for God and one's fellow human beings covers all that is required (Mark 12.28f.). Everyone understands what the 'golden rule' – a widely disseminated popular maxim – calls for; to treat everyone else as you would like to be treated yourself (Matt.7.12).

The sayings concerned with instances where fellow human beings offend against such ethical rules are characteristic. Where people suffer injustice from others, Jesus says, 'If anyone strikes you on the cheek, offer him the other' (Matt.5.39ff.). If someone passes judgment on the wrongs done by others he should be aware that the splinter in his eye is more than matched by the 'beam' in his own eye (Matt.7.1ff.).

In the context of the proclamation of Jesus this in no way amounts to subjection to the will of others. Rather, it is the expression of a sovereignty over established norms which exert social pressure and counter-pressure. If we distinguish three fundamental dimensions in our social relationships – the in-group and outsiders; those in higher positions and those beneath them; tradition and the present – we can see that in all three dimensions Jesus shows an unusual degree of freedom.

The basic in-group to which everyone belongs is the family, and the outsider group at furthest remove is its enemies. Internal solidarity and the rejection of outsiders go hand in hand. Jesus reverses the relationship. He calls on his followers to break with the family (Luke 14.26; Matt.8.21f.) but to love their enemies (Matt.5.43ff.).

The hierarchical relationship between 'above' and 'below' is also shaken: the disciples are not to behave in the way that happens elsewhere in the world: the one who wants to be first must be ready to be the servant of all (Mark 10.41ff.). The first will be last (Matt. 19.30 etc).

His attitude towards tradition is equally radical. For centuries the tradition determined what is holy. But Jesus counters 'You have heard that it was said...' with his distinctive 'But I say to you' (Matt.5.21ff.). The divine will was not established once for all in the past.

It could be said that in the proclamation of Jesus the most elementary social ordinances are stood on their head. However, independence from pre-existing social ties is also shown in other features. Only external behaviour is subject to social control. Jesus puts the accent on motivation (which is not controllable) in both ethical and religious demands – and in this way arrives at consequences which in fact specifically affect external behaviour.

On possessions he teaches that we should not just be ready to give up material objects. What matters is to have inner freedom from them, to overcome the cares with which concern for existence fetters us, from which we want to free ourselves through 'possessions' (Matt.6.25ff.)

On aggression he teaches that the guilty person is not just one who kills, but even one who hates another (Matt.5.21f.).

On adultery he teaches that one does not just commit adultery by sleeping with another woman but even by wanting to sleep with her (Matt.5.27f.).

On honesty he teaches that each of our words should be as true as though it were sworn on oath. In that case a special oath is obscured (Matt.5.33f.).

His teaching on religious conduct displays the same inner independence:

On purity he teaches that there are no intrinsically pure and impure objects, but only inward attitudes, which make something pure or impure (Mark.7.15).

On prayer he teaches that many (outward) words are superfluous. For God already knows in advance what people need (Matt.6.7f.).

As to giving, one should not give in order to make an impression on others. Rather, the left hand should not know what the right hand is doing (Matt.6.2ff.).

People should not practise ritual fasting because others expect it, but secretly, where only God can 'control' human conduct.

The sabbath may be broken if one can be of help and there is an urgent reason, without the need to justify such breaches of the sabbath with profound arguments.

Anyone who ventures on such independence of social control can also arrive at completely new evaluations of individuals and groups: Jesus is not content that what is really important should take place in secret, without any social consequences. He goes directly against manifest social judgments.

The usual view is that children are less important than adults. But Jesus says, 'Suffer the children to come to me, for theirs is the kingdom of God' (Mark 10.14). However, conversely adults must become children in order to enter it (Matt.18.3).

The usual view of tax-collectors and prostitutes is a low one. But Jesus says to the pious, 'Tax-collectors and prostitutes will enter the kingdom of God before you' (Matt.21.31).

The usual view despises foreigners and unbelievers. But Jesus proclaims: many foreigners will eat with the patriarchs of Israel in the kingdom of God, and the natives will be excluded (Matt.8.11f.).

In the usual view, sexually impotent men are despised. But Jesus says that there are eunuchs from birth, eunuchs by human hand and eunuchs 'for the sake of the kingdom of God'. In this way he clearly goes against the current derogatory view of eunuchs.

Independence from traditional norms is a persistent feature of the proclamation of Jesus. This independence can work in two directions: it can lead to making norms more radical, or to relativizing them. The characteristic feature of the preaching of Jesus is that we find both side by side, indeed even in connection with the same norms. Jesus radicalized norms by putting greater stress on external behaviour – e.g. divorce is categorically excluded – or by extending the demand to inner motivation, as when, say, erotic fascination by another woman is identified with adultery. The same norms are again relativized by the way in which Jesus has easy contact with people who do not observe these norms (cf. the story of the 'woman who was a great sinner', Luke 7.36ff.) or by assessing them in a different way from society – e.g. when he promises prostitutes entrance to the kingdom of God before the pious.

How are we to understand this simultaneous radicalizing and relativizing of Jewish norms (or accentuation and blunting of the Torah)? One probable explanation is that when norms are heightened to such a degree that they cannot be fulfilled, the conventional demarcations between 'sinners' and the 'righteous' are called in question. In the light of the radicalized norms, many, if not all, appear as sinners. But in that case no one has any right to dissociate himself or herself from them.

3. Jesus as poet

Jesus taught in parables.[13] His parables are a high point in the history of Jewish literature. They have a rural setting, do not presuppose an education (characteristic of the cities), and are addressed to simple people. In contrast to Aesop's fables there are no talking animals or plants. That may be a deliberate feature: the human world is meant to become transparent for God, rather than the world of animals and plants becoming transparent for human beings. The imagery comes from the everyday worlds. The parables tell of seed-time and harvest, seeking and finding, plans and success, masters and slaves, fathers and sons, hosts and guests – only the role of 'enemy' remains unfilled.

Why did Jesus speak in parables? It is not enough to say that he wanted to illustrate his teaching. Important aspects of his message are absent from his parables, e.g. the opposition between God and Satan – the role of the 'enemy' is missing – and the attitude of Jesus to the commandments about the sabbath and about purity. By contrast, some aspects come out more strongly in the parables than in proclamation elsewhere: above all the message of God with his amazing grace.

The form of the parable must have been particularly appropriate to its content. But what do the parables talk about? The introductory comparative questions mention two themes. Jesus asks: 'With what should we compare the kingdom of God...?' (Mark 4.30), and 'With what should I compare this generation?' (Matt.11.16). The parables deal with God and man, or more accurately, with the situation of human beings before God's judgment and rule.

They are an appropriate form of expression for this theme. There are only two ways of speaking about God's action: mythical and typological discourse. There are limits to both.

There is mythical discourse in the words of Jesus. One might think of his remarks about the fall of Satan (Luke 10.18) or the angels in the judgment of the Son of man (Mark 8.38). If someone wants to announce a new action of God in mythical discourse, it is necessary to refer to particular revelations and visions – just as Jesus drew his assurance of the fall of Satan from a visionary experience: 'I saw Satan fall like lightning from heaven.'

A second possibility is typological language. God's action is announced in analogy to his past action. This possibility is also realized in Jesus; on occasion he refers back to Old Testament types: to Noah and Lot, Solomon and Jonah. Typological language reaches the limit where it has to announce unparalleled action by God.

Parables avoid both mythical speculation and a bond with pre-existing types. They speak of God indirectly. They can make bold statements about him without their narrator needing to put forward the esoteric claim of having been specially initiated into the divine mysteries. They preserve respect for the divine reality which is not directly accessible to humanity.

Any indirect talk of God runs the risk of becoming abstract – in both senses of the word: the language declines in both content and appeal. The parable avoids both these things. It is concrete. It has the power to change people's attitudes so that the subject of the parable can be experienced as a significant reality.

The form of the parable can be defined as follows. Parables are an indirect way of speaking of God in a way that addresses others directly. They ensure both that God remains out of human hands and that he grasps humanity directly.

The content of the parables is also simple. It can be summed up as follows: God is other – and therefore human beings must behave in a different way.

God is other: he rewards different forms of work in the same way (Matt.20.1ff.). He restores the lost son to his privileged position in the house (Luke 15.11ff.). He attaches as much importance to the lost sheep as to the ninety-nine other sheep (Luke 15.4ff.). He has debts 'wiped out' in his name without feeling deceived (Luke 16.1ff.). He invites to a feast those who expect least of all (Luke 14.16ff.). But he is also harsher about mistrust than those who fail to trust him expect (Matt.25.14ff.).

Because God is other, people can behave differently. They can take greater risks. They can give up all their possessions because they have the precious pearl and the treasure (Matt.13.44f.). They may press God without being ashamed (Luke 11.5ff.; 18.1ff.). They may risk all their money to increase it (Matt.25.14ff.). They may risk great losses in sowing (Mark 4.3ff.). They may allow tares to grow up among the wheat (Matt.13.24f.).

The parables are meant to help us to see reality with new eyes and to give us courage to behave differently.

Parables are metaphors extended into narratives (or fields of metaphors). Metaphors for God also occur outside the parables. Jesus uses two central images: God is father and king. In the Lord's Prayer he combines them both: 'Our Father, thy kingdom come.' Both images have their traditional models. However, only with Jesus are they central to discourse about God. They take on new accents: the father is addressed with the familiar term 'Abba', which may have associations from early childhood. His kingdom already begins now, 'in our midst'.

Jesus probably also took up traditional imagery elsewhere and developed it into brief narratives. There could have been writers of parables other than him. We find traces of them only in the late rabbinic literature. Here the independence of the parables from scriptural exegesis (the reference to an already-existing Old Testament text) is a characteristic of the parables of Jesus.

Jesus also put new stress on literary forms other than the parables. Thus in his sayings the widespread form of the blessing is accentuated, so that it becomes an anti-blessing. It is the poor, the hungry and the sorrowful who are said to be blessed (Matt.5.3ff.), not because poverty, hunger and sorrow are valuable in themselves but because the turning point has come for the unfortunate.

In contrast to the tradition, Jesus is fond of expressing admonitions in the style of wisdom, in the plural.[14] That in itself already indicates that his teaching is addressed to everyone; however, those who are convinced of it belong to a special group.

In his sayings, Jesus opposes legal statements with bold antitheses. These antitheses not only interpret tradition but contradict it. There are no analogies for this, other than for individual elements in the formula.[15]

The Jesus tradition is fond of introducing prophetic sayings (and not only them) with the word 'Amen'.[16] Thus an asseverative formula which elsewhere serves only as a response appears at the beginning of the discourse.

All these new accents in the linguistic forms of the Jewish literature of the time reveal a great self-awareness. Though individual forms may have a great many analogies, it is remarkable for them to be combined. Nowhere else is there evidence of this combination of forms from wisdom, prophecy and law with the genre of parables and similes. While the authenticity of individual sayings may be disputed, this form of language may well, generally speaking, go back to the historical Jesus.

The question arises in connection with the whole proclamation of Jesus as to whether prophetic teaching, wisdom teaching and poetic teaching have features in common. In fact there are basic affinities in structure. Where prophecies are not fulfilled, the heightened expectation of judgment turns into an assurance of salvation: God allows both good and evil to continue to exist. He gives both a chance. Similarly, where norms cannot be fulfilled, accentuation of them becomes relativization: where norms cannot be fulfilled, the distinction between good and evil vanishes. The formal structure of the parables similarly points towards a change: parables begin from the familiar everyday world in order to show that God is utterly different, and therefore people must behave in an utterly different way. The poetic parables set out to change our perception of human beings and God; i.e precisely what happens in any transformation of certainty of judgment into certainty of salvation, accentuation of norms into the blunting of them. They make the familiar world transparent to the utterly different character of the divine reality.

4. Jesus as martyr

In his proclamation, Jesus continues the prophetic, wisdom and poetic traditions of Judaism. Even where he goes beyond the previous forms of Jewish tradition, we cannot say that he goes outside the bounds of Judaism. For Jewish prophets and wisdom teachers had always previously gone beyond the 'bounds' of the traditions which existed before them. And Jewish prophets and teachers continually came into conflict with those who controlled power in Jewish society.

Both his proximity to and difference from other religious trends in Judaism show how little Jesus can be distinguished from Jewish society.[17]

He shares a radical theocratic expectation with the revolutionary Zealots.[18] God himself will begin to rule and take the place of all other powers. However, whereas the Zealots wanted to introduce the 'sole rule of God' by violent action against the Romans and the indigenous aristocracy (even by murder and revolution), with Jesus the actions in which the kingdom of God is already beginning are healing actions: when he frees men and women from demons, the kingdom of God is dawning (Matt.12.28). Whereas for the Zealots the sole rule of God is quite unreconcilable with Roman rule, Jesus begins from a co-existence of God and the emperor (although it is transitory and provisional): one can give the emperor the coins with his image on, which belong to him, while at the same time fulfilling God's demands (Mark 12.17). God already, now, is beginning his rule in secret, while the Romans are still controlling the land. When he wholly enters on his rule, it is not so much that Israel will triumph against the external enemies of the nation. Rather, groups within Israel which are now dismissed will come to power: the poor, the weak, children and outsiders. And the Gentiles (including the Romans) will stream into the kingdom of God from all directions. They will become its subjects without war.

Jesus shares with the moderate Pharisees the basic purpose of putting God's will into practice everywhere and thus breaking through the bounds between the profane and the sacred. The Pharisaic movement did this by seeking to extend the sphere of the sacral to all everyday life. Demands made on priests were extended to the laity. A complicated casuistry, but one which bears witness to a serious purpose, attempted continually to formulate a new balance between the demands of reality and holiness. By contrast, Jesus recognizes obedience to God's will in the secular sector as the decisive factor. As a result the sacral sphere can be relativized. Holy times like the sabbath, holy places like the temple, holy objects like pure food, or holy persons who subject themselves to particular rules of piety, have only relative significance before God. Whereas the Pharisees sought to preserve the sacral in the everyday, Jesus seeks to bring everyday worship into the sacral sphere as well. However, here both are controlled by the will to take God's will seriously in every respect.

There are points of contact even with the Sadducees. The Sadducees stressed the individual subject. They attributed to him responsibility for his own destiny (Josephus, *BJ*, 2,165). They too were critical of the tradition which had been 'added' to the original will of God in the Torah. With their theology they reflected the standpoint of a privileged class which could dispense with hopes for the beyond because this world offered opportunity enough. Jesus, too, attached high significance to the human subject – not as the expression of the presence of a social reality, but as a contradiction to it. For he did not attack a privileged stratum, but worked among the lower classes in the country. He often addresses his ordinary audience with royal metaphors: they are now experiencing what prophets and kings have longed to see (Luke 10.24). They hear greater things than the 'queen of the south' who travelled to Solomon (Matt.12.42). They are worth more than the lilies of the field, whom God has clothed with more glory than King Solomon (Matt.6.25ff.). They are free princes, who need not pay any temple tax (Matt.17.25). If they rub ears of corn on the sabbath,they are claiming the same privileges as King David (Mark 2.23f.). Jesus addressed ordinary people with an awareness that elsewhere we can presuppose only among the upper classes. He also corrects the magical belief in miracles among simple people: he, the miracle-worker, does not claim the success of the healing for himself. Rather, he says, 'Your faith has saved you' (Mark 5.34 etc.). The one who is healed is the subject of his healing.

Thus Jesus represents a variant of the renewal movements within the Judaism of the first century AD. The Zealots and the Pharisees were also engaged in conflicts with society. Therefore even the execution of Jesus is no argument for seeing him primarily as a contrast to his society; on the contrary, the failure of Jesus manifests the basic conflicts of Jewish-Palestinian society of the time. That may be demonstrated from four kinds of conflict.[19]

Palestine was stamped by chronic social and political conflicts. There were no stable power structures. The Roman military administration and the native aristocracy were mistrustful of each other and expressed this in both collaboration and hostility. The Herodian princes offered themselves as an alternative form of government, not to mention the Hellenistic republics in the city states, a dense chain of which surrounded Jewish territory. Only in such a fluid situation could the Zealot resistance movement hang on so long. Only constant destabilizing conflicts could fuel messianic hopes, i.e. hopes for a native king who would drive the Romans from the land. Jesus is accused before Pilate as a messianic pretender (Mark 15.2) and executed on this charge, as the titulus on the cross shows (Mark 15.26). It is improbable that he regarded himself as Messiah. But it is probable that the messianic expectations which were alive at that time were projected on to him, expectations which he perhaps rejected firmly (as can be inferred from Mark 8.27ff.). It was not the messianic pretender, but these expectations which could endanger the ruling powers. The removal of the figure who had attracted them and kept them alive should have prevented possible unrest. That was certainly a reason for the Roman authorities to execute Jesus.

Like any other society, Jewish Palestinian society was characterized by conflicts of interest between the poor and the rich. This conflict of social and economic interests may have had a role in the conflict with the Jewish aristocracy. Jesus was accused before the Sanhedrin, whose members were above all drawn from the aristocracy, not only of being a messianic pretender but also of prophesying against the temple (Mark 14.58). The temple was the source of a good deal of income for the upper classes – and also the economic base for countless small folk in Jerusalem. Anyone who put it in question was touching on basic material interests. There was also a suspicion that a more generous interpretation of the law could raise problems about much that was of advantage to individual groups: the income of the priestly upper class was regulated by the law. Strictness in the interpretation of the law was very much in their interest. Jesus did little to allay such fears: the rumour went the rounds that he would refuse downright to pay the temple tax (Matt.17.24f.). Reconciliation with one's brother was more important to him than sacrifice in the temple (Matt.5.23f.), and duties towards one's elders were more important than giving to the 'temple treasure', the Korban (Mark 7.10ff.). The business dealings in the temple forecourt provoked his wrath.

A third conflict was also instrumental in contributing to Jesus' end: the social and economic tensions between city and country.[20] Jesus was a Galilean, who kept away from the Galilaean cities like Sepphoris and Tiberias. For the people of Jerusalem, his movement was one of those unruly country groups which caused disturbances at festivals; that was why the Roman prefect came to Jerusalem on such days with military reinforcements. The many strangers in the city contributed towards making the authorities nervous. So they wanted to execute Jesus before the festival 'because of the people' – i.e. because of the country folk who were streaming into Jerusalem (Mark 14.2). As Galileans, his followers came under suspicion (Mark 14.70); Jesus himself was arrested 'like a thief', i.e. one of those resistance fighters who found their way into Jerusalem during the feast (Mark 14.48f.). His temple prophecy is already an expression of tensions between city and country: all the prophets who prophesied against the temple – Micah, Jeremiah, Jesus son of Ananus – came from the country. The opposition against the temple among Zealots and Essenes also had its roots in the country.

Finally, social and cultural differences also played an important part in the events which led to Jesus' death. There was the ancient antisemitism which we can note on two social levels: among the Hellenistic population of the city republics in the vicinity of Palestine and among the imperial upper class. The antisemitism among the neighbouring states was in part nourished by experiences of the time in which the Jewish kings from the Hasmonaean house (in the first half of the first century BC) had subjected and oppressed the cities. The soldiers who mocked Jesus as king of the Jews and executed him recruited their auxiliary troops from these very cities. About fourteen years after the execution of Jesus they again mocked a Jewish king, Agrippa I, after his death. Their hostility to the Jews met with the approval of Pontius Pilate. There are important indications that he belonged to those sections of the Roman upper classes who were prejudiced against the Jews because the Jews would not be fully integrated into the empire. Differing from the practice of other prefects and procurators, he had coins minted with pagan symbols. Unlike them, he attempted to introduce images of the emperor or at least shields dedicated to the emperor into Jerusalem – which deeply hurt the religious feelings of the Jews quite profoundly. Until 32, Sejanus, whom Philo accuses of unbridled antisemitism, ruled at the same time in Rome: he had had a plan to kill all the Jews (Philo, *Gaius*, 160).

Both Pilate's superiors and his subordinates were antisemitic. In this sort of atmosphere the decision went against Jesus – as a messianic pretender. It is probable that the verdict is also the expression of antisemitic prejudice.

For centuries there has been discussion as to who was 'guilty' of the death of Jesus. It is now time to ask what were the actual 'causes' of his failure. Jesus was the victim of social tensions. He was torn apart in the conflicts between the empire and a subject people, between the upper class and the lower class, between city and country, between Jews and Gentiles.

Jesus came to grief in one of those social conflicts which are already present- whether consciously or not – in his preaching. His proclamation can already be understood as a response to these conflicts.

Thus in principle the kingdom of God also brings the end of Roman rule. For the moment, however, the two can co-exist. The stress does not lie on liberation from foreign rule but on the integration of disadvantaged groups within society.

Jesus' polemic against the rich is a clear stand against the economically powerful classes, and his beatitudes on the poor, the hungry and the sorrowful are clear support for the oppressed. However, here too the basic opposition is blunted: the rich man, too, can follow Jesus; he can give his goods to the poor or hand back goods which he has obtained unjustly.

Jesus' prophecy against the temple is first of all a clear declaration of war on the part of the Galilean against the capital. However, Jesus prophesies not only the destruction of the temple but a new, better temple. In this we can see a permanent identification with Jerusalem. One saying in the Jesus tradition with some justice compares Jesus' preaching to Jerusalem to a hen attracting her chicks (Luke 13.34f.).

Jesus' preaching presupposes the difference between Jews and Gentiles. By accentuating the demands of the law he makes the differentiation even greater. However, Jesus does not emphasize separatist demands, but generally accessible humanist ethical demands, while he relativizes those norms aimed at segregation (commands about purity and the sabbath).

The proclamation and the fate of Jesus are evidence of these great conflicts. This is the basis for the unity of his proclamation and his fate. It is true that we cannot describe this unity in a sequence arranged in biographical order. We do not know enough for that. We do not know why and with what expectations Jesus went up to Jerusalem. But the unity of a life can be accessible to us if we recognize that the traditions handed down to us are all related to the same problem. In his dying Jesus is a 'martyr' to the human inability to live with one's fellow human beings – not only on a personal level, but also in the context of social structures and conflicts. It is this same inability against which his preaching is directed.

After his death his disciples saw him alive. Individual appearances are handed down by three people: by Peter, who – like the other disciples – left him in the lurch at the end of his life; by James, the brother of Jesus, who possibly was sceptical about him (like the rest of his family); and by Paul, the persecutor of the Christians. In addition to this there were group appearances: before the Twelve, before all the apostles and five hundred brothers all at once (I Cor.15.3ff.) The tradition about all these appearances is old and reliable. Paul hands it down to the Corinthians twenty years after the death of Jesus as traditions which were already in existence and which he adopted. He spoke personally to the two other individual witnesses, Peter and James, some years after the death of Jesus. There is therefore no reason to doubt the internal or external authenticity of the tradition, even if it is hard to interpret its content. The disciples had to understand this appearance as a sign from God that the one who seemed to have failed had in reality proved victorious.

III

Evolutionary Aspects of Faith in Jesus

Can the New Testament conviction that God has finally revealed himself in Christ be expressed within the framework of an evolutionary theory of religion? Do we accord with the intention of the New Testament if we ask instead whether Jesus is a variant of human life which does justice to the central reality? I want to approach this conviction with three questions.

1. Is Jesus a variant (or 'mutation') of human existence in which the change of human 'heart' promised by the prophets has become reality?

2. Is Jesus the consummation of that protest against selection which was formulated with increasing clarity in biblical religion?

3. Is Jesus a permanently valid 'structure of adaptation' to the central reality to which we do justice only when we participate in its form of life?

All that sounds a 'modernist' translation of New Testament statements about Jesus. But there are some statements in the New Testament which point in that direction.

1. The New Testament does not speak of 'mutation'. But it does regard Jesus as a *new* man, into whose image we are to be changed (I Cor.15.44ff.). Jesus is the counterpart of the first Adam (Rom.5.12ff.); through him all human beings become a *new* creation (II Cor.5.17); in other words, through him the basic conditions of human life are changed.

2. Nor does the New Testament speak of selection. However, it does contrast the love commandment with animal behaviour, that devouring and being devoured which is often part of selective processes.

> For the whole law is fulfilled in one word: 'You shall love your neighbour as yourself.' But if you hate and devour one another, take heed that you are not consumed by one another (Gal.5.14f.).

3. Of course the New Testament does not speak of 'adaptation' to God. But it does describe Jesus with imagery which presupposes a

very close correspondence between God and him. He is the image of God, what man should be. He is a successful structure of adaptation to the divine reality (cf. II Cor.4.4).

Thus in some passages the New Testament itself interprets the person of Jesus as a new form of life, in which biologically pre-programmed conduct is overcome. This new form of life matches God better than all its predecessors.

We must now ask whether such statements correspond with the activity and proclamation of the historical Jesus.

1. Jesus of Nazareth as a 'mutation' of human life

Human history is a chain of 'mutations', of new beginnings, innovations and variants, only a few of which attain stability and historical effectiveness. The problem does not consist in showing that Jesus is a kind of 'mutation', but in the fact that this view of Jesus affords the possibility of seeing in him the appearance of something which has permanent validity. Modern historical awareness fights against that. It sees the historical as *a priori* relative, conditioned and immanent; in other words, it is neither completely singular nor absolute, nor does it open up a transcendent perspective.

Therefore in the first part I must demonstrate that the metaphor of mutation is in a position to integrate fully the three aspects of modern consciousness mentioned above, without barring the way to New Testament christology. I shall discuss these three points in succession.

(a) The problem of historical relativity

Historical-critical research has collected an incredible number of analogies to all the statements in the New Testament. There are parallels even to so central a statement as 'Love your enemy'. Epictetus says that the Cynic is to love as his brother anyone who strikes him (*Diss.* III, 22.54). Almost all the elements of the New Testament have their parallels. Some exegetes now seem to have made it their task to demonstrate the superiority and uniqueness of the New Testament despite such parallels. The ethically doubtful element here is that in this approach other statements are often unduly devalued. One need only think of the many derogatory judgments on the Judaism of the time, made so that Jesus can shine out against it all the more brightly. If we understand the figure of Jesus as a mutation of human life, we must reckon *a priori* with the possibility that all the elements of his activity and his proclamation are traditional through and through. By definition, mutations consist in new combinations of traditional elements. Evolution works with what is to hand, and it is capable of making amazing new things from what is to hand. Therefore we can endorse without qualification the search for analogies without having to question whether something new appeared with Jesus. It does not lie in the individual elements but in their combination. Indeed we can even evaluate the search for parallels in a basically positive way. Parallels show that in Jesus universal tendencies are expressed, those tendencies which the old apologists called the *Logos spermatikos*, which points everywhere to Jesus.[21]

Let me make the problem specific by discussing the ethical proclamation of Jesus. None of the ethical instructions of Jesus is completely without analogy. However, the combination of various ethical tendencies which are in tension and nevertheless belong together is.

Chief among them is the tension between 'You shall' and 'you may', between the radicalizing of norms on the one hand and the radicalizing of acceptance on the other. This double radicalizing is a riddle to us. For as a rule our experience is that the accentuation of norms is bound up with devaluation of those who offend against the norm. To take one example from the proclamation of Jesus: we would not expect anyone who requires absolute sexual fidelity, as does Jesus, and rejects every concession (cf. Mark 10.11ff.; Luke 16.18), to be as open as Jesus is with prostitutes, who break such strong sexual norms. Nevertheless Jesus says: 'The prostitutes and tax-collectors will go into the kingdom of God before you' (Matt.21.31). We find equally paradoxical instances elsewhere: the limitation of aggression is radicalized so that it becomes renunciation of self-defence (Mark 5.38-42), but a 'zealot' is accepted into the group of disciples (Luke 6.15). Possessions are fiercely attacked (Luke 6.24), but the rich chief tax collector Zacchaeus is among the circle of Jesus' friends (Luke 19.1-10), as are well-to-do women (Luke 8.1-3). Jesus makes a demonstration for a radicalized holiness of the temple (Mark 11.15-18), but he sits down to meals with tax collectors and sinners (Mark 2.14ff.), beyond the norms of the 'holy'. We interpreted this paradoxical relationship of demand and grace as indicating that the demand is radicalized to such an extent that in the end it is transgressed by all. No one can fulfil it completely. But in that case no one has the right to attack others for failure, for which the presuppositions are also to be found in them.

Let us note, then, that there are parallels and traditions for the individual elements in the proclamation of Jesus. There was also an accentuation and a blunting of norms elsewhere in contemporary Judaism. However, to combine them is unique. The new element lies in this combination. Here we find a 'mutation' of human life. The metaphor of mutation allows us to accept historical relativism without restraint and therefore without having to challenge the uniqueness of Jesus. The possibility remains open that his uniqueness calls for a singular decision.

(b) The problem of historical conditioning

Nowadays we become particularly aware of the problem of historical conditioning, the more we look at the social and psychological factors behind the New Testament texts. In my view it is clear that there is an intimate connection between the appearance of Jesus and a crisis in Palestinian Jewish society. The question therefore properly arises: is the proclamation of Jesus and primitive Christianity simply an illusory reproduction of the contradictions of ancient society and its slavery, as the Marxist theory runs? [22]

Now there are two good arguments against the determinist interpretation of the crisis of primitive Christianity. First, a variety of religious movements have their roots in the same situation in Palestine: Essenes, Pharisees, Zealots and the Jesus movement. Secondly, the same movement extended over various areas: the Jesus movement also expanded outside Palestine in different conditions from those in the land of its origin and took shape independently in primitive Christianity. Now if the same cause (i.e. the same social situation) produces quite different effects, while the same effect can appear in different causal connections, the recognizable social causes are not enough to explain the specific form of the new movement. Rather, the situation seems to leave room for manoeuvre, room for different possible responses.

Of course, convinced determinists need not be content with this. They can fall back on the argument from the state of the sources. This runs: if we knew more about the specific social background of the various religious movements in Palestine, we could also provide a sociological explanation for their varying form. What appears to us as openness in the situation is really deficient knowledge of the situation. This argument is irrefutable; however, it does not take us very far because the counter-argument is also irrefutable. It is a question of who can demonstrate that the burden of proof lies on the other.

With the help of an evolutionary approach we can perhaps discuss the problem for both sides in a way which does not contradict the understanding of religion which those who profess it have. On the one hand we can demonstrate the probability that the evolutionary process leaves room for the unpredictable, so that spontaneity and freedom are possible. Even if we rid ourselves of the traditional dualism between (free) spirit and (determined) society and nature, an approach from the perspective of evolution can still distinguish both spheres. On the other hand, one can see spirit, society and nature together and interpret them as different forms of adapting to the central reality, so that all those social factors and structures on which religion is dependent are in the end directed towards the same reality that is aimed at in religion.

The first attempt begins from the metaphor of mutation and makes use of an argument *a minori ad majus*. According to all that we know at present, mutations emerge spontaneously and unpredictably. Of course even with so-called 'spontaneous' mutations scientists look for possible causes – rays, warmth, enzymes – but what happens are micro-physical reactions in individual molecules which cannot be strictly determined but are subject to statistical laws.[23] All in all, even with 'induced' mutation, only the frequency can be causally determined, not the direction. Now if even within biological evolution one has to reckon with a margin which is not fully determined, indeed if the mystery of creative development is to be sought precisely in this small area, this scope for error and vagueness, that is all the more the case with cultural evolution, which displays unmistakably more openness, flexibility and delight in innovation in its pattern of phenomena. To put it as vividly as possible: we should not deny that spontaneity and unpredictability which we grant to mutations in the bacterial cultures in our laboratories to the great creative impulses of our own culture.

This is not to devalue the question of the causal connections in our own history; on the contrary, it comes up here in a new way. While in biological evolution we can only reckon with blind trial and error, human history is characterized by deliberate attempts to respond to situations and problems, though these attempts to respond still contain an element of blind trial – and error. Intended solutions of problems, however, must have not only freedom and flexibility to adapt to them (so they may not just be caused causally by them); they must necessarily show a great affinity to the problems to which they are a response. The connection with this situation would therefore have to emerge much more clearly, precisely because the situation is not just the blind work of chance but also a deliberately noted challenge (calling for a response).

In this sense the proclamation of Jesus was an absolute and necessary answer to the situation of the time. We can consider only one point of detail, the limitation of the accentuation and blunting of norms. One of the basic problems of Jewish society, faced with the advance of

Hellenistic culture, was its relationship to non-Jews. The accentuation of norm and Torah meant delimitation; the blunting of norm and Torah meant openness towards them. Society wavered between the two extremes. The resistance fighters, for example, radicalized the first and second commandment, and in so doing clearly cut themselves off from foreigners. The radical Hellenistic reformers removed the separatist norms, and in so doing opened themselves up to the new culture so much that their own cultural identity was threatened.

Both tendencies were combined in the proclamation of Jesus. The Torah was taken with the utmost seriousness. The accentuation of norms related above all to the universal norms of pro-social conduct: aggression, sexuality, possession and honesty. On the other hand norms were relativized, separatist norms like commands for purity and sabbath regulations. Independently of the accentuation and blunting of norms, however, there was a surprising openness towards those who did not live up to the norms which were demanded. In this way the proclamation of Jesus did justice to the demand inherent in the social situation: it made possible faithfulness to Jewish identity. Central norms of the Torah were radicalized. At the same time Jesus' proclamation made possible tolerance towards aliens, so that anxieties over delimitation could be reduced. This was an answer produced by the situation, but not derivable from it.

Of course experience shows that many religious people feel that such a 'sociological' interpretation of the proclamation is a threat to religious understanding – just as consistent reductionist interpretations criticize it from the other side. Therefore I must also sketch out the second approach offered by evolutionary thought, in order to overcome the problem of 'reductionism'. Religion may be largely determined by social factors and structures – but these factors and structures are themselves only part of a comprehensive evolutionary process in which new material, organic, social and cultural structures of adaptation to ultimate reality are developed and revised. In religion this comprehensive process achieves self-awareness. Even if religion, as a deliberate form of adaptation to this central reality, were completely different from other (unconscious) structures of adaptation – which I do not believe to be the case - this would nevertheless ultimately be determined by that reality to which it deliberately relates. For not only religion but the whole world is a case of trial and error in understanding the reality of God.

(*c*) The problem of historical immanence

Historical interpretations which make use of analogy and causality are immanent interpretations. They explain history from itself. The metaphor of mutation also consistently gives the figure of Jesus an immanent context; indeed it has a marked 'materialistic' feature in that it understands human history as part of general evolution. Nevertheless it is an interpretation which opens up the possibility of arguing for a revelation which goes beyond previous history, if we define revelation formally (though still in a very unsatisfactory way theologically) as a disclosure of spheres which had hitherto been inaccessible in principle. Each of the great creative mutations discloses a new sphere of life, whether through the development of new organs or through the development of new modes of behaviour which make it possible to inhabit new ecological niches. Creative mutations are improved structures of adaptation to the reality around and embrace more of it than was possible for previous forms of life. We need think only of the conquest of the land by life or the opening up of the night by warm-blooded mammals.

Here is a little fable. What would a cold-blooded dinosaur have said if a mouse had told him about the mysteries of the night – the night being as inaccessible to him as the land to a fish? Would he not have said, 'Little mouse, you are so weak and small that I could squash you without noticing it. What you are telling me is stuff and nonsense!'? Suppose that this was an intelligent mouse, a mouse who had read Paul, it might have replied, 'This foolishness is wiser than the wisdom of the dinosaurs and this weakness is stronger than the strength of the dinosaurs.' One could substitute other animals – at all events the moral of the fable is that we cannot exclude the possibility that we are in the situation of the dinosaur who finds what he is hearing incredible. For our world, too, is limited. What we experience is not the world in itself. If we accept the basic notion of a comprehensive evolution, we must also reckon with the possibility that in our sphere of life 'mutations' appear which communicate experiences from a sphere that is inaccessible to us – because they embody more appropriate structures of adaptation to this sphere than we do. Thus the metaphor of mutation contains a theory of revelation, i.e. a demonstration of possible conditions for revelation.

What are these conditions? 1. We do not live in the world-in-itself but in a specific limited environment. Everything that we experience as 'reality' is in fact assimilated to our limited equipment. 2. Like all forms of life, human beings are attempts to find adequate structures for adapting to reality-in-itself. All life can be regarded as a hypothesis aimed at forming a better picture of the transcendent reality behind our limited life. Each mutation is a new hypothesis, which possibly takes the process of adaptation one jump forward.

In the small world of our human history this phenomenon is familiar to us. New trends in painting open our eyes to the landscape or to surrealist depths within us. New knowledge suggests the unity of reality more exactly than before. New forms of life bring unknown inter-personal possibilities to bear, and so on. The objective of this infinite process of adaptation (through trial and error) is an ultimate adaptation to life which is most able to hold together all reality and be a vehicle of it. If there are such things as mutations in human life, we cannot rule out the possibility that at some point one such valid structure of adaptation will emerge in human history. The New Testament claims that this has already happened in Jesus.

To sum up provisionally: the metaphor of mutation in christology integrates all three elements in a critical modern consciousness – relativism, conditioning and immanence – and yet at the same time does not exclude the possibility of an absolute and revelatory mutation which furthers life, without being able or willing to assert that this general possibility has been realized. That is precisely what the New Testament does. It goes beyond what we could suspect and assume as a general possibility. It claims that in fact a decisive 'mutation' has come about with which a new world has begun.

2. Jesus of Nazareth as a protest against the principle of selection

It is the conviction of the New Testament that in Jesus there took place not only one new beginning alongside others, but the decisive move from a world of disaster to a new creation. Here the metaphor of mutation in christology must come up against its limits. Mutations keep happening. It seems to be arbitrary to accord one of them a decisive place, unless we have clear criteria for setting it apart.

Such criteria can emerge only from the content of what Jesus represented. The content of the proclamation of Jesus accords with the tendency which can be observed in the whole of cultural evolution, a tendency towards the diminution of selection, which in biblical religion is accentuated so that it becomes a protest against the harshness of the principle of selection, in the belief that this is a way of doing justice to the central reality. This central reality reveals itself in Jesus. Its opposition to the principle of selection assumes abrupt forms.

(*a*) Jesus' proclamation of salvation: liberation from the pressure of selection

Jesus began as a disciple of John the Baptist. His proclamation was the preaching of repentance in the spirit of the Old Testament. However, between him and the Old Testament prophets lay apocalyptic, in which judgment was universalized. It threatened not only a people, but the whole world.

What is expressed here in religious fantasies is, in my view, the apt intuition that the world of human life has no guarantee of eternity. It too is subject to the principle of selection, i.e. it too is threatened by death if it does not correspond to the basic conditions of reality. It is subject to a judgment which can not only affect individual instances of cultural evolution but also jeopardize them. In apocalyptic for the first time we have a glimmering of this idea in mythical form: the whole cultural evolution can end in a fiasco if we encourage patterns of behaviour which conflict with the basic conditions of reality.

I assume that the basic conditions which form the framework of human life find their expression in religious myths long before they are accessible to scientific reflection. The myth of a punitive judgment on the whole world which we escape only by radically changing our behaviour reflects a basic fact of our life. Like all life we are subject to a harsh pressure of selection. And we trace it most clearly when we have the impression that our behaviour is developing in a completely false direction. What gloomy prophets like John the Baptist, pronouncing the end of the world, guessed at is now commonplace wisdom: if we do not live in harmony with the basic conditions of peaceful co-existence we shall destroy our environment and leave behind the culture of *homo sapiens* as evolutionary ruins.

Jesus begins from such gloomy expectations: God's penal judgment is coming soon. But there is one basic difference between him and John the Baptist. God no longer appears as devastating power – in other words he is not the embodiment of the threat which proceeds from the pressure of selection; rather, God is described with the poetic image of the gracious father, a father who offers and makes possible life at the very point where human beings have offended against the basic conditions of reality. In biblical terms, God offers the sinner life.

We saw that the accentuation of the threat of judgment could itself bring about a change from the certainty of judgment to the certainty of salvation. If the world continues to exist although it really deserves destruction, then God must be incredibly gracious. Where the pressure of life is experienced intensively, chances of life appear clearly.

How can we interpret this change from the certainty of judgment to the certainty of salvation in evolutionary terms? The central reality encounters us on all levels of evolution and of our own life as an opportunity and pressure originating from outside, as resonance and absurdity, as success and failure to adapt. Within biological and cultural evolution so far opportunities and pressure are always related in such a way that the opportunities are available only within the framework which selective pressure allows. There is successful adaptation only in so far as the selecting factors of reality allow it. To put this in mythical language: the graciousness of God is limited by his judgment. All life is governed by the fact that it is moving towards an annihilating judgment which marks out its limits. All opportunities are limited.

In the proclamation of Jesus this relationship is reversed. God appears as the one who gives opportunities to those very people who have come under judgment and therefore should inevitably come to grief. The promise of an unconditional opportunity – independently of the threat of judgment – is the centre of the proclamation of Jesus and the New Testament.

If the basic experience of John the Baptist is the threat of the accentuated pressure of selection on life – represented in mythical fantasies of an imminent judgment – the basic experience of Jesus is the removal of the pressure of selection. Life has a chance. God is gracious. In other words, the basic conditions of reality allow much more human misconduct than any of the prophets who announced the downfall of the world supposed. This is not understood as an invitation to go on as before. The possibility of judgment continues. But trust in the graciousness of God, i.e. trust that human misconduct will not directly lead to great catastrophe, becomes the basis for a change in conduct, which is without doubt a better basis than anxiety about total collapse.

(b) The demands of Jesus: ethics directed against selection

In my view, this basic experience of Jesus – liberation from the paralysing power of the inexorable pressure of selection – explains the specific ethical tendencies of his proclamation. This basic tendency is constantly to oppose human conduct dominated by the principle of selection. If biological evolution so far has worked with mutation and selection as the two most important factors of evolution, so christological 'mutation' (together with the whole of biblical history) is singular in that it radically puts in question the second principle of evolution, the power of selection. Primitive Christian faith consists in a revolt against selection which often assumes abrupt and bizarre forms and is topical precisely in its contradiction to the modern consciousness.

Selection means enhanced and diminished chances of propagation in comparison with others. But in the New Testament eunuchs are praised (Matt.19.10ff.) and Paul encourages abstention from sexual activity (I Cor.7.1ff.).

Selection means aggression against aliens who threaten one's territory. The New Testament calls for love of enemies (Matt.5.43ff.) and promises possession of the land to the meek, i.e. to those who forswear power (Matt.5.5).

Selection means solidarity with those who are genetically akin, with one's own familiy, and aggression to outsiders. However, Jesus reverses this relationship: he calls for a break with one's own family (Luke 14.26). Inward aggression is taken into account, and solidarity is called for with outsiders – with strangers and even with the enemy (Matt.5.43ff.).

Selection means preference for those with senior positions in the hierarchy, so that those become established who have proved their capacity by getting their place in the pecking order. But the New Testament says, 'And whoever would be first among you must be slave of all' (Mark 10.44).

Selection means preference for the strong and healthy. However, the New Testament makes sacrifice for the weak a duty -love for one's neighbour (Luke 10.29ff.) – and in the miracle stories shows how Jesus identifies with the hopelessly ill.

All these basic demands presuppose a basic trust that the ultimate reality not only allows a much greater range of variations in human conduct, but also permits human conduct which according to the laws of biological evolution would have no chance.

Here a new problem arises: is there not a danger with such abrupt demands that liberation from the pressure of natural selection is replaced by even harsher cultural social pressure? Who could overcome his old 'Adam' so completely as to be indifferent to procreation, family, power and the capacity to establish himself? Do not unrealistic demands produce a new paralysing pressure of selection, a pressure which is concerned not with adaptation to the conditions of extra-human reality but with adaptation to human culture and its demands and claims?

Here we should recall that Jesus' proclamation not only begins from a change of the certainty of judgment into the certainty of salvation but additionally contains a shift from the accentuation of norms to the blunting of norms. Certainty of salvation in the face of the cosmic judgment to come signals freedom from that natural pressure of selection to which all societies and cultures succumb. However, the relativization of norms in the face of accentuated norms points to a freedom from the pressure of culture: for human beings it is the environment to which they have to adapt. To an increasing degree human society is becoming our sphere of life, and nature outside humanity is communicated only through society. Therefore as development progresses, the burden of culture becomes an increasing problem, while the conflict with nature seems to recede. But the more society becomes the 'environment', the more it is subject to social direction.

Now there is an unmistakable feature in the proclamation of Jesus: it is also aimed at limiting social pressure. His protest is also against culture, in so far as it exercises a selective pressure of adaptation.

Social pressure means that conduct is controlled from outside and takes place in order to satisfy social pressure. But Jesus says: when you give alms, pray or fast, do so in secret, where social control does not extend.

Social pressure means internalizing family, people and state as authorities imposing obligations. However, Jesus requires of his followers that they should break with their families; he presents foreigners (like the people of Nineveh) as exemplary models and makes a sharp distinction between the demands of the emperor and those of God.

Social pressure means internalizing tradition and its rules governing conduct. However, Jesus measures tradition by his insight into God's will, and disregards social norms if they go against elementary ethical demands in particular situations.

Social pressure means respect for authorities which make socially binding definitions of good and evil. This is the only way in which a society can direct the conduct of its members. But Jesus attacks the ethical and religious authorities of his society.

Social pressure means sanctions to the point of exterminating those whose conduct deviates from the norm. It functions only when people draw back in the face of this pressure, i.e. from suffering. But Jesus calls for facing up to social pressure to the point of sacrificing one's own life – and he himself was an example of that.

Thus Jesus aims at a greater freedom towards the natural and social pressure of selection. He also promises possibilities of life to people who have fewer physical and social opportunities. His proclamation is a protest against the principle of selection.

(c) The activity and fate of Jesus: overcoming the principle of selection

If we understand the activity and proclamation of Jesus as a protest against the harshness of the pressure of selection, one area of the Jesus tradition which is neglected by 'modern theologians', i.e. the miracle stories, returns to the centre of interest.[24] Whereas Goethe could still say that miracle is the favourite child of faith, modern exegetes give the impression that miracle is an illegitimate child whose existence people try to excuse in some confusion, e.g. by referring to the crude desire for miracle at the time, and saying that compared to this, miracle stories in primitive Christianity are almost a 'demythologization'. Spiritualizing interpretations made them allegories of inward changes in people and symbols of faith. However, there can hardly be any doubt that those who handed down and received these stories about Jesus understood them to be about specific, factual, saving actions. They did not seek theological profundity in them, but hope in the face of human hopelessness. For that is the point of all the miracle stories: they deny all previous experience its validity as human need to be removed and soothed. They express an unconditional protest against misery and wretchedness – against both physical distress and social isolation. We may find these miracle stories primitive, but as long as people are personally involved as they hear them and recount them, they will find the stories a weapon against the harshness of the pressure of selection. They will find that the stories speak to the sick and the disabled, the hungry and those in danger, the disturbed and the stigmatized, and they will not accept a situation in which there is little food for many and much for few; they will assert that reality could be so rich that twelve loaves would be enough to feed five thousand.

Granted, the miracle stories attest a simple, often primitive mentality. But we might compare it to quite different reactions to human hopelessness which are of equal status, e.g. to Buddha's reaction to human suffering. This is expressed in the legend of Buddha's four journeys.[25] In a chariot, the Prince Buddha left the luxurious surroundings of his royal palace which had previously protected him against unpleasant experiences. On his first journey he encountered an old man who had been abandoned in the forest. Buddha quickly had his chariot turned round and went back to his palace, to put the unpleasant picture out of his mind with sensual diversions. On his second journey he encountered a man with a diseased body. Again he had his chariot turned round, but no longer took delight in sensual pleasures. On the third journey he encountered a corpse being carried along in a funeral procession. Again Buddha had his chariot turned round, but this time he reflected on how he might be liberated from such ills. On his last journey he encountered a religious mendicant. Thereupon he resolved in the same way to renounce all sensual delight in order to lead a life of self-control and to seek 'inner quiet' in homelessness – free from passion and hate. Buddha was changed by his encounter with human suffering and he began to look for redemption.

His reaction to suffering is more philosophical and more sublime than that of Jesus. However, from beginning to end it is characterized by evasion. At the beginning he escapes to his royal palace, which is to protect him from all suffering. At the end he looks for a better refuge, for an inward royal palace which cannot be invaded by suffering. He looks for a place which is immune from all suffering. By contrast Jesus reacts by getting to grips with suffering; he is not evasive, but aggressive. He wants to do away with suffering. He makes use of a primitive technique of miracle. And he himself proves not to be immune from suffering. He dies in torment.

Buddha and Jesus both articulate their protest against the principle of selection. In both their cases it becomes clear that in the end the principle of selection works by means of suffering and death. Only because the dysfunctional has less chance of life, i.e. less room, less food, less security, only because it ultimately comes to grief, is development to greater functionality possible. Death is the price of development towards higher forms of life – and it is a high price. We should be clear what that means: all that is functional, all that is purposeful, all those hours in which we enjoy our existence are based on the suffering of countless creatures. Why can we rejoice at being able to see, whether to find our way around every day, or for the sublime enjoyment of art? Only because millions of living beings had to perish for want of better eyesight. To repeat an earlier illustration: the ape who had bad eyesight and missed the branch to which he tried to jump soon became a dead ape – and therefore could not be our ancestor. If we take that seriously, then almost Buddhist perspectives open up to us. Is not all existence suffering? Is not our happiness always based on the misery of others, not only the suffering of organisms long dead but also on the suffering imposed on other people by historical conditions? Are we not caught up in that web which used to be called original sin?

Buddhism and primitive Christianity are both expressions of a revolt against selection, even if this revolt takes almost opposite forms. Buddhist meditation overcomes suffering by transcending motivation to live. By contrast, primitive Christian faith expresses its protest against selection most clearly in belief in the resurrection of the crucified Jesus. Here a helpless man is proclaimed ruler of the world, the sacrifice is proclaimed the priest, the condemned man is proclaimed the judge and the outcast the focal point of society. What was rejected by death as dysfunctional in the process of selection here becomes the starting point for a new development and the basis for unconditional motivation to live.

3. Jesus of Nazareth – a successful 'adaptation' to the central reality?

Jesus' protest against the principle of selection takes place in the name of God. In other words, the solidarity which takes the place of the principle of selection is regarded as harmony with the central reality, as 'adaptation' to an 'environment' radically transcending the world with which human beings were previously familiar.

Jesus expresses this central reality in two images: God is portrayed as king and as father. As king he will soon establish his kingdom in the world, indeed he has already inaugurated this kingdom in secret. As father he cares for his creatures and overlooks their misconduct. The question is: Does Jesus show here an adequate grasp of the 'central reality'? Or are his attempts at approximation to it questionable?

The latter claim is often made: both 'images of God' are said to contain illusionary elements. The royal metaphor is closely bound up with Jesus' expectation of an imminent end, a decisive change that would happen soon. This expectation proved to be a mistake. The new world failed to come. Instead of the kingdom of God the church came (objectively a bitter disappointment, even if the first Christians did not experience it as such).

However, the other metaphor for God also brings us into a twilight zone: whereas the imminent expectation is an illusionary hope for the future, trust in the heavenly father seems to express an illusionary bond with the past. Human beings remain tied to infantile structures of experience. They do not look for the protection of parents in heaven in order to make life's disasters tolerable.

We should have no illusions about the magnitude of the problem: modern men and women are aware that the religious and psychological enlightenment has cast doubts on Jesus' proclamation of God. It is regarded partly as an illusionary utopia and partly as an illusionary regression. There can be no doubt about it: in coping intellectually with this problem the credibility of Christian theology is at stake – i.e. the credibility of a theology which begins from Jesus of Nazareth. If his proclamation of God is not a successful 'adaptation' to the last reality but an illusionary caricature of the harsh basic conditions of reality, then theology cannot go on according it the pride of place which it has had hitherto.

(*a*) God as coming king – an illusionary expectation of an imminent end?

The expectation of an imminent end was a mistake.[26] However, an evolutionary theory of primitive Christian faith is expecially suitable for disclosing the truth in this error: the whole of human history is a transition between biological and cultural evolution; in other words, we are always involved in both the biological and the cultural phase of evolution at the same time. The expectation of an imminent end is a mythical expression of our position in this transitional stage. Jesus and the first Christians are among the few to have expressed an awareness of this transition. That awareness is prepared for in the Old Testament and apocalyptic: a new world will come to replace this old world. The earlier animal kingdoms will be replaced by a kingdom of the 'man' (Dan.7). Jesus stands in these traditions. He proclaims the rule of God which is now already beginning in secret. The 'man' will come. The children and the poor, the halt and the lame will get their due. Primitive Christianity took over this conviction: it believed that with Jesus this new world had already begun, even if it is not yet visible. There has been a beginning. Paul detected it in creation as a cosmic longing for change: 'For the creation waits with eager longing for the revealing of the sons of God' (Rom.8.19). The Johannine community put it another way: 'It does not yet appear what we shall be' (I John 3.2). In Christ it was already there. Whatever the form of expression, the New Testament is stamped with the eschatological awareness of a decisive shift in time. This shift has cosmic dimensions; it is not just an image for inner processes.

Here it is important to note the new accents in comparison with traditional apocalyptic. Apocalyptic expectation is aimed at a new world after the decline of this world. The old world must vanish before the new one comes. In the New Testament, however, the new world begins in the midst of the old world. The rule of God comes with Jesus' activity. The new age dawns with his resurrection. The Christians are citizens of two worlds. In other words, they are on the frontier between two phases of evolution. As citizens of cultural evolution they are obliged to overcome the pressure of selection. As citizens of biological evolution they are subject to it, and put it into active practice. Both phases of evolution overlap. Just as the laws of physics continue to have an effect in biological evolution, so the laws of biology continue to have an effect in cultural evolution, even where they are transformed by new principles of organization. The communication of information through tradition takes the place of the genetic communication of information. New technologies are developed instead of new organs. Planned learning takes the place of blind trial and error; controllable institutions take the place of social relations which grow up naturally. However, we are still subject to the laws of biological evolution. We are still dependent on what happens to our organs. We die. We must still resort to blind experiment in many areas. In a word, we are still deeply rooted in the old world with our physical archaisms and social atavisms. We all live *kata sarka*, but we are all called to live *kata pneuma*, in accordance with the patterns of behaviour of this new world.

One can interpret this awareness of transition in different ways. It could be said that primitive Christianity merely became aware of the characteristics of all human history. That is not false. The tendency to reduce selection is latent everywhere in cultural history – along with opposed tendencies. In that case the kingdom of God dawning in the midst of this world would be a symbol of a timeless condition within human history, which is a transition within evolution as a whole.

However, that would not cover everything. The movement beginning from Jesus of Nazareth is something special within human history. It is the consummation of a special history: the history of Israel. It consummates a protest against selection which is expressed increasingly clearly in it. There is positive opposition to this principle of selection: solidarity – not only with those who are akin (genetically and culturally) but with all humanity, even the enemy. Here the New Testament continues Old Testament tendencies, but unmistakably goes far beyond them.

How can we describe this double character of Christianity in evolutionary terms? It is both the symbolization of a 'timeless' state and also a special turning point. We must note that the transition between biological and cultural evolution is not a once-and-for-all event, but a chain of trial and error in which people try to free themselves from the pressure of selection. This process of trial and error is aimed producing more than new variants for an environment which makes its selection, and rejects most. Rather, it is a matter of the evolution of evolution, a continued development of the factors of evolution. Human beings have arrived at the awareness of an indissoluble affinity among themselves and to all living beings. We may indeed pursue our evolution at the expense of other people and other living beings, but we do so with shame and sadness. We look for a form of life in which we develop structures adapted to our environment, not against each other but with each other, in which our less adapted fellow human beings and lower forms of life do not fall by the wayside as 'dysfunctional', but are integrated into a more comprehensive structure of adaptation. The dream of the kingdom of God expresses that. In the new phase of evolution which it symbolizes, those who were previously rejected as 'dysfunctional' – children, the disabled, reprobates, homeless and aliens (not to mention other forms of life) – are the very ones who enter the kingdom.

The objection that this goal is an illusion fails to see how many small steps have been possible in the direction of a greater solidarity. We should continually remember that compared with the millions of years of evolution as a whole, all the human history that we can survey is almost nothing, regardless of what calculations we use. We are still almost contemporary with the awakening of humanity in the civilizations of the ancient East, with their transformation in Greece and Israel, with the fusing of Greek and Jewish traditions in antiquity and their transmission and revival in European history, down to the revolutions of modern times. Basically we are still at the transition between biological and cultural evolution. As we saw, the last century made vigorous efforts to find the missing link between primates and human beings, between biological and cultural evolution, and most theologians hoped it would never be found. Our problem is different. We experience ourselves as the missing link, the transition from animals to true human beings. That may violate our anthropocentric vanity, which is fond of seeing itself as the unsurpassable crown of creation. However, it is a hope in the face of man's terrifying propensity to degeneration, which has been particularly evident in Germany. It is to be hoped that the people responsible for Auschwitz are only people in transition.

Human history is a struggle for the construction of structures of solidarity against the ever-present possibility of regression into an atavistic selection mentality. German Fascism in particular has shown that any group which gives the rejection of the weak the status of a political programme is not furthering positive developments but running headlong to catastrophe. Human beings have arrived at a stage of evolution in which they offend against the basic conditions of reality when they renounce solidarity with the rest of humanity (and with nature). We may accept the truth of the idea that God is a king whose rule brings the weak their rights, mythical though it may be, provided that we are convinced that in the end the central reality will allow only those attempts at the adaptation of human forms of life in which the outcast are the criteria for human life. In that case our attitude to them would be a matter not only of our humanity but also of the compatibility of science and life with what has given structure to all reality, God.

(b) God as heavenly father – an illusionary regression to childhood?

If the expectation of an imminent 'kingdom of God' is the expression of a truth, namely the overlap of two phases of evolution in human history in which a new stage of evolution is dawning in many 'individual leaps', then this truth points forward: it is the foretaste of future possibilities. By contrast, the proclamation of God as 'father'[27] points back to childhood. The psycho-analytical theory of regression can all too easily be applied to the proclamation of Jesus, even without esoteric interpretative skill in the psycho-analytical interpretation of symbols. Jesus himself says, 'Unless you turn and become as children you shall not enter the kingdom of heaven' (Matt.18.3). The form of address to God, 'Abba', which he coined is not free from associations with early childhood. Granted, this intimate form of address was also used by adults to adults, but church fathers familiar with Aramaic later confirmed that small children address their parents as 'Abba'. So are the criticisms of religion based on the theory of regression right, arguing as they do that the long period of childhood dependence on parents leaves permanent traces which lead to the projection of the image of parents on heaven? Is this a regression to infantile structures of experience and behaviour in situations in which people want to withdraw from a harsh reality?

Here, too, evolutionary considerations can continue to help us. Evolution does not always consist in a 'further development' in the direction of already existing tendencies, but often also means going back again to conditions before developments took place in a specialist direction. Highly developed and adapted living beings are endangered because slight alterations in their environment destroy their equilibrium with that environment, which is adjusted to the finest of balances. The greater the specialization, the less the general capacity for adaptation. 'Opportunists', who can adapt to different milieus, have a better chance here. As a rule evolution favours specialization in various environmental niches. Only the primates are spared the fate of being caught in the 'golden cage' of specialism. And among them humanity in turn has the greatest capacity for adaptation to different environmental conditions – because we have the greatest general capacity for learning.

A comparison with other primates produces the striking discovery that human beings retain throughout their lives characteristics which apes display only in their youth: young apes have a high forehead and less hair than their adult parents. To some extent human beings remain 'young' all their lives, or more accurately, they have a series of neotenic features; i.e. a living being achieves sexual maturity while in other respects remaining in a youthful state.[28]

Such neotenic features characterize not only the physical build of human beings but also their behaviour. Human beings preserve a childish curiosity long beyond their youth. Some cultures deliberately limit it. For it always brings the danger of deviation from the 'socially interpreted world'. In some cultures, however, given favourable conditions it is actually reinforced. In these cultures science could develop out of general curiosity. We owe the greatest motive power of cultural evolution to a 'regression' to childhood behaviour.

The same goes for art. Human beings preserve a childish love of playing games long beyond their youth, a love which serves no immediate purpose of survival. Here, too, there are societies which actually encourage such a 'relaxed' attitude of play and accept it as more than an extra to 'important' activities. In all of them we find the emergence of 'art', a playful way of dealing with material and forms of life which is pursued with the greatest 'seriousness'.

Something comparable may also be the case with religion. Its roots lie deep in childhood behaviour and experience. However, many societies tie themselves completely to the needs of the 'adult world'. Religion becomes social cement. But where it is deliberately articulated as a regression to childhood behaviour and experience, it emancipates itself from this function. For the child has not yet undergone socialization in society; it is still open.

In terms of evolutionary theory we could put words of Jesus like this:

Unless you again become as curious as children, you will not enter the kingdom of science.

Unless you again play like children you will not enter the kingdom of art.

Unless you again become like children you will not enter the kingdom of God.

The exhaustion of these chances given by human neoteny already took place in antiquity: Greek philosophers and scientists made youthful curiosity autonomous and turned it into a systematic investigation of the world. By playing with human forms of expression their artists created the great genres of art. In religion we find a similar 'breakthrough' in Jesus of Nazareth: he deliberately reaches back to childhood behaviour and experience in order to articulate a religious response to the whole of reality, a response which is as open as science and art in another sphere. For the basic trust of a child in its father is unconditional – yet it does not yet know what life brings. It is trust in the face of a still undisclosed wealth of possibilities.

The regression to patterns of behaviour and experience in childhood is certainly not a 'regression' in the negative sense. It is an actualization of neotenic possibilities in human life. Just as such actualization has helped human life in other spheres towards increasingly adequate intellectual and aesthetic structures of adaptation to reality, so too in religion this regression may be an opportunity. Jesus says precisely that. Anyone who goes back to childhood is taking a decisive step forward: into the kingdom of God. In this invitation Jesus combines elements from the metaphor of father (and children) with elements from the metaphor of king (kingdom of God). We also find this connection in the Lord's Prayer: 'Our Father, thy kingdom come.'

We saw that in the Old Testament, religious fantasy and experience are freed from the symbolism of the family in particular. Relationship to parents (as a parental couple) is suppressed as a model of our relationship to the 'central reality'; the mother is removed from heaven. Accordingly the metaphor of father occurs rarely in the Old Testament – rarely, that is, in comparison to the New Testament. In view of this we must ask whether the emergence of the metaphor of father in the New Testament is in fact a regression in the history of religion. Here we should remember that the regression to childhood forms of experience took place in a milieu in which monotheistic faith was secure. The reactivation of childhood patterns of experience and behaviour could no longer lead to the reactivation of the religious symbolism connected with a couple. God had no heavenly partner.

A problem arises here from our perspective. The symbolic world of biblical religion seems to be dominated by patriarchal imagery. Has this encouraged discrimination against women for thousands of years?

First of all it should be noted that for Jesus God has an explicitly 'feminine' trait, which always appears when he is fused with wisdom.[29] First, we meet this fusion with wisdom at a point where the father symbolism emerges clearly: after the unity of Father and Son stressed in Matt.11.27f. (a post-Easter passage?) there follows wisdom's gentle wooing, the so-called 'Comfortable Words': 'Come to me all who labour and are heavy laden…' (Matt.11.28-30). True, the word 'wisdom' is absent, but the parallels with wisdom literature are clear. Here wisdom woos through the words of Jesus (cf. Sir.6.24f.; 24.19; 51.23ff.). The consort of God, once suppressed, is again integrated into the image of God. She is fused with God. In Jesus' picture of God, then, despite the dominance of the father symbolism, male and female traits are combined.

That cannot be a coincidence. The connection is matched by the symbolism of childhood. Though from our perspective Jesus' invitation to return to childhood might seem regressive, it has a 'progressive' sense: childhood is a state before the differentiation of sexual roles, even when this begins early. The kingdom of God belongs to those who are not socially established in their sexual roles. The saying about eunuchs confirms this. The eunuchs are not just near to the kingdom of God because (like publicans and sinners) they are among those groups which suffer discrimination. Rather, in Matt.19.10-12 Jesus is speaking of a deliberate renunciation of sexuality for the sake of the kingdom of God.

Certainly we cannot find any feminist programme with Jesus. But we do come across features which should be noted and which point beyond a patriarchal world.

Jesus could give new life to the father metaphor without endangering monotheism. The function of this reference becomes clearer when we look at the themes connected with the metaphor: concern for physical existence (Matt.6.25ff.; 7.9ff.; 10.29) and forgiveness of guilt – i.e. 'concern' for moral existence (Matt.6.14f.; 18.14; 18.35; Luke 15.11ff.). In addition there is love for one's enemy (Matt.5.45ff.). In this connection the decisive feature is that the assurance of material existence is not everything. A corresponding feeling of 'security' is transferred to the sphere of ethical conduct.

In view of the sharpening of norms – that heightened sensitivity to ethical demands which is unavoidable as cultural evolution progresses – there must be emotional certainty about the conscience. Precisely because he goes a step further in his ethical demands, Jesus has to refer to images of emotional security. He chooses that relationship in human life which is reliable despite all its inadequacies, relationship to one's parents. It is jeopardized: in the parable of the prodigal son the younger son offends against it (Luke 15.11ff.); in the simile of the son's request, Jesus says that though they are 'evil', parents look after their children (Matt.7.11). Precisely in the light of such dangers the father relationship seems to be stable. It can symbolize that emotional certainty with which human beings can face the heightened demands made by a central reality which gradually reveals itself to them.

What does emotional security mean here? If we want to express this phenomenon in terms from the theory of evolution we might say that it is the overcoming of anxiety at the pressure from selection. The father symbolism expresses this with its themes of physical care, forgiveness of sins and love of the enemy. The pressure of selection means that resources are scarce and the weak have no chance. In view of this Jesus calls for trust in the Creator who cares for all his creatures. The pressure of selection shows itself in the social pressure which is internalized in feelings of guilt. The forgiveness of sins brings freedom from this pressure. The pressure of selection appears as aggression between human beings. However, God makes his sun rise on both good and evil. To imitate him means to love one's enemy.

The basic trust bound up with the metaphor of the father is ultimately trust that the central reality is 'love', to which one should respond by loving one's fellows. I John puts it like this: 'God is love, and he who abides in love abides in God and God abides in him' (I John 4.16). Only where the central reality 'manifests' itself as love, is the pressure of selection finally overcome. There must be two conditions here: the first presupposition is a trust in the riches of reality which gives everyone a chance without having to oppress or discriminate against others. If the central reality is 'love', extended particularly to the weak and the oppressed, then it is possibly only our lack of imagination which puts pressure on us to oppress and discriminate against one another. The central structure of reality must be made up in such a way that everyone can participate in its riches without these riches diminishing. The second presupposition is readiness for a balance between the stronger and the weaker, the more suitable and the less suitable, the privileged and the rejected. The inner riches of reality are disclosed only to those who hand them on, who participate in them. Only through mutual solidarity does humanity do justice to ultimate reality.

The basic demands of the central reality have revealed themselves in that long history of trial and error which is documented in the Bible. They are clear and simple. The New Testament formulates them as a double commandment of love: love of God and love of the neighbour. Put another way, it is expressed as trust of the inner riches of reality and as the inner power to give of them.

If cultural evolution represents a reduction of selection – i.e. an evolution of principles of evolution – protest against the harshness of the pressure of selection through the deliberate action and thought of human beings can be recognized as an obligation which is 'pre-programmed' into the structure of reality and which no one can escape who wants to accord with the ultimate reality.

To sum up. Jesus describes the central reality to which all life must adapt itself with the images of king and father. Modern consciousness often regards the statements bound up with these metaphors as illusionary, but in the light of an evolutionary approach it reveals a truth: man is on the verge of passing over to a new phase of evolution. Precisely in view of this transition he has to activate the emotional forces of his childhood past – just as in a step forward evolution often goes back to previous stages of development. By using the father metaphor (and the modes of experience and behaviour which go with it) Jesus activates possibilities which are given with the neoteny of human life.

One last thought to end with: the metaphors of father and king occur in sayings and parables. They are developed in poetic texts. That is important for our assessment of the understanding of God which they contain. Poetry gives the hearer freedom. It does not say: you must believe this or that. It seeks to change our structures of perception in such a way that in life we have those experiences for which we have not previously had a perspective. The metaphors of father and king are poetic metaphors. They are meant to stimulate us to look at reality in their light. We must discover independently where we find signs which can be interpreted as fatherly goodness and royal power. We must experience independently where that basic trust in central reality supports what we need in order to approach it in an excruciatingly slow process of trial and error. Poetic images always go far beyond reality. Anyone who takes them literally will soon suspect that they are illusions. But those who take their excesses as an invitation to explore reality will find a more appropriate attitude not only towards poetry but also towards reality. The fact that Jesus spoke of God not in dogmas but in poems should be the starting point of all our efforts to speak of God.

PART FOUR

Faith in the Holy Spirit: The Experience of the Spirit in an Evolutionary Perspective

Christian faith is based on three decisive changes in our existence – a threefold 'mutation' – in which one and the same ultimate reality has disclosed itself and continues to disclose itself anew. The first 'mutation' was faith in the one and only God who helped fugitives from slavery to survive. The second 'mutation' took place in Jesus of Nazareth as a protest against the harshness of the principle of selection. The third 'mutation' is the constant transformation of human beings as disciples of Jesus. It is faith in the Holy Spirit, i.e. the confidence that the Spirit of this one and only God who has revealed himself in Jesus of Nazareth constantly seizes people and leads them to change. This third article of faith is the 'hardest' of the three. Under the general theme of the 'Spirit' it ideals with church and community, sin, forgiveness and eternity. Common to all the statements in the third article is that they affirm the possibility of realizing what appeared in Jesus of Nazareth. They maintain that the changes in human life which take place in the biblical evidence are not an impotent dream. They continue to be possible and point to the future; indeed, in them we can see what will continue to be valid when all of history has run its course. But that raises the problem: can the new life be realized? Will it be realized?

I

The Problem: Can the New Life
be Realized?

However much we may be convinced that history and evolution
constantly bring new things into being, experience teaches us that we
overestimate the possibilities of change within our lifetime. Possibly
we underestimate them in the long term. However, this long-term
view does not determine our experience. In the short-term perspective
of everyday life there is much to tell against a belief in the possibility
of far-reaching change in humanity.

First is the doubt whether individuals can experience a far-reaching
'mutation' at all. This doubt is based on the fact that man is a natural
living being and on the recognition that his existence is governed by
society.

A look at our (biological) nature makes us doubt whether – other
than in exceptional instances – we can put into practice patterns of
behaviour which run counter to selection extending over thousands
of years. To put it in New Testament terms, we doubt whether human
beings who live in the *sarx* (i.e. in 'the flesh') can really walk 'in the
spirit'.

A look at the way in which human beings are moulded by society
does not diminish such doubts: societies want to maintain and hand
on their ways of living. They develop internal and external mechanisms
of control and compulsion for this purpose. We hear of Jesus only
through traditions which have been handed down through a particular
society. From such sources can we be stimulated to changes in
humanity aimed at liberating human beings from external social
control?

We shall have to discuss these basic questions of a Christian
anthropology: the tension between biological nature and social tradition on the one hand and the 'anti-selectionist' spirit on the other.

Closely connected with this is the problem of ecclesiology. Even if
we take the possibility of far-reaching changes in individuals into

account, that does not mean that the new possibility of life could be general. It remains an open question whether this new form of life and its spirit can fill great institutions like the church. For whereas the individual can convincingly articulate his or her resistance to a life which is determined by the struggle over the distribution of goods and opportunities, the church remains deeply entangled in this struggle. Against its will it is often determined by the intrinsic dynamics of historical self-assertion. It has to develop hierarchical structures, establish legal regulations and have sanctions at its disposal. Indeed, in modern times it sees itself exposed to the fundamental suspicion that its faith is a refined way of assuring the advantages of privileged classes and strata – and persuading the deprived strata to be content with their unjustly restricted opportunities. Hence today's question, heightened by modern criticism of ideology: can anti-selectionist motivation be institutionalized? Is not the spirit of Jesus always compromised when it becomes the basis of a great institution? Is not this institution too deeply entangled in society as a whole to be able to represent convincingly freedom from the principle of selection? Does it make sense to maintain the vision of such freedom when this freedom was compromised over a long history – most basically by the Christian churches and nations themselves? That, today, is the basic problem of Christian ecclesiology (the doctrine of the church). Motivation against selection and a church entangled in wider society, spirit and institution, seem to stand over against each other in a conflict which is impossible to resolve.

All these considerations culminate in a third question. Does that form of life attested in the Bible correspond in any way with the structure of reality? Is it really a successful adaptation? If so, it would have to preserve its validity to the end of time – indeed it would have to demonstrate in the light of the end of all history that it is an adequate structure of adaptation to the ultimate reality. This basic problem of a Christian eschatology will have to be discussed at the end of this book – on the basis of a modern evolutionary theory which cannot assume a pre-existing goal for all development but is open to the future.

So we shall go on to discuss three problems.

1. Can the individual change radically? Is his or her 'mutation' possible? Here we come up against the paradox of Christian life and the basic problem of a Christian anthropology.

2. Can social groups and institutions credibly represent an 'anti-selectionist' spirit? Here we come up against the paradox of the church and the basic problem of a Christian ecclesiology.

3. Does the whole process of the world focus on a complete 'adaptation' to the ultimate reality? Here we come up against the paradox of history or the problem of a Christian eschatology.

First of all, however, in a brief historical sketch I shall sum up what the New Testament has to say about the experience of the Spirit.

II

Experiences of the Holy Spirit in Primitive Christianity: A Historical Outline

In the New Testament there is no doctrine of the 'Spirit', but there are typical experiences which can be attributed to the Spirit. Common to all experiences is that of the Holy Spirit as a power coming from outside which is not only part of the natural endowment of humanity but discloses possibilities of conduct and experience transcending all natural possibilities.[1] Granted, human beings are also by nature endowed with human 'spirit' – and it is no coincidence that this human spirit is described with the same term (*pneuma*) as the divine spirit. However, in addition to this natural endowment, some people have a charismatic endowment, whether by permanently receiving the Spirit on their conversion to Christianity or by being temporarily seized by the Spirit and speaking and working in its power.

In the following pages I shall describe three typical experiences of the Spirit – above all through the letters of Paul, because they describe the experiences in a more sophisticated way than any other writings.

1. The Spirit in conflict with 'sarkic'[2] behaviour

In Gal.5.19ff. Paul contrasts the fruit of the Spirit with the 'works of the flesh' in the form of a catalogue of vices and virtues. The works to be overcome are sins which are forms of behaviour with a biological orientation – sexual, religious, aggressive sins and oriented on consumption – leaving aside the religious 'failings' of idolatry and witchcraft.[3] The biological conditioning of sins in the sphere of sexuality and the consumption of food is obvious. In the major group of aggressive forms of behaviour – enmity, dispute, jealousy, anger, intrigues, discord, partisan behaviour and envy – it is probable. Granted, unlike propagation and hunger, aggression has no identifiable somatic basis, but it is clearly part of the basic survival stategy of all animals, so that we have to attribute a biological root to it.[4] Paul takes this view when he dismisses aggressive behaviour in Gal.5.15 as 'bestial' behaviour: 'But if you bite and devour one another take heed that you are not consumed by one another.'

The positive forms of behaviour, i.e. the 'fruits of the Spirit', are not mirror images of the various vices. They do not begin, for example, with 'continence' as a counterpart of 'lust'. Rather, the 'catalogue' of virtues comes to a climax with eight pro-social modes of behaviour: love, joy, peace, long-suffering, friendliness, goodness, fidelity, gentleness. They correspond to some degree to the eight aggressive forms of behaviour in the catalogue of vices, which are mentioned there by Paul only in second or third place. In addition, to end with, one more virtue is mentioned, which relates to those 'vices' which are somatically conditioned: continence or self-control, a prerequisite of any pro-social behaviour.

In my view, the 'catalogue of virtues' sheds some light on the catalogue of vices. The various negative forms of behaviour are rejected because they are anti-social. Lack of sexual discipline must lead to dispute and jealousy in a primitive Christian community, i.e. a community which extends beyond the family with great emotional proximity (cf. I Thess.4.16). Idolatry is infidelity to common convictions (cf. I Cor.8-10). Luxury and drunkenness are anti-social when possessions are limited (cf. I Cor.11.17ff.).

This 'social significance' in the contrast between vices and virtues is stressed by the introduction to this paraenetic section in Galatians. Here Paul cites the command to love one's neighbour as a summary of the whole law (5.14). He contrasts it with the animal attitude of eat and be eaten. The Spirit is particularly concerned for pro-social behaviour. In this respect it is opposed to the flesh:

'But I say, walk by the Spirit, and do not gratify the desires of the flesh. For the desires of the flesh are against the Spirit, and the desires of the Spirit are against the flesh; for these are opposed to each other, to prevent you from doing what you would' (5.16f.).

Here Paul affirms a fundamental conflict between tendencies in behaviour which have a biological foundation (the works of the 'flesh') and pro-social behaviour as enjoined by the Spirit. Granted, scholars are fond of denying that *sarx* (flesh) in Paul means the biological aspect of human life – wrongly, as I Cor.15.39 shows. There Paul speaks of the different kinds of flesh of human beings, animals, birds and fishes. For him, flesh (= *sarx*) means biological life. And being sarkic, this life is something that the Christian must overcome: 'And those who belong to Christ Jesus have crucified the flesh with its passions and desires. If we live by the Spirit, let us also walk by the Spirit' (Gal.5.24f.). One can hardly give blunter expression to a repudiation of some of the tendencies towards behaviour programmed into the biological nature of human beings. In this view Paul goes directly against the modern approach which by contrast sees the origin of anti-social behaviour in the 'suppression' of biologically conditioned needs. Human beings are intrinsically good; their evil nature stems from the fact that social repression distorts, suppresses and represses the natural impulses.

We should have no illusions about this contradiction between Pauline anthropology and modern self-understanding. Not even if we may not attribute to Paul a total rejection of human nature. *sarx* (flesh) is only one concept for designating the biological aspects of human beings. It is related to impulses and aspects which have to be overcome. Sometimes the term is used neutrally, but it is never used positively. Alongside *sarx* Paul can also use the term *soma* ('body'). He, too, relates it to forms of behaviour with a biological basis like sexuality (cf. I Cor.6.13ff.) and eating (I Cor.10.16f.). In contrast to the concept of *sarx*, it often has a positive connotation: the community forms one *soma* with the Lord. The body (the *soma*) can be used in the service of the Lord – a statement which would be inconceivable in connection with the term *sarx*.[5] Whereas the term *sarx* means those impulses in human beings which must be overcome, nature which is intrinsically biological (though not exclusively so), the term *soma* denotes those biologically conditioned impulses which people can 'sublimate' and use for pro-social ends.

So we can note that in Paul the 'Spirit' shows itself to be in sharp conflict with tendencies towards anti-social behaviour with a biological foundation. However, that is only one aspect.

2. The Spirit in conflict with social divisions and the primitive Christian social mysticism

The main concern of the Letter to the Galatians is directly opposed to our modern consciousness: the subject of the controversy is law and circumcision, i.e. the norms of Jewish society. Paul warns the communities of Galatia against adopting the socially restrictive norms of the Old Testament, but binds them to the Old Testament law in respect of the central human commandment to love one's neighbour. Paul demonstrates vividly to the Galatians that the observance of the Jewish dietary laws can destroy common life between Jews and Gentiles in Christian communities; that was the reason why common meals between Jewish and Gentile Christians were done away with in Antioch (Gal.2.11ff.). However, in the communities of Galatia, as in all Christian communities, the binding principle is to be that 'There is neither Jew nor Greek, there is neither slave nor free, there is neither male or female; for you are all one in Christ Jesus' (Gal.3.28). In I Cor.12.13 this primitive Christian 'social mysticism' is directly connected with the experience of the Spirit: 'For by one Spirit we were all baptized into one body – Jews or Greeks, slaves or free – and all were made to drink of one Spirit.' The miracle of Pentecost shows how the experience of the Spirit transcends the boundaries of peoples and languages: all understand the Christian proclamation (Acts 2.1ff.). Paul, too, knows of the phenomenon presupposed in the account of Pentecost: glossolalia – a deviant way of talking which is independent of any cultural linguistic context. In the Corinthian community it was regarded as one of the most important gifts of the 'Spirit'.[6]

Thus the Spirit transcends both the linguistic barriers and the barriers created by social norms and roles. Paul refers to this experience of the Spirit when he rules out the adoption of separatist Old Testament norms by the new Gentile-Christian communities – at the same time binding them to the universal Old Testament norm of loving one's neighbour.

Circumcision had an important social function independently of its religious significance. It increased the probability that Jewish children would grow up in a home in which both parents had a monotheistic faith. Circumcision was a necessity for marriage to a Jewish woman. So a Gentile had to be converted to Judaism before he could have any influence on Jewish children. Thus circumcision reduced the probability of marriages between Gentiles and Jews (without being able to exclude them *de facto*) and therefore the possibility of religious syncretism. It provided a social basis for monotheistic faith without which this could hardly have established itself in a polytheistic environment.

In addition, circumcision was a symbol of male dominance: this religious rite was performed only on him, just as the male is the decisive figure in the handing down of the cult in a patriarchal society.

Within a Jewish household circumcision created social barriers: Jewish (i.e. circumcised) slaves were in principle temporary slaves. After six years they had a chance to be freed. Moreover, they could not be sold to non-Jews. Only Gentile slaves (i.e. uncircumcised slaves) were slaves in the full sense.

So Paul is right when he argues that on the basis of the spirit which is given to all members there is neither Jew nor Gentile, slave nor free, man nor woman – in this situation the adoption of circumcision would be a retrograde step. It would once again set up barriers between cultural, social and sexual roles.

For Paul, the building of such social barriers was behaviour according to the flesh. In Paul, *sarx* can also designate a social factor: for example, Paul calls his people 'my *sarx*' (Rom.11-14). Confidence in the *sarx* is confidence in the cultural privileges of one's own people (Phil.3.3ff.). One of Paul's boldest discoveries was that the law, which was intrinsically 'spiritual' (pneumatic) and opposed to everything fleshly (Rom.7.14), could be the instrument of the *sarx* if it again set up social barriers. In the background we have Paul's personal experience. As an adherent of the law, zealous for his people and its normative traditions, he had offended against a small minority which had proved to be open towards Gentiles. His conversion to this minority consisted in the fact that he was aware of his call to be an apostle to the Gentiles – and thus broke through the separation between Jews and Gentiles.

In the Christian communities, these and other social barriers were broken through in principle (though not completely in practice): the community formed a spiritual body (*soma*) in which all Christians were aware of themselves as members of one and the same body; indeed, this body was in a mysterious way identical with the risen Christ.[7] In practice this 'mystical communion' was realized in the common meal: because all ate of one bread, the body of Christ, they all became one body (I Cor.10.16f.).

Thus in primitive Christianity the experience of the Spirit means more than opposition to unsocial, fleshly behaviour in the name of pro-social demands as they are contained in the law. It similarly means opposition to any form of ethnocentricity – including that ethnocentricity which appeals to the law to claim itself as the sole embodiment of true life.

3. The Spirit in conflict with the finitude of human awareness and human life

The Spirit transcends not only *sarx*, not only social and cultural boundaries, but also the boundaries of psychological life generally. It is an ecstatic experience which frees human beings from being shut up in themselves. People have a share in a new dimension, in the Spirit of God. Paul specifies this ecstatic experience in two passages, pointing in opposite directions.

The Spirit of God is directly contrasted with the 'spirit of this world' which is represented by the 'rulers of this word' who crucified Jesus (I Cor.2.-6-16). To put it another way, the Spirit of God is opposition to the dominant consciousness, to existing society and the prevalent values in it, indeed to the world generally.[8] It makes accessible 'What no eye has seen, nor ear heard, nor the heart of man conceived' (2.9). It opens up 'the depths of God' (2.10).

At the same time the Spirit of God givs us profound harmony with the whole of creation (Rom.8.19-28). When the divine Spirit grasps the human spirit and leads it to utter 'inexpressible sighs', it articulates in harmony with the sighs of all creation the longing for the appearance of the 'freedom of the glory of the sons of God' (Rom.8.21). Here the Spirit opens the way to a profound harmony with tendencies of the whole of reality which are aimed at the overcoming of the dark intimations of 'guilt' (Rom.8.20) and transitoriness.

Both experiences must be seen together. The Spirit of God discloses a radically new dimension. It goes beyond any current awareness of the human world. But by taking this step beyond what exists it accords with universal cosmic tendencies. True, human beings do not know precisely where these are pointing. 'We do not know what we should pray' (Rom.8.26). But they possess the Spirit as the firstfruits of the new reality (Rom.8.23).

Because this Spirit transcends the finitude of human life, the promise of eternal life is bound up with it. Paul does not know of any nucleus in a human being which lies outside the territory of death. He knows nothing of an immortal soul. He hopes for the resurrection of the dead. But he does not hope for a resurrection without continuity between present life and eternal life. Rather, eternal life reaches into present life when human beings are seized by the 'Spirit of God' which is alien to them: the Spirit of God dwelling in them survives death and gives eternity to individual and mortal existence: 'If the Spirit of him who raised Jesus from the dead dwells in you, he who raised Christ Jesus from the dead will give life to your mortal bodies also through his Spirit which dwells in you' (Rom.8.11).

In primitive Christianity the experience of the Spirit is always a transcending of the bounds of human life. The Spirit is opposed to fundamental 'fleshly' tendencies of behaviour; it goes against the general tendency to social delimitation and extends the boundaries of the human world by new cosmic dimensions.

III

The Experience of the Spirit in an Evolutionary Perspective

1. The Spirit as a mutation of humanity and the problem of Christian anthropology

The Spirit aims at an inner transformation of humanity. Those seized by it are incorporated into the history of the protest against selection from the beginnings of Israel to Jesus of Nazareth; indeed this history becomes their own history,[9] and its struggles become their struggles. The Spirit involves them in a twofold conflict which often makes them doubt whether a far-reaching change could really take place – if not as a once-for-all change, at least as constant conversion to a new life.

The 'inner mutation' of the Spirit involves human beings in conflict both with patterns of behaviour which have a biological foundation and with the socially-conditioned pressure towards conformity exercised by tradition. Paul articulates both aspects of this conflict.

In the conflict with patterns of behaviour which have a biological foundation, the 'Spirit' is on the side of culture. For the cultural demands of the law point in the same direction as the Spirit. They seek to reduce the pressure of selection. To this degree the law is 'spiritual' and a counterpart of the *sarx* (Rom.7.14).

However, culture itself is also a system of exerting compulsion and pressure and 'compels' every individual to adapt. Although cultural institutions and norms should serve to reduce the pressure of selection, paradoxically they create new pressures: the law which was given for life proves to be a power that brings death (cf. Rom.7-10). To this degree the law can seem to be a 'letter which kills' and stands in contrast to the Spirit which brings life (II Cor.3.6; Rom.7.6).

Belief in the Holy Spirit is the conviction that despite this twofold conflict with *sarx* and law, or nature and culture, an inner transformation in humanity is possible which enables us to take a small step – perhaps only a tiny step – beyond evolution hitherto and enter a new land the dimensions of which we are only beginning to suspect.

(*a*) Renewal by the Spirit and human nature

The conflict between flesh and Spirit is the expression of the conflict between two stages of evolution which overlap hierarchically: biological and cultural evolution. This conflict is unavoidable. Paul, rather than our all-too-superficial modern awareness, is right in seeing an antagonism in principle between flesh and Spirit, i.e. between tendencies towards behaviour with a biological foundation and human culture, even if 'Spirit' is more than human culture. However, all human culture can be summed up in the command for pro-social behaviour – just as Paul can sum up the law in a command to love one's neighbour (Gal.5.14).

Biological evolution necessarily favours all forms of behaviour which give living beings an advantage over others in terms of selection, i.e. that behaviour which enhances the opportunities a particular genetic variant has to propagate itself. Conversely, a form of behaviour which reduces the chances of propagation will 'die out' in the course of time. Even a small percentage of increased chances of propagation can change the whole population over the course of generations.

There is a justified suspicion that forms of behaviour which increase the chances of the propagation of living beings need not be identical with forms of behaviour which make possible the stability of a culture. For behaviour which sets a premium on selection is always behaviour at the expense of others. Culture always begins where the pressure of selection is reduced, i.e. where people are capable of restraint in establishing themselves at the expense of others.

It could be objected that 'altruistic' behaviour can also be found among animals;[10] it would in fact be more proper to speak of analogies to altruistic behaviour, since it would be nonsensical to introduce moral categories into behaviour which is genetically controlled. Even animals put themselves at a disadvantage in favour of others. They warn other members of their species about enemies, and by so doing draw the attention of these enemies to themselves. Parents protect their young even to the point of sacrificing their own lives. Colonies of insects display a highly developed social system within which individuals sacrifice themselves for the whole. But all these modes of behaviour can only maintain themselves in the animal kingdom by ensuring those who engage in them of increased chances of propagation. They are established when they prove to have genetic advantages. That is true in particular of the insect colony: all members of an insect colony are descendants of one and the same queen; as the result of a special genetic structure they have more genes in common than human siblings and are therefore not genetic rivals. Sterilization precludes most of them from propagation. Self-sacrifice for their 'colony' is therefore the most effective guarantee of ensuring the dissemination of their genes. It is *a priori* an illuminating fact that selection in the biological sphere only favours modes of behaviour which ultimately serve to increase the genes of a species. Selection favours 'selfish' behaviour[11] – even if moral categories are quite inappropriate and this 'selfish' behaviour embraces features which we interpret altruistically.

The three groups of 'sarkic' behaviour mentioned in Gal.5 - misconduct oriented on sexuality, aggression and consumption – may correspond to patterns of behaviour within biological evolution which put a premium on selection:

Creatures which are sexually active more frequently than others have a greater chance than others of disseminating their genes and the modes of conduct based on them.

Those who practise aggression successfully, defend themselves against enemies and can prevent rival aggressors from access to propagation, have greater chances of disseminating their genes than others; this does not preclude the possibility that mechanisms which constrain aggression put a premium on selection.

The same thing is true of greater activity in the search for food and the consumption of food. Those who seek food actively and develop effective patterns of behaviour for doing so, attacking others when food is short, have greater chances of propagation than others of the species.

The riddle of cultural evolution is how genetically rival beings (like man) can develop altruistic modes of behaviour which are not just for the benefit of their kin.[12] Since the organization of human beings into larger social units – at least since the neolithic revolution (the beginnings of agriculture) – this has been the central problem of any culture. Though genetically rivals, human beings must behave towards one another in a way in which biological creatures can only behave towards genetic kin; for if animals were to behave 'altruistically' towards those who were genetically alien, these would increase at their expense and sooner or later they and their altruistic behaviour would die out.

Now there is no doubt that human beings have succeeded in emancipating themselves from the genetic law that only a pattern of behaviour which carries with it an enhanced probability of propagation can establish itself. Two examples may illustrate this.

City culture has spread, although on average the populations of cities have fewer descendants than country people. The decisive factor was not the greater probability of propagation but the greater attraction of this form of life.

A second illustration is even clearer. For centuries groups have lived ascetic lives – nuns, monks and priests – without 'dying out'. The cultural attraction of this form of life is so great – despite the renunciation of propagation, i.e. the dissemination of one's own genes – that it constantly attracts new members.

There is no doubt that unlike biological evolution, cultural evolution is no longer subject to the demand to survive and increase. More important than the increase of genes is the preservation of values, norms, insights and forms of life in which genetic rivals work together in co-operation. If we knew what made primates, who are subject to the law of genetic selfishness, into human beings who can emancipate themselves from the laws of genetic 'egoism', we would have the missing link between 'ape' and man. R.W.Burhoe puts forward the theory that religion is the missing link we are looking for:[13] through religion human beings succeeded in identifying themselves with their non-genetic fellows, treating them as though they were kinsfolk, indeed part of themselves.

How is such identification possible? It must be connected with our capacity for making symbols, i.e. with our capacity to make something a symbol for something else. For us, things, objects, creatures and people are not just our direct perception of them; we always also perceive the wider context in which they stand. They point to something else. It is enough for us to see, say, a mouse, a small, almost invisible creature, for us to be aware of the marvellous inter-connection of the whole of organic life. The little mouse becomes a symbol of life generally, in which we ourselves participate with our own individual destinies. We see its sniffing around as part of an urge to explore which we can also sense in ourselves. Its minuteness becomes a symbol of our own transitory life which is as nothing against the background of the universe, and so on. This example shows that the symbolizing of reality is not just an act of interpretation. It is closely connected with the transference of emotional and motivational reactions.

Transferred to the problem with which we are concerned, that means that people can see 'brothers' and 'sisters' in others even when these are neither brothers nor sisters genetically. By virtue of a symbolic action – a transference of the imagery of the family to a particular partner – the other person becomes a brother or sister. With the symbolic transference, at the same time those emotions and motivations which otherwise are only associated with genetic kindred are transferred to the reality symbolized.

The symbolism of brother and sister (and the symbolism of the heavenly father which is closely connected with it) is part of the basic imagery which makes possible specifically human pro-social behaviour, i.e. behaviour which does not just benefit those who are genetically akin. Other symbolism appears in the New Testament, e.g. the image of the body and its members. This can also be found elsewhere in antiquity, but in primitive Christianity it takes on a special intensity. All are members of the exalted Lord, who in a mystical way is present in the members of the community, indeed in the whole cosmos. Here, too, a biomorphic symbol is applied to relations between human beings. If we experience the other person as a member of the same body, then we can love him or her as ourselves. We experience his or her happiness as part of our own happiness and his or her grief as part of our own grief. It should be mentioned in passing that such identification with others brings problems arising from inadequate demarcation, but that should not obscure the fact that here there is a quite decisive act going beyond previous evolution.

Accordingly, religious faith consists in the capacity to transfer symbols – and in the power to use these symbolic interpretations to transfer to the reality symbolized those modes of behaviour and obligations which were once associated with the images. The other person is experienced as a brother and sister, as the member of one's own body. Genetic rivalry with him or her is ruled out – by virtue of the infinite passion of faith which experiences the symbolic pictures as a compelling power. Through this capacity to make and transfer symbols, human beings have been able to take that small step beyond previous evolution which allows them to have inklings of a freedom from the power of genetic and social egoism.[14]

It is a small step – but it represents a profound mutation of human life which can happen again and again, however improbable that might seem. Let me stress this improbability once again. We must be clear that the capacity to make symbols and identify with them is part of the basic equipment of the human mind. It is a constantly recurring 'miracle' that all this is actualized as pro-social motivation: it is our spirit being grasped by the 'Holy Spirit' of anti-selectionist motivation. The capacity to make symbols and identify with them is not a necessary presupposition, nor is it an adequate condition for universal pro-social behaviour. On the contrary, it can be realized in quite a different sense.

These specifically human capacities can often be realized in the service of one's own group towards others. Here the 'alien' (the one which is not genetically and culturally akin) is interpreted symbolically as a 'demon' and there is an almost mystical identification with members of the in-group in warding off the alien. The same capacity for symbolism and identification also makes possible the improbable, namely that the enemy is experienced as brother and sister, indeed as part of an overarching whole in which all human beings are bound together as closely as members in an organism.

It has not yet proved possible for any society to make this improbable possibility the basis of human society. It does not appear anywhere as an expectation which forms the basis of reliable secure conduct. Nevertheless, it is constantly realized by individuals and select groups, so that probably every individual in his or her life comes up against this improbable possibility, is seized and fascinated by it.

In this way they have irrevocably become the citizens of two worlds. They have taken the first step into a new phase of evolution without being able to be permanently at home in it. For as biological creatures they are still subject to the laws of biological evolution. However, as cultural beings they are confronted with the possibility of universal pro-social behaviour. As biological creatures they are determined by tendencies to behaviour which have the objective function of furthering life at the cost of non-genetically kindred members of the species. As cultural beings they see themselves exposed to the demand of furthering life through an increasingly comprehensive solidarity with those very people who are the losers in the fight for the distribution of opportunities.

Even if we cannot see the whole of this human conflict, we can make an attempt to analyse it. There is rightly a dispute as to how far human conduct is genetically conditioned. So it may be a myth that there are certain genes for certain kinds of conduct. However, the capacity to learn which is given with the whole organism is indeed genetically conditioned – not only as a general, but also as a specific capacity to learn: as a capacity for motor, sensory and linguistic learning. Here there are genetic predispositions, which means that there is an enhanced probability of the appearance of particular tendencies of behaviour if they are required or encouraged through cultural environmental conditions, or at least not hindered by them. For without doubt we have the possibility, indeed often the duty, to suppress predisposed tendencies towards behaviour within us.

Suppose we take sexual behaviour as an example: human beings with marked sexual activity – even outside cultural norms – will probably have more offspring than others. In so far as sexual activity is genetically predisposed, it will extend further among the descendants of those who are sexually active than other forms of behaviour aimed at sexual control. Perfect ascetics are excluded as possible ancestors. In so far as every culture calls for sexual discipline, it will always have to direct its efforts against 'natural' dispositions.

So it could be that a double moral standard is constantly reinforced genetically: women can bear and bring up only a limited number of children and depend on men for their support. By contrast, men can beget an abundance of children, provided that they are not obliged to bring them up. They effectively ensure the chances of the propagation of their genes by having their children brought up by others – i.e. by committing adultery and abandoning pregnant mothers. Therefore they claim liberal sexual norms for themselves and at the same time expect unconditional marital fidelity from their own wives: males would diminish the chances of the propagation of their genes were they to bring up the children of others unnoticed. To avoid any misunderstanding: no human being arranges his or her sexual behaviour on the basis of genetic calculations. However, the *de facto* result of behaviour necessarily seems to be calculated – over many generations. Here a double moral standard is an explicitly successful strategy: it is more likely that we have males with a dual morality than model husbands as our ancestors.[15]

It is clear that aggression is a form of conduct with a premium on selection. It is true that restraint on aggression is also favoured by selection. However, with human beings, deadly aggression towards fellows seems to be constantly favoured in the long pre-history of humanity. Our variant of humanity was able to establish itself because it exterminated other variants by force. We are all descendants of Cain – and have this predisposition to fratricide in us. However, quite apart from warlike oppression it is true that human beings whose aggression is restrained perhaps have fewer descendants than others. They 'conquer' fewer women (the metaphor is an apt illustration of the aggressive element in human wooing) and are less successful in warding off competitors. As we exist, we may be quite sure that we descend from people with a sufficiently aggressive disposition. At the same time we live in a culture in which the limitation of aggressive behaviour has become a fundamental problem.

In specific instances we may arrive at other results. But a series of arguments suggests that the truth could be what liberal theologians love to deny, that we have a 'natural' inclination to sin, in other words that we have pre-programmed tendencies of behaviour which are held in check by strong cultural control in the opposite direction and that when the cultural systems of restraints collapse they unleash a terrifying 'proneness to degeneration among human beings'.[16] We are citizens of two worlds, on the frontier between two eras. We experience the tension within us between biological and cultural evolution as 'guilt'. We are aware that we need not automatically follow predisposed tendencies to behave. We can direct them. But all too often we are defeated by them. We are predisposed to sin. 'Original sin' is certainly not a good term, but the repression of the inner disposition of human beings towards degeneration is a dangerous illusion.

Paul's remark that flesh and spirit fight against each other is very old-fashioned, but it might be true. The experience of the Spirit makes it certain that it is possible to be 'driven' by the Spirit in the conflict between tendencies towards anti-social behaviour with a biological foundation and the basic demands of pro-social behaviour. Granted, such activity by the Spirit is improbable, but it can never be excluded. Of course no society can take into account universal pro-social behaviour as a reliable model for conduct – social regulations must make compromises and rules of conflict for social and individual egoisms – but any society would be inhuman if unplannable and unforeseeable mutations of conduct did not take place in it: the improbable change of the human heart, in which it becomes open to pro-social behaviour and an ultimate realiity is disclosed by which all human beings are bound together more deeply than we can realize in our limited world.

(*b*) Renewal by the Spirit and human tradition

Our culture is stamped by a fundamental contradiction: it depends for the transmission of its values on possibilities of behaviour and experience which it cannot hand on by tradition. That is true of both our conduct and our experience.

Human social life continually aims at unplannable acts of solidarity between human beings in which individual and social egoism are overcome. However, at best a social structure is a balanced interplay of egoisms, made up of ordered compromises between conflicting interests. This prompts the question how a society can preserve and hand on the possibility of radical pro-social behaviour, which is so important for its life, if it may not presuppose the reliability of such pro-social behaviour in achieving its on-going basic tasks.

The same goes for the experience of reality. Every culture loses a decisive dimension unless there are always people in it who have limit-experiences in which they encounter a 'wholly other' reality. Such experiences escape the collective interpretations of the world. Yet every culture must offer its individual members a relatively well-ordered structure of interpretations which promises and suggests the certainty that it is protected against irregular upheavals.

The handing on of biblical faith, i.e. the possibility of a radical change of conduct as a response to a completely different reality, is in itself a paradox. The handing on of faith and its power to convince depends on unplannable 'mutations' within human beings. It is impossible to preserve these inner 'changes' once for all in the same way as we preserve and can hand on scientific insights or technical skill. Religious and ethical insights must constantly be rediscovered.

At this point we must take another look at biological evolution. What sees to it that creative variants do not get lost? Basically there are only two ways: inheritance and repetition. Mutations which improve the fitness of an organism are handed on by inheritance to successive generations. Mutations which are dysfunctional are excluded – but not for ever. Rather, there is a degree of probability that they will arise again by chance. At some point they may have adaptive value in different environmental circumstances. Thus biological evolution 'preserves' in two ways, if one can call the second way preservation. Either it takes mutations into the genetic repertoire or it allows blind chance repetitions without 'learning' from previous mistakes.

Cultural evolution can susbstitute tradition for inheritance, i.e. through the non-genetic transfer of information from one generation to another. This transfer of information works comparatively reliably in handing on knowledge and skills. However, human beings and cultures constantly find themselves powerless to transmit central values and norms to the next generation. In the most important spheres there are insights which each individual has to acquire anew, as though he or she were the first to discover it – just as there are follies in life which no one may escape and which cannot be avoided even by the advice of those who have already learned from corresponding follies of their own. In cultural evolution, too, as well as the unproblematical transmission of acquired knowledge there is a wealth of valuable insights, important possibilities of conduct and experience, which can only be handed on by unplannable and spontaneous repetitions.

However, in contrast to biological evolution, these unplannable 'insights and changes' are expected: they are there as an invitation or as examples in the cultural tradition. No one begins life without tradition being there already. However, the appropriation of this tradition escapes the usual technique of tradition.

Here the Christian churches openly confess that they are faced with a dilemma. They concede that the usual techniques of tradition are not enough to communicate the decisive element of faith. Rather, the handing on of faith is dependent on unplannable changes within human beings, on changes which cannot be brought about with any certainty by any method, any handbook, any training. The Holy Spirit must open men's eyes to new things and change them. Without this miracle the message of the Bible does not come alive. Without it the church cannot communicate any faith, but at best contributes to 'religious education'. In other words, what was disclosed in the two great 'mutations' of the Old and New Testaments can only be handed on if it evokes constantly unplannable 'mutations' within each individual, that change which the Christian tradition calls being grasped by the Holy Spirit.

The church is therefore a paradoxical institution. It is a plannable institution which aims at offering opportunities for an unplannable event that escapes all institutionalizing: the event of the Holy Spirit who blows where he wills.

What does that mean for the disclosure of new possibilities of experience? For that 'illumination' which at a stroke often puts the whole of reality in a new light? What does it mean for that new mode of behaviour with which alone we do justice to the newly disclosed reality?

There are features here which recall chance 'mutations', and do so necessarily: the experience of the Spirit provides an opening to a transcendent reality. By definition it lies beyond our familiar world. Only the Spirit opens up access to it. From the perspective of the limited world in which we live, events which open up this access must be fortuitous. They are not *a priori* meaningful and related to that ultimate reality. The call of this reality can touch us all: in the stillness of nature or in the bustle of the city, in abrasive conflicts or in inner peace. A beloved face, or the sight of an unexpected tree, can be the medium for it. No one can say where it will encounter us. All disclosure situations[17] are unpredictable. They are chance variants of life which involuntarily come up against another reality. It remains impossible to plan for someone so to change in them that these chance disclosure situations become transparent to an ultimate reality: 'The Spirit blows where it wills' (John 3.8).

Fortuitous as the disclosure of a 'wholly other' reality may be, in retrospect it seems necessary. Indeed the whole of life, in all its variants and variations, looks for harmony with this ultimate reality. Through chance disclosure situations it simply becomes aware of what has necessarily always already determined life.

However, it is not only this subsequent meaningfulness and evidence which distinguishes the experience of the Spirit from the blind mutations of pre-cultural evolution. Human beings already know in advance of the possibility of religious experience: tradition offers them many roles in religious experience.[18] As a result, the individual finds himself or herself in a precarious situation: the religious tradition indicates insights and forms of behaviour which can become clear and credible only on the basis of unplanned disclosure situations. Without the prior intimation of religious tradition, it might be possible to pass by such disclosure situations without noticing them. However, without an inner transformation in them the tradition becomes a 'dead' social convention: the letter that kills.

Consequently, human beings who are sensitive to the inner significance of religious tradition often find themselves pressed to decide. They feel forced to adopt an attitude towards them, although they do not have sufficient grounds for such an attitude. Only the intrinsic evidence of chance and unplannable disclosure situations could in fact lead them to an affirmative decision.

This pressure to decide is made even more urgent by the claim of ethical norms in the religious tradition. Both the disclosure of a 'wholly other' reality and the obligation to 'wholly other' conduct, to 'conversion', are one and the same for biblical faith.

Without an encounter with a wholly other reality which requires and makes possible a radical change in behaviour, the radical commands of the religious tradition are felt to be an inhuman and excessive demand, whether they are played off against the actual behaviour of religious people, whether there is a rebellion against their unrealistically strict formulation, or whether they are pushed aside dispassionately as postulates alien to the world.

In this situation it is important that we should be clear about the inevitability of such a pressure for decision. It has its foundation in the chance nature, the plurality and the borderline character of religious traditions.

If faith in historical 'mutations' of our existence is related to the history of Israel leading up to Jesus of Nazareth, it is related to 'chance' events. By that I mean that there is no reason why a decisive turning-point in the history of evolution should have taken place in Israel, of all peoples – and not in another. There is no need for this turning point to have taken place in a small strip of land between the sea and the wilderness in the eastern Mediterranean – away from the cultural centres of the old world. There is no reason why these events should have happened when they did – between the great migrations of peoples in the Mediterranean about 1200 BC and the establishment of the Roman empire under the first emperors. However, all that is no argument against the belief that if we approach and adapt ourselves to the central reality only through unplannable mutations, any alternative to biblical faith is no less fortuitous than this.

Now there are alternatives in the history of religion. Different 'revealers' present themselves to us side by side. This plurality of religious experience may be fairly unconscious in homogenous cultures. In pluralistic cultures like those of Graeco-Roman antiquity and the modern world, however, it confronts ordinary people with decisions. Buddha and Jesus are alternatives, at least from our limited perspective. Of course in principle one can endorse this plurality: it is good that human efforts to adapt to the central reality did not follow the same course. In evolution everything was not staked on one card. If an attempt failed and got into difficulties, the whole undertaking did not come to grief. However, for the individual the pluralistic situation brings with it a pressure to decide.

Yet even if we assume that a complete adaptation to central reality has appeared in our history, we can never be certain that it is a *perfect* adaptation. For that to happen we would have to be able to compare it with the reality to which it is adapted. We cannot do that. The same argument goes for our knowledge: it is bound up with our form of life. We shall never be able to test independently of the conditioning of our life whether we have arrived at an adequate intellectual adaptation to or picture of the world. Here too we come up against the limits of certainty.[19]

The pressure to decide emerging from religious traditions is therefore not a phenomenon characteristic only of religion. In so far as human life is historical and dependent on chance variants of trial and error, in so far as it develops pluralistically in alternative variants, in so far as it is limited and is precluded from absolute certainty, it is everywhere exposed to a pressure to decide. Anyone who denies this is deceiving himself about the human condition. Therefore our decisions must not be arbitrary: we can explain by arguments why there are limits to compelling arguments in life and in religion. We can explain our decisions of faith. Like the whole of culture, the creative 'mutations' of religious faith reveal a direction: a 'selection' which provides a direction takes place among 'mutations' – within human culture a selection aimed at the reduction of selection. In this tendency towards the reduction of selection we have a criterion by which we can examine all variants of religious life and all decisions of faith.

To sum up these thoughts on the paradox of Christian life: if Christian faith has taken possesion of an unpredictable inner mutation of humanity then this person will immediately come into conflict with both his nature and tradition. The experience of the Spirit will make him take a step beyond everything that is programmed into the biological rules of life; indeed it will come into tension with these 'rules'. We experience the obligation to take this step beyond nature in the religious and ethical tradition, but in fact it really cannot be handed on, as it must carry inner conviction in unplannable disclosure situations which make human beings open to a completely different reality. In a single sentence: this new life is constantly present in individual 'mutations', but it escapes our attempts to incorporate it in a reliable way into that repertoire of human possibilities which we can hand on.

2. The Spirit as motivation against selection and the problem of ecclesiology

If the new life constantly becomes reality in individual 'mutations' but is not a form of life which can be handed on with security, how far is it possible to build a whole institution on this possibility which is not at our disposal? Is there not here a conflict between Spirit and institution which cannot be resolved? Or more accurately, between the Spirit as motivation against selection and the unavoidable hierarchical, legal and economic structures of the church?

All these questions are accentuated by the modern criticism of ideology. It expresses the suspicion that religion is not at all ensouled by a Spirit directed against selection. Rather, religion appears as a refined 'instrument' in the fight over social distribution which independently of the subjective will of its representatives has the objective function of legitimating privileges and offering consolation over opportunities withheld.

Now it cannot be denied that religion is caught up in the historical struggle over resources among peoples and classes. In that it is not alone. The dialectic of culture consists in the fact that all the means which emancipate us from the pressure of natural selection heighten our capacities to assert ourselves more successfully at the expense of others in the historical struggle for resources and privileges. That is true of technology, economics and organization just as much as of religion: cultures with better military, technological and economic resources, with more effective structures of organization, with greater capacity to ground motivation for co-operative action in the social system, will spread better than others, whether through enhanced chances of increase and survival, through the greater attractiveness of their form of life, or through power and compulsion.

Religion has always served (albeit unconsciously) as an instrument in this historical struggle over the distribution of opportunities. But its functions have not just been ideological, aimed at legitimating rule. Religious support has always been claimed by both sides, not just by those with the upper hand. Rather, religion has also supported protest against oppression. Indeed, it has articulated visions which point beyond this historical fight over resources.

In the following pages I shall demonstrate this ambivalence of religion in both the social forms of biblical faith, in Israel and in the church. In the history both of the Old Testament and Judaism and of primitive Christianity we find a struggle over the true social form of faith. Nowhere is it protected from an 'ideological' function. But we always find tendencies in the opposite direction, so that religion usually seems to be ambivalent.[20]

(a) The social ambivalence of biblical faith in Israel

When we read the Old Testament it is unmistakable that religion often serves to strengthen various social systems – clans, people and classes – at the expense of others. Here biblical faith serves to create better chances of survival for those social groups which are its vehicle. That can be demonstrated in succession through the three social units I have already mentioned: clan, people and class.

1. The fundamental social group is the family and the clan. The patriarchal narratives illustrate the function of religion within the Israelite clan. As the clan has no state functions in this social framework, it is relieved of the functions of war and rule.[21] That is why we find the patriarchal narratives sympathetic: here everything is peaceful. Sagacity and good fortune, humanity and patience, faith and despair stamp the figures of Abraham, Isaac and Jacob. But we can also observe the selective value of religion in this peaceful history: the most important themes of clan religion are the promise of descendants, and, closely bound up with this, the danger to the mother of the clan and the promise of land. It is immediately obvious that groups with a high motivation for descendants and the promise of land (the material basis for descendants) have greater chances of establishing themselves in history than groups with lesser motivation for these aims. Moreover, the stories of the danger to the mother of the clan show how much these tribes thought in 'genetic' categories: only the physical descendants are to enjoy the blessing. In all this the Israelite tribes do

not fall outside the general framework of the history of Near Eastern religion: descendants and the possession of land were goals also legitimated elsewhere by religion.

New accents may be felt in what follows: the clans whose chances of survival were strengthened by promises with a religious motivation were not victors. Rather, the patriarchal narratives are full of hopeless situations. The descendants do not appear, the patriarchs are strangers in their own land, we see them as fugitives and beggars who have to make their way by deceit. On one side they have the Canaanite cities with a more highly developed culture, which they mistrust – one has only to think of the story of Sodom and Gomorrah – and on the other the wild hunting tribes of Esau, of which they are afraid. Here religion appears as a way for groups to survive when confronted with hopeless situations. It is understandable that these stories were read and told again in exile: people again found themselves in the situation of Abraham, who believed against all appearances that his descendants would be as the sand on the sea shore.

However, even in this role – as help for the weak to survive – biblical religion is not an explanation of clan ethics. Many narratives show us the fragility of the solidarity of the clan: Cain kills Abel; Abraham is ready to kill his son; Jacob deceives Esau; the brothers hand over Joseph. And yet the blessing rests on Abraham and Jacob. It is with Jacob in particular that we can see that God is also with those who emancipate themselves from strict ties to the clan. From here a line leads to Jesus' terse remark, 'If anyone comes to me and does not hate his own father and mother and wife and children and brothers and sisters, yea, and even his own life, he cannot be my disciple' (Luke 14.26). Whereas selection as a whole encourages a combination of higher internal solidarity (with the family and the in-group) and aggression towards outsiders, here the relationship is reversed: Jesus calls on his disciples to make a radical break with the family – but at the same time to love the outsider and the enemy. The tendency of biblical religion to go against selection can hardly be expressed more sharply than this.

2. A second (larger) social group relating to religion is the people of Israel. We can trace in the Old Testament how this people grew up out of various tribes and how religion encouraged this process by creating a collective readiness for defence against the enemy and demanding solidarity between all the tribes. Religion served as a factor in military mobilization: in times of danger the 'spirit of Yahweh' came upon a gifted army leader who freed Israel from its enemies. In these wars Yahweh himself fought for his people.[22] In my view there

can be no doubt that here religion has the function of securing better chances of survival for national groups.

And yet biblical religion is more than a strategy for survival at the expense of others. It is at its most authentic in giving chances of survival to a people which was in hopeless slavery. When Israel came on the historical scene about 1200 BC, well developed city cultures and empires had already existed for a long time. It was hard for this people, with a far less developed civilization, to find a place among them; Israel was constantly threatened by the powerful empires in the south and north and its immediate neighbours in the west and east. In this situation it became a central experience of Israel that it had a power which was superior to the military, technical and economic culture of the Egyptians, the Canaanites and the Philistines: the religious faith of Israel in Yahweh proved to be stronger. Yahweh was stronger than horses and riders – than the divisions of chariots in the Egyptian military machine (Ex.15.1). Yahweh was stronger than the armies of the kings of the Canaanite city-states (Judg.5). Yahweh helped David with his stone-age weapons against the ironclad Goliath, the representative of the newly-emerging Iron Age with its armour (I Sam.17). Israel discovered that while it might be inferior in every respect, it could compensate for its inferiority with the power of its faith. No wonder that religion assumed a singular place in the life of the nation and that some people recognized that the future destiny of the people depended on it. The all-important question was whether people obeyed Yahweh's commandments or not.

Now we could conclude that to a much greater degree than elsewhere the religion of Israel was an instrument in the historical fight for the distribution of opportunities. However, that would be very wide of the mark. Only in Israel do we know the phenomenon of prophets announcing inexorable doom to their own people in the name of the God of the land (Yahweh). With the great prophets of doom, religion has freed itself from its ideological function in order to reinforce motivation for the struggle with others in the historical battle for resources. Rather, religion turns against its own people with the aggressiveness of the absolute. Yahweh himself summons the other peoples to punish Israel. No one in Israel is safe from his wrath. From here there is a direct line to the New Testament prophets: John the Baptist played off God's judgment of wrath against the ethnocentric consciousness of the children of Abraham. Jesus proclaimed that in the kingdom of God it would be the aliens, the Gentiles, who would stream from all the corners of the earth to eat with the patriarchs of Israel, while the real 'sons of the kingdom of God' were excluded

(Matt.8.11f.). Without doubt, the Holy Spirit which spoke through all prophets down to the time of Jesus was a spirit which spoke out against the ethnocentric assurance of salvation: anyone who waits for judgment on the enemies of Israel will have to experience judgment on himself.

3. Religion has a function expressly oriented on selection in a third social context: it regularly serves to ensure superior opportunities for the dominant groups within a social system. The Old Testament gives us the unique chance of being able to join in the experience of the way in which a central government imposes itself on an 'acephalous' society without state direction – and with it a group of officials, soldiers and landlords which becomes increasingly influential. In this context religion has an additional function: it serves to legitimate rule. Following traditional ancient Near Eastern ideologies the king is interpreted as 'son of God', who is appointed to his office by God (Ps.2.7), sits alongside God and participates in his power (Ps.110.1). His rule is to extend geographically over all peoples (Ps.72.11) and his dynasty is to reign for all eternity (II Sam.7.14). It is not surprising that he is addressed as 'God' (Ps.45.7). That is open religious backing for the ruler. Attempts to find criticisms of the king in such statements seem to me to be meaningless.

Without doubt, then, biblical religion had the function of legitimating rule. However, characteristically, to an even greater degree it legitimated resistance against misrule.[23] In the period of the judges, Israel lived for about two hundred years without a central government. There was no place in its own religious traditions for a king. The legitimation of rule had to be imported from 'outside'. The royal ideology cited above may have found its way into the Old Testament world through traditions from the royal city of Jerusalem, which was conquered by David. A series of rebellions as early as the first century of the monarchy (*c.*1000-900), in which we can see a complete rejection of the kingdom on the basis of traditions preceding the state, shows its insecurity. In the second century of the monarchy, Ahab and his Phoenician wife Jezebel also tried to advance the claims of Canaanite kings in Israel, but they came up against the Yahwistic opposition embodied in Elijah. His successors were wiped out by a bloody revolt. In the Hellenistic period, citizens of Jerusalem with modernist leanings tried to make the Jewish society of the rural hinterland into a Hellenistic city republic. This was again a rebellion with religious motivations. The Jewish revolts against Roman rule in the first and second centuries AD are to be seen in this context. It is certainly the case that religion had the function of providing ideologies in class conflicts; however, it did not just support the rulers. In the biblical tradition we can see the opposite tendency. God is not on the side of the Pharaoh, but on the side of the slaves who are fleeing from him.

The revolt against the principle of selection which, left uncorrected, usually favours the more powerful becomes clearer when we pursue the history of the 'royal ideology' in Israel. The prophets take it up, but not in order to support the rule of the present king; it is rather to develop the utopia of a quite different rule. The royal ideology turns into the utopia of the Messiah. This Messiah increasingly loses his features as a ruler. He becomes the 'impotent' Messiah, who rules without force.[24] The climax of this development is reached in Zechariah:

> Rejoice greatly, O daughter of Zion! Shout aloud, O daughter of Jerusalem! Lo, your king comes to you; triumphant and victorious is he, humble and riding on an ass, on a colt the foal of an ass. He will cut off the chariot from Ephraim and the war horse from Jerusalem; and the battle bow shall be cut off, and he shall command peace to the nations; his dominion shall be from sea to sea' (Zech.9.9f.).

This messianic king has no repressive features directed inwards. He himself belongs to the 'lowly people' over whom he rules. He himself is 'lowly'. He has no outwardly aggressive features. He abolishes all weapons. He does not establish peace by force, but proclaims it. Even if we think that such a 'domination-free' rule is purely utopian, we must pay attention to this dream. There is a direct line from it to the New Testament. Jesus' proclamation undermines all structures of domination. Anyone who wants to be first must be the servant of all – Jesus says this in explicit contrast to the usual forms of political rule (Mark 10.42). He himself becomes the embodiment of the 'impotent messiah': the disciples recognize the hidden ruler of the world in the crucified Jesus. Here religion has lost for the moment any taint of being a legitimation of rule. It does not explain the power of the rulers but recognizes in their sacrifice the ultimate standard by which all conduct has to be measured.

In the history of religion we recognize the conflict between the unholy spirit of religious behaviour oriented on selection and the 'holy Spirit' of a deliberate opposition to the principle of selection. We constantly find convincing evidence that religion (Old Testament religion, Christian religion, Islamic religion, and so on) is aimed at securing the survival of clans, peoples and classes at the expense of others. In this respect religion proves to have a force which favours aggression and repression. But we can constantly note features going in the opposite direction.

Counter-tendencies can be seen in biblical religion in two respects: in so far as it creates advantages for its social vehicles, it provides the possibility of survival for weak groups which in 'normal' circumstances would have inevitably gone under because they would have been destroyed by neighbouring cultures with superior civilization and military resources.

In addition, however, at some points we find an even more radical conflict with the 'principle of selection', in that it is directed specifically against its own people: nowhere else do we find the phenomenon of prophets prophesying the downfall of their own people. Here religion does not reinforce the people in its fight for self-assertion, but becomes a disturbing factor.

Biblical religion gives the runaways and the weak a chance of survival – yet it threatens the same groups with their downfall if they get caught up in illusionary fantasies of power.

Thus an evolutionary theory of religion like the one outlined here takes up the ideological-critical argument against religion: religion is clearly an instrument (functioning unconsciously) in the struggle over the distribution of opportunities. However, it is in religion above all that the protest against the domination of the principle of selection is expressed. It can already be perceived in the earliest biblical traditions of the exodus of the people from their slavery in Egypt, and finds its clearest form in Jesus of Nazareth.

(*b*) The social ambivalence of biblical faith in the church

The decisive difference between the social forms of biblical faith in Old and New Testaments (and in rabbinic Judaism) is that faith no longer has its *Sitz im Leben* in the context of a whole society but in the framework of small 'sub-cultures' in more comprehensive social systems. Thus religion is at least in part relieved of some functions relating to society as a whole. Granted, it must argue with economics, law and power, but it is aware that the shaping of these tasks do not lie with it and its representatives.

This change from a 'people's religion' bound up with the whole of society to a universal 'community religion' begins in the post-exilic period, when Judaism consolidated itself afresh in the context of larger empires. It comes to an end in the New Testament period with the schism between rabbinic Judaism and pagan Christianity, in so far as in the first and second century the dream of the political independence of biblical religion (political messianism) is rejected: synagogue and church understand themselves as religious communities which are at a critical distance from society as a whole. They do not aim at political rule.

This new *Sitz im Leben* has led to a change of function which is not to be underestimated, or better, to a shift of function within religion. We saw that religion had constantly given those groups which were its vehicles advantages in selection through aggression towards outsiders and solidarity within. It mobilized defensive powers against the enemy and reinforced inner cohesion. The two belong closely together. There has always been a co-evolution of aggression and solidarity in both biological and cultural evolution.[25] Many modes of behaviour in solidarity were practised where there was a common front against the enemy. Solidarity and aggression are functionally interwoven. So we cannot evaluate the sensitivity of Old and New Testament to solidarity between human beings without seeing their functional involvement in religiously legitimated aggression. This function is evident in the Old Testament but it can also be traced in the New Testament in sublimated forms of human aggressiveness.

Now if the aggressive aspect of religion becomes dysfunctional in a particular historical situation, the furthering of inter-human solidarity can become the primary function of religion. At least there is a chance of that. This situation arose when Israel lost its political independence. Now religion was freed from the task of legitimating military aggression abroad and repression at home. This was the concern of others. Wars were waged by alien rulers, and they practised repression. Within these over-arching empires sub-cultures could arise with unmilitary and non-repressive features. In this situation the impulses in biblical religion which favoured solidarity could gain the upper hand over the aggressive motives, so that solidarity was freed from its involvement with external aggression and could even include the outsider and the enemy.

In this situation Jesus could give love for the enemy a preferential position over family ties and thus raise the co-evolution of aggression and solidarity to a new level: the bond between aggression outwards and solidarity inwards was replaced by the demand for solidarity outwards and detachment from one's closest relations.

In this situation Jesus could proclaim the fulfilment of the ethnocentric dream of the kingdom of God – but as a radical criticism of this ethnocentricity: the Gentiles will stream into the kingdom of God from all over the world but the 'sons of the *basileia*' will be excluded (Matt.8.11f.).

In this situation Jesus could stand all structures of rule on their head

and proclaim that rule is demonstrated not by oppressing the weaker
ones but by serving them. The kingdom of God belongs to children,
the despised and the meek, all those who are certainly not predestined
to rule.

The first Christians continued this form of life in principle. When
Paul says that there is neither Jew nor Gentile, slave or free, man nor
woman, he is addressing those three social contexts within which
religion has always exercised ambivalent functions: people, class and
family. If sexual roles are unimportant, then the significance of family
and descendants is relativized. The struggle for opportunities for one's
own family is over. If there are no longer masters and slaves, then
there can be no more repressive rule. It cannot have a foundation in
Christ. If the boundaries between Jews and Gentiles have been
overcome, then competition between peoples is replaced by solidarity.

As I have said, these are statements of principle. From the beginning
reality looked different. We can understand the history of the Christian
church as a conflict between the motivation of the 'Spirit' against
selection and the compromising of it by the demands of church
practice. This compromising is inevitable. It does not begin after an
undisturbed primal period. Earliest Christianity already knows the
'Spirit' only in compromises with the world.

Let us begin with the positive side of motivation against selection:
the love commandment. It stands at the centre of the three most
important social forms of primitive Christian belief: Synoptic, Pauline
and Johannine Christianity. It always takes first place: as the supreme
commandment (Mark 12.28ff.), as the fulfilling of the law
(Rom.13.8ff.) and as the central message of the heavenly ambassador
(John 13.34f.;15.12ff.).

It receives its most radical formulation in the Synoptic tradition: as
love of one's enemy (Matt.5.43ff.) It seems to be bound up with a
radical form of existence, with homeless wandering charismatics, who
disseminate the new message throughout the countryside.[26] These
outsiders could make a credible presentation of the Synoptic ethos,
which does without family, possessions and protection. However, the
very formulation of the commandment to love one's enemy shows the
possibility of the misuse of this commandment. Segregation from
other groups appears here as a reason for loving one's enemy: those
who only love in order to be loved in return are no better than
publicans, Gentiles and sinners. A commandment which seeks to
overcome all boundaries between men and women becomes the
instrument of a sublime concern for segregation, namely the self-
segregation from others of those who want to be as perfect as God

(Matt.5.48). If we add other Synoptic sayings, we can note an often terrifying aggressiveness: for example, people living normally are condemned in the light of the sinful generation of Lot and Noah – statements which may even go back to Jesus himself (Luke 17.26ff.).

In Paul the love commandment appears in three contexts. In Galatians it expresses the conflict with the selfish mode of sarkic behaviour. It goes against 'nature' (Gal.5.12ff.). In Romans it appears in tension with state paraenesis (Rom.13.1-7). Whereas the state appears as the avenger, to whom one is obliged to pay all that is 'due', love renounces vengeance (12.19) and owes nothing other than love (13.8). Here the love command goes against society. In I Corinthians it appears in contrast to the community: in the light of a squabble over prestige on the basis of spiritual gifts, all religious gifts are relativized by love (I Cor.13). If we look at specific solutions of conflicts within the Pauline sphere, it is striking that they take into account the inequality of members of the community. Certainly there is no difference in principle between man and woman (Gal.3.28), but *de facto* Paul himself insists on distinction which were not absolute requirements in the world of the time (I Cor.11.3ff.).[27] A balance is certainly struck between rich and poor, but in such a way that account is taken of the superior position of the rich. At the eucharist they must not share in all the food that has been brought, but are asked to fill themselves up at home (I Cor.11.17ff.).

The Gospel of John also shows the element of compromise in Christianity. Here the love commandment is the only ethical commandment that the heavenly envoy gives to his own followers. It is not a commandment to love the enemy. Love is restricted to the brethren. We find quite different attitudes to outsiders. The Gospel of John adopts an ambivalent attitude towards 'the Jews'; at some points they are condemned in a terrifying way, as when all Jews are stamped as children of the devil (John 8.44). There must be a close connection between this abrupt segregation from outsiders and great internal solidarity. Because the world rejects Christians, it brings them closer together. However, the converse is probably also the case: because people come closer together, they tend to part company with outsiders.

We can see that even in early primitive Christianity, forms of life in solidarity always appear in compromises with tendencies which do not lead to solidarity. There can be no doubt of that in the case of the love command, and it should sharpen our perception that even supreme ethical values have a dark periphery. The conflict between the old world and the new similarly runs through both individuals and through the church. The church never belongs completely to the new world. Even with the best of intentions, it is continually entangled in those behavioural connections which it wanted to escape. It is directed towards justification, at the very point where it shows its best side. The revolt against selection is not pursued by saints. It is impossible to divide human beings into just and unjust, into children of light and children of darkness. Matthew, who formulates the ethical teaching of Jesus with the least compromise, is most aware that the church is a mixture. Given the dual nature of human beings as citizens of two worlds – or more accurately, of a transition between two worlds – anything else would be improbable.

The church is an institutionalized compromise with human inadequacy. And for that reason it contains a latent conflict within itself. The 'Spirit' to which it appeals is always critical of the church. This criticism can flare up wherever the Spirit wills. But in the ancient church there are also 'institutionalized' forms of protest against selection, pneumatics who enjoy particular respect and evade the church's institutions, i.e. ascetics and martyrs.

Ascetics embody a contradiction against the principle of natural selection. They voluntarily forgo procreation. They evade the rivalry for increased chances of propagation which stamps the behaviour of all creatures. They are reminders that human beings are citizens of two worlds and can at least make a start on entering a sphere in which the principle of selection has been overcome. In my view the usual Protestant denigration of asceticism is quite inappropriate.

Martyrs embody the conflict against social selection in its most merciless form, the execution of those whose modes of behaviour and convictions differ. By their martyrdom they demonstrates their freedom from this social pressure. Those who marvel at them demonstrate that physical annihilation of the 'chances of propagation' do not diminish faith but enhance it: the blood of the martyrs became the seed of the church.

Asceticism and martyrdom are extreme forms of behaviour directed against selection. Evil motivations may sometimes flow into both forms of behaviour. Nevertheless we should not deny that asceticism and martyrdom can be an expression of solidarity between human beings.

In some people sexual asceticism can perhaps become convincing because they succeed in transferring that restraint over sexuality which we find easiest to achieve towards our physical kindred, to all people, to all 'brothers' and 'sisters', so that their capacity to love takes on a much greater range than that of others.

Martyrdom for a group symbolizes a deep bond with it: anyone who, like Maximilian Kolbe, voluntarily dies for another sets up (even in the midst of Auschwitz) a convincing sign of love in the face of the most brutal exaggeration of the principle of selection applied by human beings, as happened in the Nazi mass murders.

The protest of the Spirit can take many forms in the church. It is continually made against the church, which is necessarily burdened with compromise. For all their darker side, the fact that the Christian churches have produced and keep producing this self-criticism of their own accord is one of the most positive statements that one can make about them.

To sum up: anti-selectionist motivation (the Holy Spirit of biblical faith) can only be institutionalized with many compromises. These compromises are unavoidable. Without them there would continually be no chance of those unplannable 'mutations' of individuals in which there is a clear expression of what an institution can express only in a contradictory form.

In my view this suggests some criteria which mark out the limits of compromise.[28]

1. The obligation to make tolerable compromises with human inadequacy does not mean adaptation to whatever contradicts the spirit of biblical religion. Rather, we must constantly see and understand what spirit is 'compromised' – only in this way does the Spirit have a chance of becoming effective despite all compromises.

2. The church loses its identity where it clearly supports selectionist processes with its faith – e.g. the policy of apartheid, which with a crude one-sidedness distributes opportunities according to a biological criterion; or a policy which seeks to maintain the power of a ruling class by violating human rights.

3. The church loses its identity where it stands in the way of the working of the Spirit in individuals and small groups. It must allow some people constantly to take a risky course, to live and act in the spirit of Jesus, free from the compromises of the institutional church. The church is called to live as an exception. Without it the salt would lose its savour.

3. The Spirit as adaptation to the ultimate reality and the problem of eschatology

If inner transformation through the Spirit cannot be planned, and happens only in individuals, and if it appears in our traditions and institutions only as being burdened with inner contradictions, we must ask all the more urgently whether this Spirit, the Spirit of the monotheistic revolution, the Spirit of Jesus of Nazareth and his followers, corresponds to the basic conditions of reality. Is it the 'Spirit of truth' (John 14.17), i.e. the Spirit which accords with the ultimate reality? Is it a successful structure of adaptation to it, or a dream? Is it an impotent desire of living creatures rebelling against the harshness of the principle of selection?

More specifically, is a society possible in which the natural and cultural pressure of selection is cushioned to a far greater degree than now happens? In which new forms of life are developed not against the weak but along with them? In which the losers in our society are not lost? Anyone who believes that must reckon with the possibility that the 'Spirit' brought into the world by the monotheistic revolution and by Jesus of Nazareth is in closer accord with the basic conditions of reality than the biological and cultural systems known to us, which always represents only transitory structures of adaptation to this reality.

It seems reasonable to attempt to undergird faith in the possibility of realizing new life with the theory of evolution, by interpreting evolution as a purposeful process. And of course that happens regularly: either belief in secular progress (which need not necessarily be connected with belief in a goal to this process) is supported by considerations from the theory of evolution – or a religious hope for the fulfilment of history is articulated with the help of evolutionary categories (here we need not necessarily assume a continuous approach to this goal).[29] Belief in progress and eschatology (as faith in the fulfilment of history) will constantly make use of evolutionary categories.

However, we should have no illusions about this point: in both cases we have a pre-modern evolutionism.[30] In both cases it is a matter of going beyond what can be said in the context of evolutionary thought. The great progress in the modern theory of evolution lies precisely in the fact that it explains as an interplay of chance and necessity what was earlier interpreted teleologically by analogy with purposeful action, namely the miraculous order, purposefulness and higher development of organisms. Even if we are still not completely clear about what factors are chance and what are necessary to this process, in the present state of our knowledge we are compelled to assert that it is meaningless to smuggle teleological thought into the theory of evolution. Evolution is open. No one knows where it is leading. No one can guarantee that it will lead to more differentiated and higher forms of life. No one knows whether observable tendencies towards a reduction of entropy and selection are moving towards a culmination. Of course no one can assert that this is ruled out. But anyone who wants to argue for faith in the perfection of the world must draw on other sources than modern evolutionary thought. No one can be precluded from this belief in the perfecting of the world. However, in what follows I shall try to remain as far as possible with our paradigm of the theory of evolution (as it is valid at present).

That means that I shall regard the history of nature and humanity as a history of trial and error determined by chance and necessity. In this way we shall move a long way from that optimism about belief in progress which many people wrongly regard as a characteristic of evolutionary thought.

'Trial and error' means that new attempts fail. Without this failure there would be no further development, if there is any at all. However, the failure of variants of life does not tell against these variants: some came at the wrong time. In different conditions they could be valuable for life. 'Trial and error' does not mean justifying failed variants as a necessary sacrifice to progress. There is no reason why the first attempt should not succeed. There is no need for many attempts to fail before we find a solution (blindly or through deliberate insight). That is only a probability. But we must be ready for failure if we are to have success.

However, even if our trial and error should be temporarily successful, there is no guarantee that we are developing in the right direction. Evolution has constantly led into dead ends. No one knows whether our cultural evolution, too, is not such a dead end. No one knows whether we too shall not fail by being unable to control our tendencies towards aggressive behaviour.

All that sounds pessimistic. The question is, can one express hope at all within the context of the theory of evolution? Does not the 'heat death' of the universe lie at the end of the world process, on the basis of the law of entropy? May we not be certain that life will come to an end on our planet long before that? Does not our transitory life seem increasingly clearly to be meaningless in the unfathomable dimensions of the cosmos?[31]

To speak of the Holy Spirit in the context of evolutionary theory means to contradict such hopelessness and resignation. But how can that be possible? How can what contradicts our experience be true?

In the context of evolutionary thought, truth is the adaptation of cognitive structures to reality. Here truth is subject to two criteria of adaptation: it must be 'adapted' to the totality of our knowledge, i.e. it must be logically coherent with it, and it must be 'adapted' to external reality, i.e. to the experience that streams in from outside. In both respects the search for reality is a continuation of a general tendency of life to adapt to the reality around it.[32] However, there is a decisive difference between biological and cultural evolution. In biological evolution anything that is not adapted 'inwardly' has no chance, even if it has greater opportunity of adaptation to the outside world. Limits are set to the increase in size of the human brain (and the greater chances of adaptataion to outward reality which are connected with it) by human anatomy: an embryo with too large a head will not survive birth. Internal coherence with one's own system. is the necesary (though not all-sufficient) condition for enhancing externally conditioned chances of adaptation. This relationship has shifted in the human quest for truth: in their cultural systems of adaptation, human beings can adopt elements which are in marked contrast to the existing cultural system. With the extension of knowledge they even deliberately look for dissonant elements because only these are capable of bringing progress in knowledge by shattering the inner equilibrium of previous knowledge. Thus the inner coherence of cultural systems is not in every respect the necessary condition of an enhanced opportunity of external adaptation. Human beings can develop tolerance towards ideas and notions which do not fit into their system of convictions – not least because they suspect that these could disclose new aspects of reality which were previously hidden from them.

To this degree the experience of the Holy Spirit is a specifically human experience. It brings human beings into conflict with the biological, cultural and cognitive systems in which they live: Spirit and flesh, Spirit and law, Spirit and tradition can become rivals which threaten to tear human beings apart. However, such dissonances in human life are still not sufficient ground for rejecting the experience of the Spirit as an illusion. Rather, these dissonances could point to the pressure of a problem which works on human beings from outside, which starts from a reality that is still always inaccessible to them.

Thus conflict with our experience does not allow us to say that this Spirit does not correspond to the truth. However, this conflict is a challenge to our thought, a challenge for us to look for possible correspondences. There are such correspondences. The hope for a realization of the new life must not just be maintained against experience. Anyone who examines experience in its light will, rather, find confirmatory signs of hope. That is particularly true if one interprets our experience in a (modern) evolutionary framework of thought.

In all probability, evolution has no pre-existing goal. At least, such a goal cannot be formulated within an evolutionary framework of thought. However, the properties of the system of all reality may have been created in such a way that tendencies in particular directions are constantly strengthened.[33] Here we need not assume any guiding hand. Chance can be at work. Whatever direction a flyer may take by chance at the North Pole, he will always eventually arrive at the same point, the South Pole, regardless of his intention, simply because of the properties of a sphere.

So we cannot rule out the possibility that the world-process has an intrinsic goal, which follows from properties of the system which are still hidden from us. Trial and error can also bring us nearer to it.

(a) Hope in 'chance'

There can also be hope in chance. The result of a game of dice is a matter of chance. But if we know that the die has a 'six', we shall not stop hoping for a six – even after a long losing run. It will only be a matter of time before a six is thrown. And yet on any individual throw, no one can guarantee that we shall get a six. It is the same with the creative 'mutations' of human thought. The decisive thing is for us to be certain that they are part of the great game of the world. Some time we shall hit on them, even though we know that the realization of such 'mutations' depends on many factors which are chance and not the result of our intentions. It is basically only a matter of time before these favourable circumstances come about.

But how can we be sure that there is a 'six' in the repertory of reality – that God does not play with loaded dice? That is part of a basic trust in reality generally. But it is no blind trust. A look back on evolution hitherto suggests that there is a 'six' in creation. The origin of life was a 'six' and the same may be said of the development of the nervous system or the humanization of mankind. We keep coming up against creative variants of human life in our cultural evolution. The prophet from Nazareth, too, is another improbable 'six'. What was once possible for him is not excluded as a possibility for the whole future. It can be repeated. It accords with the basic conditions of reality.

However, that prompts the sceptical question: if something has appeared in Jesus which does not contradict the basic conditions of reality – why has it yet to establish itself? Why over a history of almost two thousand years has it continually been compromised, betrayed, and turned into its opposite?

Here too the evolution of life gives us a pointer. New forms of life can emerge which show their true value only much later. Any creative mutation has an anticipatory dimension. As an illustration I might mention the industrial melanism of moths.[34] As a result of industrialization in some areas of England the birchwoods became grey and black. The salt and pepper moth, which otherwise had the best protective colouring and chance of survival, became more easily recognizable and a prey to its enemies. Now from time to time black mutations of it had already appeared. As long as the birchwoods were white, these fell victim to selection. Now, however, they had the better chances of survival. Gradually the moths became darker. In a different situation their dark colouring, which was once dysfunctional, gave them a chance of survival. One is tempted to add a moral to the illustration: Jesus is such a black moth. He was done away with, but his mode of existence could later offer a chance of survival. Jesus' love of his enemies seems to have been an impracticable dream in world history so far. But the time could come – indeed is already here – when our survival depends on how far we are successful in reducing aggression between human beings and changing our ways of reacting to enemies.

The Spirit is always the anticipation of what could perhaps happen one day. We shall only be able to say whether the form of life shaped by it has a chance when the whole of evolution has run its course. Then we may see whether it was possible among human beings to replace selection with solidarity, war with peace, aggression with co-operation. According to sayings in the New Testament the 'Spirit' is an anticipation of future possibilities. It is called a 'pledge', a first payment. It is the 'sighing of creation' which longs for its own transformation and awaits the appearance of the new human being. This Holy Spirit is the intuitive certainty of human beings that their present form of life, too, need not be final. There is still more to come in the game of the world! 'It is not yet clear what we shall be' (I John 3.2). Or more exactly, it has already appeared – in Jesus. Recollection of him keeps alive that intuitive certainty that human beings can still change in unknown possibilities.

(b) Hope in 'necessity'

For many people it will be too risky a business to trust in such a future possibility. Therefore I should add that it is not a matter of blind trust. In respect of experience so far we can note those tendencies that evolution has 'favoured'. 'Favoured' is of course an anthropomorphic expression. Evolution has no purposes. More accurately, we must say that looking back, we can have some idea which new beginnings and mutations so far corresponded with the basic conditions of reality so that in fact some tendencies were positively reinforced.

Three tendencies should be mentioned here: the tendency of smaller units to combine, the tendency towards greater independence and the tendency towards a deeper capacity for suffering. These tendencies can be recognized quite independently of the Bible, but in the light of biblical faith they become significant in a new way.

To illustrate the first tendency I shall quote the creed by the molecular geneticist C. Bresch (1977), which Christians can take over without any qualifications:[35]

> Elementary particles attract each other.
> Atoms enter into bonds.
> Cells become humanity.
> In all phases of evolution there is the goal that is eternally the same,
> that of the part becoming More through union.
> Readiness for integration is the primal force of all development.
> At the human level that is called 'love'.
> Mankind needs more love for humanity,
> more readiness to put itself in the place of others,
> more mercy towards those in need,
> more solidarity for the weak,
> more responsibility from each individual for the whole.

It needs no commentary. If this confession describes a feature which is really present in reality, the prophets, Jesus and primitive Christianity would have an important place in evolution as a whole. For here we find an overall interpretation of reality in which love is the foundation and meaning of the universe. Moreover, should we not find traces of this reality everywhere in human history, in the faith and dreams of mankind?

The second tendency seems to contradict the first. It is the tendency towards sharper delimitation and independence.[36] Material evolution already leads to elements and forms which can 'assert' themselves as entities over other unities. Single cells develop barriers between interior and exterior. More complicated organisms increasingly develop their independence from the environment. As the most complex form of life, human beings are aware that they must lead their lives responsibly – even going against pre-programmed natural tendencies and widespread tendencies in society. Again, biblical religion is one of the strides forward in this history. In it Jesus took a decisive step when he called on the one hand for independence from external social direction in his 'You have heard – but I say to you' and on the other for freedom towards one's own inner nature, by spontaneously incorporating sexual and aggressive impulses into the sphere of personal responsiblity (Matt.5.21ff.).

The third tendency goes against the charge which is continually expressed, that evolutionary thought is too optimistic. All progress has its price. So in evolution there is an unmistakable tendency towards a greater capacity for suffering. With the move from a single cell to many cells death comes into the world.[37] Without it there would be no evolution. Only the succession of generations – and that means the death of a generation – makes possible that unconscious process of trial and error by which life has gone on developing down to the present day. The development of an inner division of function in the organism leads to the central nervous system and thus to pain. Pain furthers life when it announces danger. But it means more conscious suffering. Cultural evolution offers the capacity to transcend the immediate temporal and spatial present through systems of symbols – and thus the awareness of the inevitability of death and the possibility of experiencing the suffering of others as one's own. The industrial revolution brings not only prosperity for many but also for the first time the possibility of human beings destroying themselves by their own products. From now on we have to live with this completely new anxiety. Each step in evolution brought increased suffering. And probably no further progress will be possible without new forms of suffering. Is it not deeply significant that Christ – as an anticipation of a possibility of life not yet disclosed – came into this world as one who suffered? It is the conviction of the New Testament that where God finds a perfect image, he shows himself in the form of a crucified figure. Where human beings find a more perfect match to the central reality, they will probably learn new possibilities of suffering which are now still hidden from them. Those who have the Spirit articulate the 'sighing of all creation', which runs through the whole of reality as a comprehensive cosmic tendency and which no one can penetrate to the depths.

Today the three observable tendencies of evolution towards greater solidarity, responsibility and sensitivity to suffering are all coming together. We have the responsibility to see that a minimal solidarity between all human beings prevents the great catastrophe. The course of further evolution on our planet lies in our hands. We are responsible for it. We are responsible for seeing that cultural evolution continues and that the earth remains habitable. In this respect we are learning new forms of apocalyptic anxiety, new tides of meaninglessness and new dangers of external and internal self-destruction. Yet our situation is not without analogy. We are repeating in a global context the experience of Israel. The promised land is given only conditionally, on condition that certain ethical and religious demands are fulfilled. Failure to observe the commandments leads to exile. Except that if we do not observe the commandments that preserve life, no exile awaits us, but the end – the destruction of the sphere of human life by a global war which, however probable it may seem, is still not inevitable. If we want to continue to take part in that great process of trial and error by which we seek after increasingly adequate structures of adaptation to the central reality, then we must take a step beyond all that has happened hitherto: renunciation of war and annihilation. That has never come about. But looking back, it seems as though the command to love our enemies – formulated about two thousand years ago – anticipates a situation with which we must cope today in a quite special way. We should have no illusions about this: without a capacity for peace we shall fall victim to the primal laws of selection. The revolts of biblical faith against selection will have failed. Jesus will have lived in vain.

(c) Hope as justification

Religious hope is directed beyond the continuation of tendencies observable hitherto. It seeks a fulfilment, an end to evolution. However, all the evolutionary tendencies that we can observe have no pre-given goal. There is no guarantee that the experiment of human happiness will succeed – but there is no need for it to fail, either.

However, an evolutionary interpretation of the world-process also allows further statements. The properties of the system in the evolutionary process suggest an 'inner goal': an adequate adaptation to the basic conditions of reality, either by exhausting their hidden possibilities and configurations through the transformation of objective reality into subjective experience or through hardly conceivable limit values of the reduction of entropy and selection. We do not know what a completely adequate adaptation to the basic conditions of reality could be; on the basis of previous tendencies we only suspect that they are to be sought in this direction. We suspect an inner goal of evolution which is immanent in the evolutionary game of trial and error, even if no teleology guarantees that it will be attained objectively. The whole evolutionary process is moving objectively towards this goal. Common to all the manifold forms of matter, life and culture is that in a powerful process of trial and error they look for increasingly adequate structures of adaptation to a central reality which is still unknown. They are all hypotheses which, consciously or unconsciously, are related to God. They are conscious only in human beings.

We are the only living beings in which this unconscious process of trial and error has arrived at consciousness of itself. We recognize the inner goal of the whole of evolution which is independent of any possible realization. We experience this process not only as destiny but also as a task which we have not set ourselves but which has been set us by the central reality which determines everything. It is programmed into the structures of our existence.

The assumption of such an inner goal (without external teleology) is adequate for an interpretation of primitive Christian eschatology from an evolutionary perspective. Evolutionary theory allows us to say that the goal immanent in the properties of the evolutionary process consists in adaptation to the basic conditions of reality. Primitive Christian belief makes a comparable statement: the eschaton fully accords with God. It speaks of the appearance of the freedom of the glory of the 'children of God' (Rom.8.21), of the transformation of human beings into the image of God (I Cor.15.49). It speaks of this goal with great certainty. But it interprets the goal of history with mythical imagery which contains a correction, indeed a criticism of any teleological certainty. The end is coming with a judgment to which all human beings are subject. The mythical picture of the final judgment says that it is by no means a matter of course that human life will achieve its intrinsic goal. Granted, in apocalyptic we constantly find the optimistic view that a select group will achieve this goal. But this question is put in question in the New Testament: 'All have sinned and fall short of the glory of God' (Rom.3.25) – that glory which God's image should have.

There is a dark side to the rising awareness of human beings that the inner goal of evolution has become conscious in them and is their lifework: while human beings anticipate the intrinsic goal of the evolutionary world process, they experience alienation from it all the more intensively. They can experience life as a dead end which takes them increasingly far from this goal. They experience separation from that central reality to which all their thought, action and being is consciously or unconsciously related, as grievous omission and failure. They call this separation sin: insufficient capacity to realize adequate structures of adaptation to the ultimate reality.

The New Testament begins from this insight: in their lives all human beings have the 'pre-programmed' task of living in harmony with God, i.e. adapting themselves to the central reality, but none of them achieves this aim. Harmony with God is achieved in quite another way: God takes the questionable attempts of human beings to adapt as being successful. He affirms them independently of their success or failure. That is the content of the doctrine of justification. It is already contained in the basic certainty of Jesus that despite the judgment that all human beings, good or bad, deserve, God lets them live before him. It is developed again by Paul, who bases it not on the proclamation but on the fate of Jesus: because God recognized the accursed one on the cross and found an adequate image in the one who was crucified and rose again, he is ready to accept every other person as an image, however much he or she may have gone wrong. In Christ, anyone can be the image and likeness of the hidden reality of God.

The justification of the godless offers everyone that harmony with the ultimate reality which is the inner goal of evolution – regardless of how near to this goal they may be – or how far from it. This offer can therefore be already made now. It holds for every point of evolution regardless of the one at which we find ourselves. There is nothing that can transcend it: even the most final end could not give us more than this certainty, of complete harmony with the central reality. This offer is the 'dawn of eternity' in the present.

So will the evolutionary process in the future universally reach that 'intrinsic goal'? But who knows whether this harmony with the central reality can take place at all in time? Time is indeed itself part of that reality which has to accord to the unknown central reality. Harmony with it would have to embrace all of time. But that goes beyond the conceiving of a living being whose existence is temporal through and through.

The decisive thing is that the ultimate reality which manifests itself in justification has always determined all being: at one point it allowed elements to become matter in chemical evolution. Through the interplay of mutation and selection in biological evolution it takes the development of organisms to an heightened state of differentiation. In cultural evolution it reveals itself as the invitation and obligation to go beyond the game of biological evolution which is so cruel for beings capable of consciousness. It is identical with that reality which revealed itself in the history of Israel leading up to Jesus of Nazareth. It is this to which all recognizable reality has to adapt.

Human beings suspect that if complete harmony with this central reality could be achieved, their transitory individual life would participate in something eternal, in that information which directs and determines everything. They would experience something eternal in themselves and could identify themselves with it as their true self – not a nucleus which had already been there, but a new structure and dynamic bestowed by the central reality. The Spirit of God would dwell in them as perfect harmony with God.

This is precisely the possibility which Christian faith seeks to open up. Although human beings are deeply alienated from the central reality, they may regard themselves as its successful 'image'. They have been given the Holy Spirit. The central reality offers its unconditional support to their imperfect trial and error. It also accepts their failed attempts and their unsuccessful efforts. It gives them the possibility of experiencing, now, already – within a transitory and often unsuccessful life – the intrinsic goal of the whole of evolution: harmony with God. At those moments when this awareness fills them, they are freed from identifying their true selves with the transitory constellations of organic and cultural elements. They experience a peace which is higher than reason: something of eternity.

Abbreviations

BiBe	Biblische Beiträge
BS	Biblische Studien
BWANT	Beiträge zur Wissenschaft vom Alten und Neuen Testament
CTM	Calwer theologische Monographien
CH	Calwer Hefte zur Förderung biblischen Glaubens und christlichen Lebens
EvTh	*Evangelische Theologie*
FRLANT	Forschungen zur Religion und Literatur des Alten und Neuen Testaments
FZPT	*Freiburger Zeitschrift für Philosophie und Theologie*
GTB	*Gütersloher Taschenbücher*
KuD	*Kerygma und Dogma*
RLA	*Reallexikon der Assyriologie*
SBS	Stuttgarter Bibelstudien
SIDA	*Scripta Instituti Donneriani Aboensis*
SNT	Studien zum Neuen Testament
TDNT	G.Kittel, *Theological Dictionary of the New Testament*
ThExh	*Theologische Existenz heute*
TRE	*Theologische Realenzyklopädie*
UB	Urban Taschenbücher
USQR	*Union Seminary Quarterly Review*
UTB	Uni-Taschenbücher
VT	*Vetus Testamentum*
VuF	*Verkündigung und Forschung*
WMANT	Wissenschaftliche Monographien zum Alten und Neuen Testament
WPKG	*Wissenschaft und Praxis in Kirche und Gesellschaft*
WUNT	Wissenschaftliche Untersuchungen zum Neuen Testament

ZAW   *Zeitschrift für die alttestamentliche Wissenschaft*
ZTK   *Zeitschrift für Theologie und Kirche*

Notes

Part One

1. The hypothetical character of our knowledge was worked out above all by the representatives of 'critical rationalism'; cf. H.Albert, *Traktat über kritische Vernunft*, Tübingen 1968; id., *Konstruktion und Kritik*, Hamburg 1972.

2. Cf. e.g. the account in K.D.Schmidt, *Grundriss der Kirchengeschichte*, Göttingen ⁵1967, section 9, 'Die Konsolidierung der Kirche in festen Formen', 72ff.

3. The dependence of religious belief on 'social support' is one of the themes in the books by P.L.Berger on the sociology of religion, e.g. *A Rumour of Angels*, New York 1969 and London 1970, 50ff. Berger speaks of a 'plausibility structure'.

4. Cf. K.R.Popper, *Objective Knowledge*, Oxford ²1979; K.Lorenz, *Behind the Mirror*, London 1977; G.Vollmer, *Evolutionäre Erkenntnistheorie*, Stuttgart 1975; R.Riedl, *Biologie der Erkenntnis. Die stammesgeschichtlichen Grundlagen der Vernunft*, Berlin and Hamburg 1979; cf. also C.F. von Weizsäcker, 'Der Rückseite des Spiegels, gespiegelt', in *Der Garten des Menschlichen*, Munich 1977, 187-205.

5. A good account, which is the basis for the following remarks, is G.Osche, *Evolution – Grundlagen, Erkenntnisse, Entwicklungen der Abstammungslehre*, studio visuell, Freiburg and Basle 1972. In my view, the best introduction to the dialogue between biology and theology is J.Hübner, *Biologie und christliche Glaube*, Gütersloh 1973.

6. There is a collection of the characteristics of cultural evolution in G.Osche, *Evolution*, 110ff., and G.Vollmer, *Evolutionäre Erkenntnistheorie*, Stuttgart 1975, 84-6. The independence of cultural evolution is evident as early as the Stone Age; cf. G.Freund, 'Evolution der Kulturen', in R.Siewing (ed.), *Evolution*, UTB 748, Stuttgart 1978, 397-410.

7. D.T.Campbell, 'On the Conflicts between Biological and Social Evolution and between Psychology and Moral Tradition', *American Psychologist* 20, 1975, 1103-26 = *Zygon* 11, 1976, 167-208, and J.C.Eccles and H.Zeier, *Gehirn und Geist. Biologische Erkenntnisse über Vorgeschichte, Wesen und Zukunft des Menschen*, Munich 1980, 100ff., have been basic to my understanding of biological and cultural evolution. The opposite view, that cultural evolution is an extension of biological evolution – without any opposition to its tendencies – has been put forward e.g. by E.O.Wilson, *Sociobiology – The New Synthesis*, Cambridge, Mass. 1975.

8. Cf. R.W.Kaplan, 'Die Mutation als Motor der Evolution', in

H.v.Ditfurth (ed.), *Evolution* II, Hamburg 1978, 13-28; R.Siewing, 'Die genetischen Grundlagen der Veränderung von Arten', in id., *Evolution*, UTB 748, Stuttgart 1978, 319-36; H. v.Ditfurth, *Kinder des Weltalls*, Hamburg nd., section 'Der Motor der Evolution', 213-34.

9. Strictly speaking, the concept of mutation should be limited to genetic changes. However, in the present context it is more than an appropriate, but optional, metaphor. It is used 'analogously', as e.g. in K.R.Popper, 'The Rationality of Scientific Revolutions', in R.M.Hare (ed.), *Problems of Scientific Revolution*, Oxford 1975, 72-101. Variations of gene structure, the repertoire of behaviour or of scientific theories, take place as a 'response' to external demands. At the genetic level these are mutations and recombinations of the coded instruction; on the level of behaviour they are exploratory variations and recombinations in the repertoire, and on the scientific level they are new and revolutionary theoretical approaches. On all three levels they receive new tentative instructions, in short, they are tested (74). Popper rightly, in my view, puts forward the theory of a 'fundamental similarity of the three levels' (73). A.Alland, *Evolution and Human Behaviour*, New York 1970, similarly sees an analogy, indeed a continuity, between biological and cultural evolution. His view is that the process of evolution is the same: theory requires no more than that there should be variation mechanisms (which produce new variables) and mechanisms of continuity (which produce the maximum effect) and that these systems should be exposed to the selection of the environment. At the same time, however, he is sceptical about analogies between the mechanisms of process which demonstrate cultural and biological characteristics and believes that to call the process of innovation in culture a mutation is to depart from the logical model of evolution. Mutations are somatic; they also recur in negative selections and they are fixed in a population only through genetic transference. One can clearly see these distinctions, but nevertheless it may be said that in cultural evolution, cultural innovations perform the function of mutations in biological evolution. They provide a choice of variants.

10. By way of qualification it should be said that mutagens produce certain preferred types of mutation, but this does not apply to the mutagens of adapted types, cf. R.W.Kaplan, 'Mutation', 21.

11. Some favourite examples of the use of the metaphor of mutation for phenomena of cultural evolution are e.g. the discovery of human imagination (H.v.Ditfurth, *Kinder*, 226); the appearance of new kinds of tools in the Stone Age (G.Freund, *Evolution*, 409); the protest of the young against the culture of their parents (K.Lorenz, in F.Hacker, *Aggression*, rororo 6807, Hamburg 1973, 138).

12. For the dangers of such an anthropomorphistic way of talking cf. A.W.Ravin, 'On Natural and Human Selection, or Saving Religion', *Zygon* 12, 1977, 27-41, esp.29f.

13. For the transference of the concept of selection to cultural phenomena I would again refer to K.R.Popper, 'The Rationality of Scientific Revolutions' (above n.9). For him the next stage is the selection from the available mutations and variations: the new attempts which are badly

adapted are eliminated. This is the stage of the elimination of error. So it is possible to speak of adaptation by the 'method of trial and error' or better by the method of 'trial and the elimination of error'. The elimination of error, or of badly adapted trial instruction, is also called 'natural selection'; it is a kind of negative feedback. It works at all three levels (74). Cf. also J.Monod, *Chance and Necessity*, London 1972, 150f., and D.R.Hofstadter, 'Metamagikum. Virusartige und andere sich selbst-replizierende Gebilde', *Spectrum der Wissenschaft*, 1983, 8-15.

14. Thus K.R.Popper, e.g. *Objective Knowledge*, 261: 'Thus, while animal knowledge and pre-scientific knowledge grow mainly through the elimination of those holding the unfit hypotheses, scientific criticism often makes our theories perish in our stead, eliminating our mistaken beliefs before such beliefs lead to our own elimination.'

15. Cf. A.Munk, *Biologie des menschlichen Verhaltens*, UB 831, Stuttgart 1972 (Danish 1971).

16. I have borrowed the phrase 'evolution of evolution' from N.Luhmann, 'Geschichte als Prozess und die Theorie sozio-kultureller Evolution', in K.G.Meier and C.Meier (eds.), *Historische Prozesse*, dtv 4304, Munich 1978, (413-40) 426.

17. See n.4 above.

18. D.T.Campbell, 'On the Conflicts between Biological and Social Evolution', see n.7. above.

19. A.Hardy, *The Divine Flame*, London 1975.

20. R.W.Burhoe gives a summary account of his 'scientific theology' in 'The Human Prospect and the "Lord of History"', *Zygon* 10, 1975, 199-375, and replies to his various critics in 'What does Determine Human History? Science Applied to Interpret Religion', *Zygon* 12, 1977, 366-89.

21. H.v.Ditfurth, *Wir sind nicht nur von dieser Welt. Naturwissenschaft, Religion und die Zukunft des Menschen*, Hamburg 1981.

22. Cf. K.Lorenz, *Behind the Mirror*, Ch.1: adaptation is a process of knowledge, for every 'adaptation to' a particular datum of external reality means that a mass of 'information about' it is incorporated into the organic system. Cf. also the chapter, 'Life as a Process of Knowledge'.

23. Cf. H.v.Ditfurth, *Der Geist fiel nicht vom Himmel. Die Evolution unseres Bewusstseins*, Hamburg 1976, esp. 297ff. Cf. 313: 'The reality which we experience is so dependent on the structure of our thought that it seems reasonable to say that it is the creation of our brain. However, our brain does not produce this reality in freedom either, but as far as we know, does so in interaction with a real world, though this remains hidden from us under the facade of our reality.'

24. Cf. the same argument in P.L.Berger, *A Rumour of Angels*, 64: 'The mathematics that man projects out of his own consciousness somehow corresponds to a mathematical reality' (i.e. in nature).

25. Cf. my *On Having a Critical Faith*, London and Philadelphia 1979, 39ff.

26. A.Munk, *Biologie des menschlichen Verhaltens*, 87f., derives affirmation of life from what he calls a 'psychological selection': 'Quite certainly pessimists are not subject to greater mortality; it is much more likely

that optimists sometimes experience misfortune. But there have been pessimists right through the history of our culture who have refused to bring children into this vale of tears. In other words, the more terrifying it has become to live in the changing orders of human society, the more strongly has there developed in genetic culture a type of man capable of seeing the bright side of existence. In my view this is the only real explanation for the indomitable will to life which characterizes human beings even in the most desperate circumstances.' A sceptical comment: selection certainly put a premium on intelligence – but that also encourages sensitivity to the absurdities in life.

27. H.v.Ditfurth, *Im Anfang war der Wasserstoff*, Hamburg 1972; id., *Kinder des Weltalls. Der Roman unserer Existenz*, Hamburg ⁵1976; C.Bresch, *Zwischenstufe Leben. Evolution ohne Ziel?*, Munich 1977, are fascinating accounts of evolution as a whole.

28. The best-known is the version by J.W.v.Goethe in *Zahme Xenien*, Book 3:

> Were not the eye sunny,
> it could never look on the sun;
> were there not God's own power within us,
> how could the divine attract us?

The image can be traced right back to antiquity. Cf. Plato, *Republic* VI, 508B; Manilius, *Astronomica*, II, 115f.; Plotinus, *Enneads*, I, 6,9: 'Had the eye never seen the sun, it would not itself have a sunny nature.'

29. Cf. H. v.Ditfurth, *Der Geist fiel nicht vom Himmel*, 318: 'From this perspective, then, eyes are proof of the existence of the sun, just as legs are proof of the existence of firm ground and wings are proof of the existence of air. So we may also suppose that our brain is proof of the real existence of a dimension of the spirit independent of the material level.'

30. A.Einstein, *Ideas and Opinions*, New York 1956, 40.

31. R.Musil, *Der Mann ohne Eigenschaften*, Hamburg 1952, Ch.62, 249f.

32. R.Burhoe, 'Natural Selection and God', in *Zygon* 7, 1972, 30-63, shows 'parallels between the religious concepts of, or characteristics ascribed to, God and the scientific concepts of, or characteristics ascribed to, nature and natural selection' (30). He stresses that selection can work within cultural evolution without the death of individuals: '...if in the trials or mutations there must be a certain number of errors or deaths per successful adaptation, it will cost that many deaths of whole organisms (and of their genetic patterns) for each successful or adaptive trial. But in the case of trials by a modifiable model maker like the brain, where it is only the bad models which are "killed" and not the total mechanism for making the models, the cost is measured in terms of the time and energy taken to weed out bad models' (48).

33. D.T.Campbell, 'On the Conflicts', 1103: 'On purely scientific grounds, these recipes (sc. the traditional belief systems) for living might be regarded as better tested than the best of psychology's and psychiatry's speculations on how lives should be lived.'

34. The best-known example of such a replacement theory is A.Comte's three-stage law, according to which there follow in succession a theological-fictive, metaphysical-abstract and a positive stage of human thought; id., *Die Soziologie*, Jena 1923.

Part Two

1. In my view, it makes no sense to restrict divine action to particular stages of the evolutionary process (e.g. to creation or the origin of life). All of reality has a theological dimension, from two perspectives.

(a) The basic conditions of reality, the structure of matter and the natural laws are perceived as a wonder by any unprejudiced person. Behind everything we detect a unitary 'programme' which directs everything.

(b) The latent possibilities of structure have been realized in increasingly complex forms, in an infinite evolution. We also experience this dynamic as wonder. 'In this view God participates in the world as it evolves, as the possibilities for the world become concretely realised from the organisation of electrons, and the like, into atoms; and the organisation of atoms and cells into living organisms.' Thus the biologist C.Birch, 'What does God do in the World?', *USQR* 30, 1975, (76-84) 83.

2. F.Hacker makes the following calculation; although one can of course challenge individual figures, it is a good illustration of the dimensions of evolution. Suppose human history – this last minute – to be a period of fifty years, *homo sapiens* will have lived for thirty-nine years in caves, will have begun agriculture only three years ago, founded the great religions two years ago, invented printing presses fifteen months ago and discovered electricity ten days ago (the illustration is taken from F. Hacker, *Aggression*, rororo 6807, Hamburg 1973, 351).

3. G.Vollmer, *Evolutionäre Erkenntnistheorie*, 84, speaks of an 'alteration in the principles of selection'; however, in my view the examples he collects on p.85 result in a reduction of the biological pressure of selection.

4. E.Schrödinger, *Was ist Leben?*, Munich 1951. Cf. also N.Wiener, *Mensch und Menschmaschine*, Frankfurt and Bonn 1964, 34f.

5. Reduction of entropy and selection takes place in stages. The construction of the first elements still required an enormous amount of energy. Thousands of millions of stars burnt out in space. The construction of molecular bonds releases warmth, but a million-fold less energy than in the nuclear reactions within stars and suns. The brain can construct the most complicated of structures with a minimum of energy. With evolution and the increasing complexity of structures entropy diminishes (cf. C.Bresch, *Zwischenstufe Leben. Evolution ohne Ziel?*, Munich 1977, 279). Similarly, hard selection – i.e. selection at the expense of other lives – takes place in stages. Culture is not an 'overcoming of selection' but a tendency towards a reduction of selection.

6. The remarks in A.W.Ravin, 'On Natural and Human Selection, or Saving Religion', *Zygon* 12, 1977, (27-41) 40, point in this direction: 'Religion must countervail against the naturalistic mode of selection in human affairs.'

7. The following account is based above all on M.Smith, *Palestinian Parties and Politics that Shaped the Old Testament*, New York 1971, ch.2, and B.Lang, 'Die Jahwe-allein-Bewegung', in *Der einzige Gott. Die Geburt des biblischen Monotheismus*, Munich 1981, 47-83.

8. By 'henotheism' I mean here the temporary adherence to one god. 'Monolatry' would be the permanent and exclusive bond to a god without the denial of other gods, while 'monotheism' would be the recognition that there is only one God. The inscription from Kuntillet Ayrud quoted in the text below, which accompanies a mysterious picture, is interpreted by F.Stolz, 'Monotheismus in Israel', in O.Keel (ed.), *Monotheismus im Alten Israel und seiner Umwelt*, Freiburg 1980, (143-84) 168ff.

9. Cf. W.H.Schmidt, 'Alttestamentliche Religionsgeschichte', *VuF* 14, 1969 (1-11) 7: *'Mutatis mutandis*, the ironic verdict of J.Wellhausen that "it does not make much difference whether monotheism was imported from Egypt, where it is not to be found, or, rather more reasonably, dropped down from heaven", still holds. There is no real analogy, nor even a model, for the first commandment, especially when it is taken in conjunction with the prohibition of images.'

10. Cf. M.Weippert in a review of P.D.Miller, *The Divine Warrior in Early Israel*, Cambridge 1973, *Biblica* 57, 1976, (126-32) 132: ' "Israel" in the later sense with which we are familiar therefore arose through a kind of "conversion" in which the tribal alliance committed itself to the worship of Yahweh, whose cult had been handed down by a group which had emerged in Israel (which one might call the "Sinai group").'

11. Cf. W.H.Schmidt, *The Faith of the Old Testament*, Oxford and Philadelphia 1983, 60-5: 'Was Yahweh God of the Midianites?'.

12. Cf. S.Herrmann, *A History of Israel in Old Testament Times*, London and Philadelphia ²1981, 76f. However, *Yhw'* could also be a geographical or ethnic designation. Cf. M.Weippert, 'Jahwe', *RLA* 5, 1976/80, 250.

13. For the historical probability cf. W.H.Schmidt, 'Jahwe in Ägypten', *Kairos* 18, 1976, 43-54.

14. Cf. the Merneptah Stele (about 1219 BC), in D.Winton Thomas (ed.), *Documents from Old Testament Times*, London and New York 1958, 137ff.

15. Thus E.Otto, *Jakob in Sichem*, BWANT 110, Stuttgart and Berlin 1979, 219-23.

16. Thus A.H.J.Gunneweg, *Geschichte Israels bis Bar Kochba*, Stuttgart ⁴1982, 24.

17. Cf. M.Weippert, 'Israel und Judah', *RLA* 5, 1976/80, (200-8) 202: 'The rapid socio-economic development of Israel (i.e. the Northern Kingdom) in the transition from "patriarchal" society to a kind of "market capitalism", presented in the Old Testament as a conflict between the gods Yahweh and Baal and their adherents, led to relatively unstable political conditions which can be recognized, for example, in the numerous revolutions (ten dynasties in the two hundred years of Israel's existence).'

18. M.Rose, *Der Ausschliesslichkeitsanspruch Jahwes*, BWANT 106, Stuttgart 1975, has shown that previously Yahweh was a national god; the claim to exclusiveness was connected with his relationship to the

people as a whole. In private matters people of all classes turned to Canaanite deities.

19. Deuteronomic traditions, sometimes even the original book itself, are often dated back to the Northern Kingdom: the North Israelite heritage moved to the South with refugees after 722 BC. W.H.Schmidt, *Introduction to the Old Testament*, London and New York 1984, 124.

20. A.van Selms, 'Temporary Henotheism', in *Symbolae Biblicae et Mesopotamicae*, FS F.M.T.de Liagre Böhl, Leiden 1973, 341-8.

21. Cf. the Mesha inscription (about 840 BC) in D.Winton Thomas (ed.), *Documents from Old Testament Times*, London and New York 1958, 'The men of Gad had always dwelt in the land of Ataroth, and the king of Israel had built Ataroth for himself.'

22. *ANEP* 538. Cf. B.Hartmann, 'Monotheismus in Mesopotamien', in O.Keel, *Monotheismus im Alten Israel und seiner Umwelt*, BiBe 14, Fribourg 1980, (49-81) 50.

23. For the preceding discussion cf. above all H. Weippert, *Schöpfer des Himmels und der Erde. Ein Beitrag zur Theologie des Jeremiabuches*, SBS 102, Stuttgart 1981. For the breakthrough of monotheism in the exile cf. H.Vorländer, 'Der Monotheismus Israels als Antwort auf die Krise des Exils', in B.Lang (ed.), *Der einzige Gott*, 84-113: 'Monotheism did not arise as a theoretical idea but served to overcome the religious crisis sparked off by the exile'.

24. Cf. R.Albertz, *Persönliche Frömmigkeit und offizielle Religion*, CTM A9, Stuttgart 1978, esp. 178ff.: 'The deliverance of Israel by personal piety in the exile'.

25. H.Vorländer, *Der Monotheismus Israels*, 103-6, 'External Stimuli to the Development of Monotheism', who concludes: 'The Israelites were prompted and supported by the Persians in the shaping of their monotheistic faith. The Persians in turn saw monotheistic faith in Yahweh as a kind of kindred religion' (106).

26. M.Weippert, 'Fragen des israelitischen Geschichtsbewusstseins', *VT* 23, 1973, 415-42.

27. Cf. Y.Amir, 'Die Begegnung des biblischen und des philosophischen Monotheismus als Grundthema des jüdischen Hellenismus', *EvTh* 38, 1978, 2-19.

28. Cf. M.Hengel, *Judaism and Hellenism*, London and Philadelphia 1974.

29. Text with commentary in M.Stern, *Greek and Latin Authors on Jews and Judaism* I, Jerusalem 1974, no.115, 294ff.

30. R.Pettazoni, *Der allwissende Gott. Zur Geschichte der Gottesidee*, FiBü 319, Frankfurt 1957, 117. O.Keel, 'Gedanken zur Beschäftigung mit dem Monotheismus', in id., (ed.), *Monotheismus im alten Israel und seiner Umwelt*, BiBe 14, Fribourg 1980, (12-30) 21, takes a slightly different line: 'The model of a chain of revolutions, following one another in relatively rapid successions, in the direction of monotheism, seems to me to be unavoidable.'

31. N.Lohfink, *Unsere grossen Wörter*, Freiburg 1977, 138: 'If I am right, monotheism only arrived in Israel when it was also announcing

itself everywhere else. This fruit was also growing on the tree at that time in Persia and in Greece. Zarathustra and the pre-Socratics could in fact be regarded as contemporaries of Deutero-Isaiah.'

32. B.Lang, 'Die Jahwe-allein-Bewegung', 83.

33. For the dissemination of the 'institution' of the Holy War in antiquity generally cf. M.Weippert, 'Heilige Krieg im Israel und Assyrien', *ZAW* 84, 1972, 460-93.

34. Cf. E.Hornung, 'Monotheismus im pharaonischen Ägypten', in O.Keel (ed.), *Monotheismus im Alten Israel und seiner Umwelt*, 83-97.

35. Cf. F.Stolz, 'Monotheismus in Israel', in O.Keel (ed.), *Monotheismus im Alten Israel und seiner Umwelt*, 143-84, who rightly brings out the anti-polytheistic character of biblical monotheism.

36. A.D.Nock, *Conversion. The Old and New Religion from Alexander the Great to Augustine of Hippo*, Oxford 1933, who rightly distinguishes 'attachment' to new cults from conversion proper. In a polytheistic milieu it is possible to join basically new cults without having to give up others. Therefore there is 'conversion' in the strict sense only when someone turns towards Judaism, Christianity, and some philosophical schools.

37. Cf. E.Hornung, 'Monotheismus im pharaonischen Ägypten', 86: 'The absolutizing of the one and only God, whose claim leads to the obliteration of other gods, corresponds to the absolutizing of the king, who is now the only mediator.'

38. E.O.Wilson, in *Sociobiology – The New Synthesis*, has interpreted religion in the framework of his socio-biological approach as a survival mechanism. In his view, traditional religious convictions have been undermined, not so much by disheartening refutations of their myths as by the growing awareness that such convictions in fact are mechanisms which make survival possible. Like other human institutions, religions develop to the degree that they further the survival and influence of their adherents. This thesis is criticized by W.A.Austin, 'Are Religious Beliefs Enabling Methods for Survival?', *Zygon*, 15, 1980, 193-201.

39. I have developed more fully the theory sketched out in what follows, that religious experience is based on a specifically human transformation of animal behaviour towards the environment, more fully in *On Having a Critical Faith*, 14ff.

40. What follows relies on H.v. Ditfurth, *Der Geist fiel nicht vom Himmel*, 255f.

41. Cf. J.C.Eccles and H.Zeier, *Gehirn und Geist*, 163.

42. Cf. J.Lamprecht, *Verhalten, Grundlagen – Erkenntnisse – Entwicklungen der Energie*, studio visuell, Freiburg 1972, 37 and 39.

43. The prohibition of images was established only gradually in Israel. The images (or image) of the bull in Bethel are first criticized by Hosea (8.6f.). Such strict followers of Yahweh as Jehu and Amos did not find them offensive, though Amos strongly attacks the cult in Bethel. Hosea seems to have provided the stimulus towards the 'iconoclastic' tendency in Yahwism. Cf. T.Mettinger, 'The Veto on Images and the Aniconic God in Ancient Israel', *SIDA* 10, 1979, 15-29.

44. E.G.d'Aquili, 'The Neurobiological Bases of Myth and Concepts

of Deity', *Zygon* 13, 1978, 257-75, seeks to locate Western and Eastern (kerygmatic and mystical) forms of religion in the dominant or non-dominant spheres of the brain.

45. The term derives from the Swedish theologian and psychologist of religion H.Sundén, *Gott Erfahren. Das Rollenangebot der Religion*, GTB 98, Gütersloh 1975 (Swedish 1961), 59f.

46. Cf. H. v.Ditfurth, *Der Geist fiel nicht vom Himmel*, 183.

47. The 'phase-shift' in religious experience is certainly not to be explained by the dependence of a person on passive 'shifts of mood', but also by the active 'restructuring' of our perception, cf. H.Sundén, *Gott erfahren*, 59f.

48. For a thorough discussion of Freud's theory of religion I would refer to the introduction to my book, 'Psychologische Aspekte paulinischer Theologie, FRLANT 131, Göttingen 1983, 26ff.

49. For what follows cf. H. v.Ditfurth, *Der Geist fiel nicht vom Himmel*, 202-6.

50. B.Lang, 'Die Yahweh-allein-Bewegung', 80ff.; id., *Frau Weisheit – Deutung einer biblischen Gestalt*, Düsseldorf 1975.

Part Three

1. The concept of 'hermeneutical conflict' comes from P.Ricoeur, *Conflict of Interpretations* (1965), Evanston 1974; id, *Freud and Philosophy: An Essay in Interpretation*, New York and London 1970.

2. Cf. E.Troeltsch, 'Über historische und dogmatische Methoden in der Theologie' (1898), in *Gesammelte Schriften* II, Tübingen 1931, 729-53. Troeltsch mentioned three principles of historical consciousness: criticism, analogy and correlation (734), which lead to a relativizing of claims to absoluteness. In what follows, the first point, criticism of the historicity of what is contained in the sources, will not be discussed. What is being discussed is not the historical Jesus, but New Testament chronology. It is not necessary to go behind the texts to establish what the New Testament says and believes about Christ.

3. G.E.Lessing, 'Über den Beweis des Geistes und der Kraft' (1777), in *Lessings Werke* III, ed. H.Wölfel, Frankfurt 1967, 307-12. I am aware that Lessing did not have in mind the problems discussed above. His 'enormously deep ditch' between chance truths of history and necessary truths of reason is something different.

4. Of the numerous accounts of Jesus I mention here only G.Bornkamm, *Jesus of Nazareth*, London and New York 1960, which is still one of the best and most balanced accounts of Jesus.

5. Cf. W.Bauer, 'Jesus der Galiläer', in *Aufsätze und kleine Schriften*, Tübingen 1967, 91-108.

6. Cf. K.Müller, 'Apokalyptik/Apokalypsen III', *TRE* 3, 202-51.

7. There is a summary comparison in J.Becker, *Johannes der Täufer und Jesus von Nazareth*, BSt 63, Neukirchen 1972.

8. There is a dispute as to whether Jesus ever spoke of the 'Son of man'.

However, most people would think that at least the sayings about the future Son of man should be regarded as genuine.

9. The sun which shines on good and evil is a reminiscence of Noah: although human beings are evil, the rainbow guarantees that the earth will remain. I am grateful to R.Rendtorff for this concept.

10. Cf. U.B.Müller, 'Vision und Botschaft. Erwägungen zur prophetischen Struktur der Verkündigung Jesu', *ZTK* 74, 1977, 416-48.

11. For P.Vielhauer, 'Gottesreich und Menschensohn in der Verkündigung Jesu', in *Aufsäze zum Neuen Testament*, Theologische Bücherei 31, Munich 1965, 55-91, this was a reason for regarding all the Son of man sayings as spurious.

12. H.Braun, *Jesus. Der Mann aus Nazareth und seine Zeit*, Themen der Theologie 1, Stuttgart/Berlin ²1969. There is a new summary outline in M.Hengel, 'Jesus und die Thora', *Theol.Beitr.* 9, 1978, 152-72.

13. Here, too, I must content myself with a reference to two recent works: H.Weder, *Die Gleichnisse Jesu als Metaphern*, FRLANT 120, Göttingen 1978, and D.Flusser, *Die rabbinischen Gleichnisse und der Gleichniserzähler Jesus. 1.Teil: Das Wesen der Gleichnisse*, Judaica et Christiana 4, Berne and Frankfurt 1981.

14. Cf. D.Zeller, *Die weisheitlichen Mahnsprüche bei den Synoptikern*, Würzburg 1977, 38.

15. Cf.E.Lohse, 'Ich aber sage euch', in *Die Einheit des Neuen Testaments*, Göttingen 1973, 73-87.

16. Cf. J.Jeremias, *New Testament Theology* 1, *The Proclamation of Jesus*, London and New York, 1971, 35f. For a discussion of the authenticity of the non-responsory Amen cf. R.Riemer, *Jesus als Lehrer*, WUNT 2,7, Tübingen 1981, 379-82.

17. There is a summary comparison of Jesus with the groups in Judaism in G.Baumbach, 'Die Stellung Jesu im Judentum seiner Zeit', *FZPT* 20, 1973, 285-305.

18. The relationship of Jesus to the Zealots is dealt with by O.Cullmann, *Jesus and the Revolutionaries*, New York 1970; M.Hengel, *Was Jesus a Revolutionist?*, Philadelphia 1971.

19. There is an account of these kinds of conflicts in my book *The First Followers of Jesus*, London 1978 (US title *The Sociology of Early Palestinian Christianity*, Philadelphia 1978).

20. Cf. my article 'Die Tempelweissagung Jesu. Prophetie im Spannungsfeld von Statt und Land', *ThZ* 32, 1976, 144-58 = *Studien zur Soziologie des Urchristentums*, WUNT 19, Tübingen 1979, 142-59.

21. Cf. the evidence in E.Spiess, *Logos Spermatikos*, Leipzig 1871, 2-5.

22. As an example of a Marxist account which unfortunately falls far short of the potentialities of a Marxist analysis, mention should be made of M.Robbe, *Der Ursprung des Christentums*, Leipzig 1967. For a non-Marxist sociological analysis of primitive Christianity I would mention my books *The First Followers of Jesus* and *Studien zur Soziologie des Urchristentums*.

23. Cf. R.W.Kaplan, *Die Mutation als Motor der Evolution*, 27f.

24. For what follows cf. my book *Miracle Stories of the Early Christian Tradition*, esp.287ff.

25. I have taken over this comparison from my article 'Synoptische Wundergeschichten im Lichte unseres Sprachverständnisses. Hermeneutische und didaktische Überlegungen', *WPKG* 65, 1976, 289-308. The legend of the four journeys can be found e.g. in *Buddhist Scriptures*, ed. E. Conze, Harmondsworth 1959, 39-44.

26. There is a summary in W.G.Kümmel, 'Die Naherwartung in der Verkündigung Jesu', in *Zeit und Geschichte*, Festschrift R.Bultmann, Tübingen 1964, 31-46.

27. The basic study is J.Jeremias, 'Abba', in *The Prayers of Jesus*, London and Philadelphia 1967, 11-65.

28. Cf. A.Munk, *Biologie des menschlichen Verhaltens*, 55f.

29. Of course, H.Wolf, *Jesus der Mann. Die Gestalt Jesu in tiefenpsychologischer Sicht*, Stuttgart 1975, exaggerates when she says that 'Jesus allows feminine values to predominate in the image of God' (121), but her insight is correct.

Part Four

1. The basic work is still H.Gunkel, *Die Wirkungen des heiligen Geistes*, Göttingen 1888.

2. 'Sarkic' (from the Greek *sarx*, flesh) here means behaviour conditioned by our biological nature. Paul also uses the term *sarx* to denote behaviour which is communicated socially.

3. Witchcraft was usually connected with invocation of gods and demons.

4. Opinions here do diverge widely. The assumption of an impulse with a biological foundation (thus K.Lorenz, *On Aggression*, London 1966) is countered by the opposite theory of the social conditioning of aggressive behaviour (thus A.Bandura, *Aggression. Eine sozial-lerntheoretische Analyse*, Stuttgart 1979). At all events, only the capacity for learning aggressive behaviour is conditioned. How, when and where it is learned is largely connected with the cultural environment. However, it is improbable that aggressive behaviour would be learnt at all if there were no biological basis for it.

5. For both concepts cf. the two articles by E. Schweizer, *sarx*, *TDNT* VII, 98-104, 108f., 118-51; *soma*, *TDNT* VII, 1024-91.

6. Cf. my *Psychologische Aspekte paulinischer Theologie*, FRLANT 131, Göttingen 1983, especially the chapter on 'Glossolalia – Language of the Unconscious?', 260-340.

7. Cf. my article 'Christologie und soziale Erfahrung', in *Studien zur Soziologie des Urchristentums*, WUNT 19, Tübingen ²1983, 318-30.

8. I have developed these thoughts in *Psychologische Aspekte paulinischer Theologie*, in the chapter on 'Wisdom for the Perfect as a Higher Awareness (I Cor.2.6-16)', 340-89.

9. Cf. the illuminating analyses by D.Ritschl/H.O.Jones, *'Story' als Rohmaterial der Theologie*, ThExh 192, Munich 1976.

10. Cf. the account of the problem of altruism in D.E.Zimmer, *Unsere erste Natur. Die biologischen Ursprünge menschlichen Verhaltens*, Munich 1979, 142-52, who gives a clear account of the various explanations of animal altruism in the context of a Neo-Darwinian theory. There is a survey of various theories of altruistic behaviour (including non-biological theories) in E.Staub, *Entwicklung prosozialen Verhaltens. Zur Psychologie der Mitmenschlichkeit*, Munich 1982, 1-43.

11. Cf. the title of the book by R.Dawkins, *The Selfish Gene*, Oxford and New York 1976.

12. G.Breuer, *Der sogenannte Mensch. Was wir mit Tieren gemeinsam haben und was nicht*, Munich 1981, 174-80, rightly sees the central problem as summed up under the heading 'the evolution of compassion'. One can explain the origin of morality partly in Darwinian terms, 'but any morality of this kind, whether implicitly or explicitly – draws a distinction between those people who are preferred (kinsfolk, members of the same group, one's own people, and so on) and other people' (177f.). 'There are also many other examples of people being capable of developing moral conceptions which go far beyond the framework of a "genetically reasonable" altruism which calls for certain fellow human beings to be preferred' (178). It is a fact 'that man – *and only man* – is capable of identifying himself with any other member of the species. We do that much too rarely, but at the same time we have at least put a toe over a threshhold which animals cannot cross' (180). Breuer sees this threshhold crossed in the New Testament call for universal love.

13. R.W.Burhoe, 'Religion's Role in Human Evolution: The Missing Link Between Ape-man's Selfish Genes and Civilized Altruism', *Zygon* 14, 1979, 135-62.

14. After analysing nature and culture as a competition for survival between genes and memes (i.e. ideas), R.Dawkins, *The Selfish Gene*, ends with an impressive confession of the human capacity to transcend natural and social 'egoism': 'We are built as gene machines and cultured as meme machines, but we have the power to turn against our creators. We alone on earth can rebel against the tyranny of the selfish replicators' (215).

15. The argument can be found in brief in D.T.Campbell, 'On the Conflicts', 1112: 'Mates are in genetic competition, with different interests in the sex of the offspring produced, and a motivation for a double standard because interest in the monogamous loyalty of their spouse is positively selected, while one's own fidelity usually is not.'

16. Campbell alludes in so many words to traditional theological anthropology. Cf. 'The Conflict between Social and Biological Evolution and the Concept of Original Sin', in *Zygon* 10, 1975, 234-49. Campbell does not think that 'natural' and social conduct point in fundamentally different directions. There is also clearly 'natural altruism' within bio-social optimism, whereas the ethical commands – to some degree by way of compensation – lie above this optimism.

17. The dependence of religious evidence on disclosure situations is a basic notion of the philosophy of religion put forward by I.T.Ramsey, *Religious Language*, London 1957.

18. This is the central theory of H.Sundén, *Die Religion und die Rollen*, Berlin 1966; id., *Gott erfahren. Das Rollenangebot der Religionen*, GTB 88, Gütersloh 1975.

19. Cf. the considerations to this effect in G.Vollmer, *Evolutionäre Erkenntnistheorie*, 118-37: 'The degree of correspondence between the world reconstructed by theoretical knowledge and the real world remains unknown to us, even if it is complete' (137).

20. The following remarks are an attempt to take up and qualify from an evolutionary perspective the correct insight in the Marxist criticism of religion. In principle I could assent to the famous formulations of the young Karl Marx with slight reservations. Religion (not the need for religion) 'is both an expression of real misery and a protest against real misery. Religion is the sigh of the oppressed creature, the feeling of a heartless world, as it is the spirit of conditions without spirit.' It is not just the opium but the 'opium and hope' of the people (cf. K.Marx, 'Critique of Hegel's Philosophy of Right. Introduction', in T.B.Bottomore (ed.), *Karl Marx: Early Writings*, London 1963, 43f.).

21. For the 'religion of the fathers' cf. especially R.Albertz, *Persönliche Frömmigkeit und offizielle Religion. Religionsinterner Pluralismus in Israel und Babylon*, CTM 9, Stuttgart 1978.

22. Cf. M.Weippert, 'Heiliger Krieg in Israel und Assyrien', *ZAW* 84, 1972, 460-93.

23. F.Crüsemann, *Der Widerstand gegen das Königtum*, WMANT 49, Neukirchen 1978.

24. Cf. W.A.Schmidt, 'Die Ohnmacht des Messias', *KuD* 15, 1969, 18-34.

25. For biological evolution cf. H.Markl, *Aggression und Altruismus. Coevolution der Gegensätze im Sozialverhalten der Tiere*, Constance 1976.

26. Cf. my articles 'Wanderradikalismus. Literatursoziologische Aspekte der Überlieferung von Worten Jesu im Urchristentum', *ZTK* 70, 1973, 245-71 = *Studien zur Soziologie des Urchristentums*, WUNT 19, Tübingen 1979, 79-105, and 'Gewaltverzicht und Feindesliebe (Mt 5,36-38; Lk 6,27-38) und deren sozialgeschichtlicher Hintergrund', *Studien*, 160-97.

27. Cf. my examples in *Psychologische Aspekte paulinischer Theologie*, excursus on '1 Kor.11.3-16: Die Hülle auf dem Kopf der Frau', 161ff.

28. I refer to the criterion that is given by U.Duchrow, *Konflikt um die Ökumene*, Munich ²1980, 32: 'As long as a church makes it clear in faith, praxis and organization that it is fighting to correspond to the characteristics of the true church of Jesus Christ, it is fighting for sanctification. As soon as a church in faith and/or praxis and organization notoriously contradicts the characteristics of the true church or puts other principles in its place and in so doing actively fights against the true church, it must itself be fought against as a false church.'

29. That would be the approach of Teilhard de Chardin. Cf. e.g. his book *The Phenomenon of Man*, London 1959. Karl Rahner's thoughts should also be included here, cf. 'Christology within an Evolutionary View of the World', *Theological Investigations* 5, London and New York

1966, 157-92; id., *Foundations of Christian Faith*, London and New York 1978, 178-203.

30. S.Toulmin, *Human Understanding, I, The Collective Use and Evolution of Concepts*, Princeton 1972, ch.5, 'Evolution and the Humane Sciences', distinguishes between evolution oriented on providence and evolution oriented on progress, which emerges with the basic assumptions of 'variation and selection for continued existence'.

31. Cf. J.Monod, *Chance and Necessity*, for a combination of an evolutionist interpretation of reality with an existentialist philosophy of the absurd: man must recognize his 'total solitude, his fundamental isolation. He must realize that, like a gipsy, he lives on the boundary of an alien world, a world that is as deaf to his music and as indifferent to his hopes as it is to his suffering and his crimes' (160).

32. For the distinction between internal and external adaptation in organisms and societies cf. A.Alland, *Evolution and Human Behaviour*, 108ff.

33. For what follows cf. C.Bresch, *Zwischenstufe Leben. Evolution ohne Ziel?*, Munich and Zurich 1977, 265ff., 276ff.

34. Cf. G.Osche, *Evolution*, 58.

35. C.Bresch, *Zwischenstufe Leben*, 298.

36. Cf. H.v.Ditfurth, *Im Anfang war der Wasserstoff*, Hamburg 1972, 336ff.

37. Cf. C.F.von Weizsäcker, 'Der Tod', in *Der Garten des Menschlichen*, Munich and Vienna 1977, 145-66.

Index